THE LIFE AND ART OF ELINOR WYLIE

THE · LIFE · AND · ART · OF
ELINOR WYLIE

Judith Farr

LOUISIANA STATE UNIVERSITY PRESS

BATON ROUGE · AND · LONDON

The author is grateful to those listed below for permission to quote from the works indicated:

Excerpts from *Collected Prose of Elinor Wylie*. Copyright 1933 by Alfred A. Knopf, Inc. Reprinted by permission of the publisher.

Excerpts from *Collected Poems of Elinor Wylie*. Copyright 1932 by Alfred A. Knopf, Inc. and renewed 1960 by Edwina C. Rubenstein. Reprinted by permission of Alfred A. Knopf, Inc.

Elinor Wylie's unpublished poem "O what have you done . . . and milk" is printed by permission of the Collection of American Literature, Beinecke Rare Book and Manuscript Library, Yale University, and of Mrs. Sydney Schiffer.

Library of Congress Cataloging in Publication Data

Farr, Judith.
The life and art of Elinor Wylie.
Includes index.
1. Wylie, Elinor Hoyt, 1885–1928.   2. Authors,
American—20th century—Biography.   I. Title.
PS3545.Y45Z66   1983   811'.52   [B]   83-7987
ISBN 0-8071-1107-4

Frontispiece: Elinor Wylie, portrait by Nicolas Muray, 1926, courtesy Collection of American Literature, Beinecke Rare Book and Manuscript Library, Yale University.

To my husband, George F. Farr, Jr.,
and to our son, Alec Winfield Farr

The only engine which can fabricate
Language from spirit is the heart of each

ELINOR WYLIE
"A Red Carpet for Shelley"

CONTENTS

Acknowledgments   xi

Introduction   1
I · The Life of Elinor Wylie   12
II · *Jennifer Lorn*: An Argument Against Decadence   36
III · Debut as Aesthete: The Early Poems   58
IV · *Black Armour*: Emotional Defeat and Artistic Success   84
V · *The Venetian Glass Nephew*   102
VI · The Chosen Image: Shelley as Better Self   113
VII · *The Orphan Angel*   127
VIII · *Mr. Hodge and Mr. Hazard*   144
IX · *Trivial Breath*   163
X · *Angels and Earthly Creatures*   181
Afterword   207

Index   213

ACKNOWLEDGMENTS

This book could not have appeared without the help of others. For suggesting the topic to me and for patiently and wisely enlarging my understanding of it, I owe thanks to Professor Louis L. Martz of Yale University. To Professors Cleanth Brooks and Maynard Mack of Yale I also owe deep thanks for excellent advice and assistance over the years. My husband, George F. Farr, Jr., provided affectionate concern and daily support as well as his scholarly knowledge of the nineteenth-century literature Elinor Wylie knew well. The poet Léonie Adams generously shared her recollections of Elinor Wylie in the 1920s. Wylie's niece, Edwina Schiffer, in letters that bespeak a family gift for eloquence, acquainted me with her aunt's upbringing. Professor Thomas Walsh of Georgetown University graciously passed on to me Katharine Anne Porter's memories of Elinor Wylie. Roland Harmon, professor emeritus of English at Georgetown, recalled Thomas Wolfe's impressions of her. Professor Pamela Askew of the Department of Art, Vassar College, advised me about the style of Bernardino Luini. Sheila Cudahy Pellegrini, poet and novelist, took an abiding interest in the book, consulting her own and her friends' acquaintance with biographical and linguistic matters germane to it. The Reverend James A. Devereux, S.J., of the Department of English of Georgetown University, made valuable suggestions about the sonnets of Shakespeare.

To the directors, curators, and staff of two great libraries, I also offer heartfelt thanks. Donald Gallup, curator emeritus of the American Literature Collection of the Beinecke Rare Book and Manuscript Library of Yale University and a noted scholar in American letters, not only helped me to use Yale's Elinor Wylie Archive but discussed with me her importance as a writer. To David Schoonover, present curator of Yale's Collection of American Literature, and his staff, I am grateful for hospitality and for help in reproducing the

Nicolas Muray portrait of Wylie. Donald Anderle, associate director for special collections of the New York Public Library, enabled me to profit from the library's Berg Collection of English and American Literature. His considerate interest in my work, together with that library's traditional generosity to the individual scholar, made my days at the Berg serene and fruitful and the expense of reproducing their holdings minimal. Dr. Lola L. Szladits, curator of the Berg Collection, and Brian McInerney, librarian, answered questions, found manuscripts, and offered encouragement.

I am grateful to Random House and Alfred A. Knopf, Inc., for permission to publish excerpts from the *Collected Poems* and *Collected Prose* of Elinor Wylie and from her *Last Poems*.

Beverly Jarrett and John Easterly of the Louisiana State University Press have been cordial and solicitous in guiding the translation of my manuscript into a book. My copy editor, Trudie Calvert, has provided me with help that is beyond price. She has understood what I wished to say and, when I failed to say it, reminded me of what it was. This book is better for her perspicacity, her sympathy, and her exactitude.

To the American Council of Learned Societies, I am indebted for a grant that made it possible for me to travel to and use the Elinor Wylie Archive. The New York State Research Foundation gave me a fellowship that permitted a summer of writing and research.

Finally, I should express gratitude to the memory and the spirit of my mother, who so respected the language of Elinor Wylie.

THE LIFE AND ART OF ELINOR WYLIE

INTRODUCTION

hen I was seventeen and devoted to the poetry of Emily Dickinson, my indulgent mother (perhaps hoping to make our trips from Manhattan to the Dickinson house and grave in Amherst less frequent) gave me the *Collected Poems* and *Collected Prose* of Elinor Wylie. "You should have another interest among women writers," she said. I replied instinctively and ungraciously, "I'm not interested in *women* writers, only in good writers." But my mother, who admired the crisp elegance of Wylie's language, insisted, "Read Elinor Wylie. She does things differently from Emily Dickinson but she's good."

Years later Louis Martz remarked to me, "Somebody should write a book about Elinor Wylie. She's been neglected." I was then writing on Dickinson; but Martz's comment piqued my interest. I took out my old volumes and spent weeks and then years with them and with the Elinor Wylie Archive of the Beinecke Rare Book and Manuscript Library at Yale University and the Berg Collection of the New York Public Library.

Elinor Wylie's fame was chiefly earned as a poet, but I began at that second beginning by rereading her novel *The Venetian Glass Nephew*. I had first enjoyed the book as a sophisticated fairy tale about eighteenth-century Venice and France, glass blowing, spectacular clothes, passion, and magic into which Greek history, the writing of Lawrence Sterne, the ideas of Voltaire, church Latin, and the adventures of Casanova had been wonderfully and gracefully introduced. I had had no idea of the book's meaning except that real love demanded sacrifices if it were to triumph in the end and that the author thought being a porcelain figure might be much safer than being a woman. On rereading it in a small first edition delicately printed and bound according to

Elinor Wylie's instructions, I found *The Venetian Glass Nephew* a witty parable about the rivalry between art and nature. The book's confident erudition, its dexterous comedy of surprises and metamorphoses supported a vision that was also poignant: Elinor Wylie's regard for and fear of the flesh. The body, her novel taught, might be vivid, pliant, and soft. An artifact, however, was ageless and symmetrical and did not feel pain or behave ignobly. In her syllogism one discerned both respectful commitment to art and reluctant distrust of humanity.

The Venetian Glass Nephew had fresh whimsy and an urbane sense of humor. It was clearly the work of one who experiences literature, art, and history as richly as life itself: the work of a mind that had been in the old aristocratic way "cultivated." The book's pages could of course be precious with their golden griffins, azure glass, Chinese lacquer, and Sèvres—the artificial landscape of the literature of the 1890s. Yet it was constantly challenged by a natural one of flowers, grass, and a girl's quick running. The book brought to mind the writing not only of the Aesthetes but of Exquisites such as Ronald Firbank or Edith Sitwell, whom Wylie knew. Like them, she seemed to have a taste for *chinoiserie*, elaborate silver, *verres agatisés*, even elaborately bound books in the Beardsley manner. Interestingly, however, she had placed that taste in a critical perspective. It triumphed in the pages of her fantasy, where life is defeated by art when the heroine Rosalba becomes porcelain to please her glass husband. But Wylie was explicitly illustrating the horror of such a choice, for the girl sacrifices vitality to an art that is not heroic but merely decorative. The masculine-feminine antagonisms of *The Venetian Glass Nephew* were subtle yet manifest and seemed to say something about women who became victims, forced to surrender their true natures for love. I wondered if the book were autobiographical to some extent. Yet what persistently engaged my interest was Wylie's preoccupation with art. She was writing about a theme of permanent significance in English and American letters, one prominently developed in the art of her day. In her own way, in a special voice, she was as concerned with what good art could do and bad artists fail to do, with what life offered of value and what art could preserve as were Henry James, Virginia Woolf, Wallace Stevens, the young Ezra Pound, and the young (and old) William Butler Yeats.

My eye fell on a line: "His sauve voice delicately divided silence, as one cuts a precious fruit."[1] It was highly wrought and showed care. Its writer knew what was literate, alliterative, charming. It was also studiously mannered, and its manner was indeed different from Dickinson's. (Yet such was Wylie's reputation in her day that with lavish impropriety the journalist Joseph Auslander had exalted her above both Dickinson and Brontë, eulogizing her as "Blake in chain mail, and *both* Emilies!"[2]) By chance I saw another line: "Upon the day of her birth a golden peach knocked at the door and a white rose flew into the window" (279). That line showed not only skill and taste but the flexible eloquence of the fabulist.

Why had Elinor Wylie been neglected? During her lifetime, she had achieved fame easily and had won not merely popularity but the respect of important artists. Yeats had praised the music of her poems. William Faulkner spoke of her intelligence. Max Beerbohm and Aldous Huxley admired her style in fiction.[3] She had won important prizes, given readings, lectured students, and been discussed in critical journals. Her death was lamented in critical apostrophe and in the worshipful verse of schoolchildren, but later she was in many ways neglected. There was, for instance, no adequate criticism of her work. Thomas A. Gray's *Elinor Wylie*, published in 1969, for example, is short and unsympathetic.[4] Nevertheless her poems were continually anthologized, often with accompanying notes that deplored the failure of real critical interest in her. Magazines like the *New Republic* sometimes reprinted a sonnet. Her lovely, puzzling figure still moved through biographies of her

1. Elinor Wylie, *Collected Prose* (New York, 1946), 266. Because Wylie's novels are easily accessible only in this omnibus volume, I shall cite it hereafter in this book. Subsequent references appear in the text.

2. Auslander's verse memorial containing these lines is preserved in the file of newspaper clippings of the Wylie Archive of the Beinecke Rare Book and Manuscript Library of Yale University.

3. For Yeats's praise of Wylie, see Chapter I, at note 36; for Beerbohm's, see Chapter II, note 1; and for Huxley's, Chapter VI, note 4. Faulkner, congratulating Anita Loos on the success of *Gentlemen Prefer Blondes*, wrote, "I am still rather Victorian in my prejudices regarding the intelligence of women, despite Elinor Wylie and Willa Cather and all the balance of them." See Joseph Blotner, *Faulkner: A Biography* (2 vols.; New York, 1974), I, 496.

4. Since this book was completed, Donald Pizer published an appreciation of Elinor Wylie's novels as (in her phrase) "'romances of the mind' of a permanent density and charm" that reflect "a coherent response to life and a successful attempt to create forms appropriate to that response" ("'Symbolic Romances of the Mind': The Novels of Elinor Wylie," in *Centennial Review*, XXIV [1980], 284–301).

fellow artists. My students asked me about her life because they were reading about the lives of her friends, Ernest Hemingway or Edmund Wilson.

Thus I spent some time rereading the poems and novels published by Elinor Wylie in her lifetime. Few writers, perhaps, are judged by what they have written in seven years; yet she must be. And what seems from first to last to preclude disinterested judgment of her merit as an artist is what two writers, Carl Van Doren and John D. Gordan, have called the "legend" of Elinor Wylie: her personal history. When I first came to Elinor Wylie the only biography of her was her sister Nancy Hoyt's *Elinor Wylie: Portrait of an Unknown Lady* (New York, 1935). This affectionate, blithe account, deplored by Wylie's admirer Edmund Wilson as mindless, discourages interest in her art. It reflects a peculiar set of American upper-class assumptions about life and labor—that both must be taken lightly—which was common also to the circle that surrounded the young Edith Wharton. It betrays as well a loyal desire to conceal or dismiss the scandal and misery of certain interludes in Wylie's life. Hoyt gives the impression, for example, that with courageous ease Wylie ran away from an unfortunate early marriage to a life of tea gowns, weekends in Paris, and tranquillity in the English countryside with intermittent moments of pain provoked by others' knowledge of her unmarried state; for she was for six years the scorned common-law wife of Horace Wylie. Only at the end and then without adequate seriousness does Hoyt's biography suggest what Wylie herself spoke of as her salvation through art: "This stern ascetic habit of control / That industry has woven for my soul." [5]

Stanley Olson's biography *Elinor Wylie: A Life Apart* (New York, 1979) clarifies the reasons for the unhappiness that marked Wylie's early years: marriage at twenty to a schizophrenic and cruel man whose suicide was a lasting reproach to her and an initially unsteady alliance with Wylie, to whom she bore one stillborn infant and a son who died at the age of one week. Neither her third marriage, to William Rose Benét, nor fame brought satisfaction, and she fell in love with an Englishman whose identity Gordan disclosed in 1964: a country squire much surprised by the desire he had unwittingly kindled in so celebrated a woman. Olson's book, with its concentration on the disappointments of Wylie's life, does much to explain why at the end of it she

5. Elinor Wylie, *Collected Poems* (New York, 1932), 308, "Sonnet." Unless otherwise stated, all references to Wylie's poems are to this volume.

craved solitude; or why, as her sister said, she "often valued fine porcelain above humanity."[6]

Yet Olson's decision that Elinor Wylie "turned herself into a writer when she discarded the idea, and hope, of being simply a woman"[7] does not explain—and implicitly devalues—the inner forces that fostered her literary achievement. And at this point my mother's old phrase "a woman writer" returns to mind. For Elinor Wylie did have to win her way beyond assumptions about women's lives maintained in her lifetime. An excellent student, particularly gifted in drawing and literature, she was not permitted to aspire to a college education, and though her mother encouraged her to write verses, it was as another form of divertissement or refined accomplishment. As Virginia Woolf's antifeminist Tansley puts it in *To the Lighthouse*, "Women can't write; women can't paint"; or as others have put it, women—particularly a Hoyt debutante—ought to *be* a poem, *be* a painting. In her first novel, *Jennifer Lorn*, Elinor Wylie was humorously to reveal the results of this point of view, her depersonalized heroine Jennifer, who is undoubtedly herself, serving the male protagonist as a source of artistic satisfaction alone. And since child is father to man, or woman, all her life Wylie strove, sometimes ludicrously or pathetically, to fulfill expectations of aristocratic femininity formulated for her in youth. The designer clothes and chic coiffures, the period furnishings of her homes, even her frightened attempts to write a flourishing hand show that she felt responsible to be beautiful as "simply a woman." This desire to create beauty and to embody it was both praised and held against her; at its worst it resulted in paranoid tantrums when her efforts fell short of expectation, and at its best it emerged, transfigured, in her art.

Regardless of motivation, however, one does not "turn oneself into a writer"—certainly not a writer who has commanded as much esteem as Elinor Wylie—without the requisite genius. My own view of Wylie's life supposes that she was not suited to eros. Certainly she was unsuited to the routines of marriage and motherhood. Hers was a volatile, self-assertive, and romantic sensibility. Like Shelley, on whose life she ultimately tried to pattern her own, she loved risks and required excitement. Ambivalent toward her own desires, she was often physically unable to withstand their effects. Yet her

6. Nancy Hoyt, *Elinor Wylie: The Portrait of an Unknown Lady* (New York, 1935), 129.
7. Stanley Olson, *Elinor Wylie: A Life Apart* (New York, 1979), 259.

need for romance, preferably without much sexual expression, persisted in her life until its close.

A charcoal self-portrait that she presented to her second husband, Horace Wylie, which is now preserved in the Berg Collection, is entitled in her hand, "Une blonde que l'on connaît." The portrait, though a memento, implies Wylie's confidence in the powers of appearance and artifice. Like a painting's, its stillness is meant to force reflection. The eyes are cold and measuring; the arch of the neck is charming. Perhaps because of the bows in her hair, Wylie's face seems vulnerable. In an accompanying note, she tells Horace that the face is "silly" but adds, "I drew it from myself in the glass." Her comment is illuminating to the biographer and to the student of her verse; for Wylie's fascination with her own image, seen in the "glass" of her mirror or in the various mirrors she contrived in art, is crucial to an understanding of her life and work. Her use of the French "une blonde" with its underlying suggestions of danger and allure is also telling. Horace Wylie preserved two locks of Elinor's hair—one from 1909 when they were first in love, another from 1920 before they parted. The locks are red, like those of her heroine Jennifer Lorn. That she called herself "une blonde" implies an ideal of personal beauty, the need to be "une blonde," from which only recognition of her genius could free her.

Like many women of her time and class, Elinor Wylie married early because marriage seemed a decorous and inevitable career. It could provide access to a life of wider fulfillment. Evidence suggests that she regarded her first marriage as an escape from a confining girlhood. To Horace Wylie, she was indebted for broad, general knowledge and the encouragement to write poetry. ("To breathe the same air [with him]," she told her family, "is educational."[8] To William Rose Benét, a published author when they met, she owed both faithful protection and the practical assistance that brought her poetry notice. Her marriages were accompanied by different degrees of pain and disillusionment. She abandoned her only child, by her first husband. Guilt probably led her to try to have other children. In the crucible of failed maternity she seems to have learned the value of another form of creativity:

8. *Ibid.*, 88.

"Une blonde que l'on connait"

Elinor Wylie, charcoal self-portrait, *ca.* 1909, sent to
Horace Wylie before their elopement in 1910

the "slow miracles of thought" (*Collected Poems*, 199) that initiate artistic vision. Thus in a vague yet steady if self-obsessed way, Elinor Wylie moved by means of marriage toward the achievement of a life in art. At the end, her devotion to art was absolute and, unlike many of her other efforts, it bore fruit. Yet so much has been written that is hostile toward Elinor Wylie as a person—regarding her as trivial-minded, corrupt, or even demented—that it may have challenged serious interest in her art. Like her friend Dorothy Parker, she has appeared to many merely as a literary personality.

Another hypothesis for the critical neglect shown Wylie's work is that it is not experimental. She was a traditionalist who chose to preserve the conventions of the nineteenth-century lyric and novel. Yet she lived and wrote at a time when formal innovations were being introduced in fiction and verse. Writers of novels such as Virginia Woolf (who envied Elinor Wylie's financial success) were experimenting with stream of consciousness and associational techniques that contrast with her own habit of writing in the three-volume format of the late eighteenth century and in a fantastic but representational and expository mode. In poetry the art of T. S. Eliot in particular resulted in new respect for a complicated metaphysical or at least tough and intricate style that gratified scholarly analysis and disputation. As her last collection of poems, *Angels and Earthly Creatures*, demonstrates, Wylie could adopt a metaphysical style, yet it was not her customary voice but chosen to accommodate a specific subject. As a poet she was, even in 1928, a practitioner of what may be called the classical lyric—its subjects, love, death, and nature; its manner, direct and melodious, consciously graceful if witty. One of my colleagues, hearing that after years of intermittent attention to Elinor Wylie, I was at last writing a book about her, objected, "What in the world will you say about her poems? They are hopelessly traditional." His remark brought to my mind objections to such a bias made by Richard Wilbur in his defense of a lesser poet of the 1920s, Witter Bynner—that it reflects fidelity to the "inexorable" "prescription" of experimentalism accepted after Eliot whereby an "open sort of song" was scorned. And I remembered Wilbur's other remark, justified by my own experience with practicing poets, that traditional poetry always retains its importance for the working artist. "I can think of one thoroughly 'experimental' poet," he wrote, "on whom Elinor Wylie has been a recent influence."[9] Furthermore, although to a student of schools and movements of the 1920s Wylie's art may seem old-fashioned, in the larger context it represents a pattern of constancy to proven stratagems and insights that characterizes the greatest artists. Eliot observed that the good writer must have a "historical sense, which is a sense of the timeless as well as the temporal," and that he must "develop or procure the consciousness of the past and . . . continue to develop [it] throughout his career."[10] Elinor Wylie possessed that consciousness. Indeed, one aspect of her work—her assumption of the masks and accents of such varied writers as Austen, Donne, Shakespeare, and others—reveals a sense of tradition that lent itself to the especially "modern" practice of quotation for ironic or dramatic purposes.

Fifty years have passed since Elinor Wylie's death. It is a reasonable interval after which to attempt a critical assessment of her art and its importance. And there are good reasons for doing so. Of those American poets capable of excellence in the "open song," she was one of the best and most literate. Her themes—which include the sexual antagonisms of one who, "being woman [was] hard beset" (65)—are both enduring and of her time. They shed light on the nature of the lyric and on the concerns of poets of the 1920s. Because her art was fostered by Aesthetic art but respectful of that Romantic art that she thought the greatest expression of human achievement, her work reveals the consistent influence in American letters of other traditions than the metaphysical. Pehaps more significantly, the intellectual and verbal sophistication of her writing testifies to what one admirer, Sinclair Lewis, thought of as America's coming of age,[11] or more particularly, to the fact that urbane Americans might choose to write about important things with accents and assumptions that were cosmopolitan. Wylie's writing displays the same enthusiasm for refined civility that is perceived in the art of

9. Richard Wilbur, Introduction, *Selected Poems of Witter Bynner* (New York, 1977), lxxxii.

10. T. S. Eliot, "Tradition and the Individual Talent," *The Sacred Wood* (London, 1928), 49, 52.

11. Lewis wrote to Wylie after *Jennifer Lorn* appeared, "I wonder if there has ever been written a more distinguished first novel? I am so interested in it as an American phenomenon that I can scarce think of it in relation to you. . . . Books like it mean definitely that for the first time America has ceased to be a Colony, has become a Power" (quoted in Mark Schorer, *Sinclair Lewis: An American Life* [New York, 1961], 380).

Henry James and Edith Wharton. She deserves attention as another representative of the aristocratic tradition in American literature.

The legend of Elinor Wylie is still remembered. At a party in Washington, D.C., where she lived and married and from which she fled, I recently heard a famous hostess recite "Little Elegy." She had learned it thirty years before at school and recalled that it was then described as the good poem of a bad woman. "Van Wyck Brooks," she complained, "calls Elinor Wylie practically 'reptilian'[12] in his autobiography but she wasn't. She was tortured and vulnerable." One of the guests, a noted historian, commented, "People should remember how well Elinor Wylie wrote, not what she did and how she looked. *Jennifer Lorn*—what a wonderful novel! A brilliant rendering of the influence of eighteenth-century ideas." (And, I thought, an examination of the fatuities of false art, a study of the imprisonment of women in assigned and cosmetic roles, a vision of cruelty and decadence, and a revelation of the failure of marriage to satisfy Wylie's need for knowledge and adventure. For like most of Wylie's fiction, *Jennifer Lorn* is rich in these qualities. Hostess and guest at the party I attended were regretting the intrusion of the notoriety of the legend of Elinor Wylie on the accomplishment of the artist. Still, like the legend of the shy "Myth of Amherst" in her white dress, the legend of the haughty Elinor in her silver gowns must be acknowledged; for Wylie, like Emily Dickinson (to whose poetry she never alluded) created, fostered, and wrote about her own legend. Perhaps at last, however, the superficial fascinations of that legend will give way to serious acknowledgment of the art of Elinor Wylie.

This book is written in that expectation.

In the following chapters Elinor Wylie's works are treated in the order of their publication with certain exceptions dictated by the nature of her career and imagination. Most of her work (apart from juvenilia and posthumously published poems) appeared within the space of seven years. It does not describe a

12. See Van Wyck Brooks, *An Autobiography* (New York, 1965), 376. Brooks's recollection of Wylie was not pleasant. "At our Westport house," he wrote, "I met the author of *Black Armour*, a phrase that evoked for me an image of herself; for there was something metallic about her and, if not reptilian, glittering and hard, as of some creature living in an iridescent shell. She enters a room with clanking scales, full panoplied for war, like Bonduca or an elegantly slim Valkyrie."

wide arc of development. Thus I have not felt it awkward to place discussion of *Jennifer Lorn*, published in 1923, before *Nets to Catch the Wind*, which appeared in 1921, especially since *Jennifer Lorn* is an effective paradigm of themes contained in the poems and other novels and a serviceable introduction to Wylie's way of seeing and writing. I have postponed discussion of her imaginative debt to the art of Percy Bysshe Shelley until Chapter VI because that debt became significant only after 1924, increasing in importance until her death in 1928.

CHAPTER I · THE LIFE OF

ELINOR WYLIE

There is a form of Mask or Image that comes from life
and is fated, but there is a form that is chosen.

W. B. YEATS,
The Trembling of the Veil, Book III

All creative activity depends on the energy to assume a
mask. . . . Something of the theatrical element, of affec-
tation even, is necessary to all active virtue.

GRAHAM HOUGH, *The Last Romantics*

But you have a proud face
Which the world cannot harm,
You have turned the pain to a grace
And the scorn to a charm.

ELINOR WYLIE, "Proud Lady"

n December 19, 1928, a small group gathered at the
apartment of William Rose Benét at 36 West 9th
Street in New York City. The apartment's appearance
suggested the elegance of the woman who had deco-
rated it and who was Benét's second wife. Mourning
her as Sylvia Chantry in his autobiographical poem *The
Dust Which Is God*, Benét recalled her arrangement of the "lovely high-ceiled
room in the old house,"

with the tall mantel-mirror   the flower-prints
the long low book-cases   the mellow lamp
with white shade   blue Wedgwood ornament
the silver lamp on the mahogany lowboy
the rug of Orient colour[1]

1. William Rose Benét, *The Dust Which Is God* (New York, 1941), 339.

Her friend Edmund Wilson associated Mrs. Benét's taste for formal furnishings with her past as a daughter of a fashionable family. Those who assembled in the Benét apartment that day represented two aspects and stages of her life: relatives from Philadelphia and Washington, where she had spent a childhood ordered by the assumptions and conventions of society; and members of New York's literary establishment who knew her as a hardworking writer. Both groups were aware that literary fame had never entirely compensated her for the pain of a complicated personal life, and both doubtless felt shock as well as bereavement. For Benét's wife—the poet and novelist Elinor Wylie—had died suddenly of a stroke two days before at the age of forty-three. Having finished proofreading her last volume of poems, *Angels and Earthly Creatures*, she asked for a glass of water, said, "Is that all it is?"[2] and died.

An Episcopal minister read a short service from the Book of Common Prayer to which she was devoted. In an adjoining bedroom lay the body of Elinor Wylie, dressed in a favorite silver gown by Paul Poiret whose metallic cloth she liked to think of as armor against the world. In death she seemed more beautiful than ever, though in life she had been a famous beauty. Her dead face, her editor Carl Van Doren said, was "lovely and serene and proud." The paralyzed left cheek that had given her a pinched look about which she fretted was now smooth. Acknowledging her legendary vanity, Van Doren wondered later whether she had not been secretly ready to die: "Her beauty had been a part of her career, and she felt that she could not bear to be disfigured, however slightly."[3]

Literary people who attended the service included Edna St. Vincent Millay, Franklin P. Adams, Henry Seidel Canby, Christopher Morley, Carl Van Doren, and Mary and Padraic Colum. Also present were Blanche (Mrs. Alfred) Knopf and Douglas Moore, the latter one of several composers who

2. This account of Wylie's death is from Nancy Hoyt, *Elinor Wylie: The Portrait of an Unknown Lady* (New York, 1935), 187. Variations appear in Edmund Wilson, "The Death of Elinor Wylie," *The Shores of Light: A Literary Chronicle of the Twenties and Thirties* (New York, 1952), 392; and John D. Gordan, "A Legend Revisited: Elinor Wylie," *American Scholar*, XXXVIII (Summer, 1969), 468. See also Benét's fictionalized account in *The Dust Which Is God*, 377–78.

3. Carl Van Doren, *Three Worlds* (New York, 1936), 240; *Dictionary of American Biography*, Vol. IX, Pt. II, 580.

had set her poems to music. Her family was represented by her sister Nancy Hoyt, whose cheerful fiction Wylie loyally encouraged; her mother, Mrs. Henry Martyn Hoyt, described by newspapers as a proud old lady for whom Elinor's death was the last of a long series of tragedies; and the one mourner who had known her least well and had never before been in her apartment: her twenty-one-year-old son, Philip Hichborn III, whom she had abandoned eighteen years earlier.

Elinor Wylie's mother had asked Benét to make her daughter's funeral as private and as discreet as possible. Daughter of a banker, wife of a lawyer who was assistant attorney general and then solicitor general of the United States under Theodore Roosevelt, Anne McMichael Hoyt was loyal to her children but had been much tried by their unconventional conduct—she once called them "a generation of vipers"[4]—and grieved by the early deaths of three of them. Considerable notoriety had attended the suicide of her son Henry Martyn Hoyt, classmate of Benét and an aspiring painter; the suicide of her daughter Constance, Baroness Strumm; and the rumored suicide of a younger son, Morton, whose leap from the steamship *Rochambeau* on July 6, 1928, was explained by the New York *Post* as either "harebrained deviltry" or an attempt to follow in the self-destructive pattern of his siblings. The early death of her eldest child, Elinor Morton Hoyt, then Elinor Hichborn, next Elinor Wylie, last Elinor Benét, provided a new unhappiness and a cause of fresh gossip. For on December 16, 1910—eighteen years to the day on which she died—Elinor Hoyt Hichborn committed an unforgivable act in the Washington society in which her family moved: she left her young husband Philip and their three-year-old son and went away with a married man.

Horace Wylie was the son of Andrew Wylie, judge of the Supreme Court of the District of Columbia and husband of Katherine Hopkins, daughter of a member of the House of Representatives. A lawyer and millionaire, he was the father of four children and sixteen years older than Elinor. That he had left his wife once before for a younger woman and that Elinor's marriage to Philip Hichborn had been mocked in Washington's *Town Topics* as stormy and quarrelsome made their alliance more newsworthy. Not quite two years later, while in the process of divorcing Elinor Hichborn and gaining custody of their

4. Gordan, "Legend Revisited," 462.

child, the deserted Philip Hichborn shot himself in the head. His suicide seemed especially pitiable because he left a note attributing it to his fear that he was mentally ill. Those acquainted with the romances he had written about Elinor thought him in despair at their separation.

As might be expected at a time when divorce was rare, when openly conducting an affair merited ostracism, the press made Elinor Hichborn's name scandalous. Although at the time of her death she was acclaimed for literary achievement and credited with having twice regularized her marital status, she was also remembered as the young wife who had run away. The day after her death, the Chicago *Journal* and syndicate papers carried the headline, "Elinor Wylie, Poet, Figure in Sensational Elopement, Dies."

The obsequies of Elinor Wylie were thus designed to avoid publicity. She was buried quietly in her family plot at the Forty Fort Cemetery in Wilkes Barre, Pennsylvania, commemorated in her poem "As I Went Down by Havre de Grace." Her tombstone read, "*Elinor Wylie* (Elinor Morton Hoyt)"; for Benét—like Harold Nicolson who buried his wife as "Vita Sackville-West"—seems to have wished to establish her separateness of identity. He inscribed two quotations on the monument: one, from the *Epipsychidion* of Shelley, the poet she loved best, "An Image of Some Bright Eternity"; the other, an encomium that puzzled those who thought her worldly: "Well done, thou good and faithful servant." Thus Benét insisted on what he considered Elinor Wylie's "deep faith" and her adherence to the virtue she most respected, honesty. He would soon isolate courage as her chief personal merit, saying that she had come to "worship courage" because "she . . . had suffered deeply, and still [at the end] suffered proudly from early recklessness."[5]

"Recklessness" was a word that even associates such as Mary Colum who respected Elinor Wylie's earnestness as an artist sometimes used in describing the way she conducted her life. Colum praised Wylie both for her art and for breaking down "the conventional ideas of what was to be expected from a woman poet";[6] but she agreed with Padraic Colum in thinking Wylie personally dangerous, narcissistic, affected, and, as a wife and mother, heartless. She recalled that this supposed heartlessness was evoked at Elinor Wylie's funeral:

5. Benét, letter, *Commonweal*, XI (February 13, 1929), 432.
6. Mary M. Colum, "In Memory of Elinor Wylie," *New Republic*, LVII (February 6, 1929), 318.

I could not look at Elinor's dead body without giving way; I wept openly as I knelt beside her, for something had passed away from the earth, spirit and fire, and a sort of emotional power hard to qualify. As I rose from my feet a hand was held out to me: I gazed into a boyish, Celtic-looking face. . . . As he pronounced his name I caught only the last name, "Hichborn," and I realized strangely that this freckle-faced boy . . . was Elinor's son, the son of her first husband, the child and husband she had eloped from. As far as I knew, except for one meeting . . . she had never seen her son since she had left him. . . . We stood side by side . . . looking at the wonderful dead face of her who had been his mother but to whom he had meant so little. My mind . . . kept itself fastened on the man, Horace Wylie, who had flung away his life for her, to be abandoned also by her. Now penniless, I knew, he was making a living in Chicago teaching society women to play bridge. I had never seen him, this man who had been so recklessly in love with Elinor laying flesh and spirit in her hands. . . . How would Horace feel when he heard of her death? . . . His absence from that room seemed the strangest absence of all.[7]

If Elinor Wylie would always be remembered for having left two husbands, her desertion of her son was best remembered. It was chronicled, for example, in Kathleen Coyle's novel *Immortal Ease*, in which the poet-heroine Victoria Rising leaves an infant boy without regret. Edna St. Vincent Millay attributed Wylie's rejection by the League of American Penwomen to her abandonment of her child. Speaking, near the end of her life, of her girlhood, Wylie said that in deserting her son she had been "a bad woman."[8] Public feeling concurred. She received more censure for her apparent indifference to young Philip than for living abroad with Wylie for six years, unmarried and shunned by society, under the pseudonym "Waring"; for her eventual estrangement from Wylie and marriage to Benét (described by gossips as the discarding of an elderly, now impecunious man for a young one who could help her in publishing); and for her temperamental conduct after she won fame. Reared by his father's sister, Martha (Mrs. Paul) Pearsall, Philip was invited to visit Elinor Wylie once when he was eleven. She saw him once again at her mother's request. She failed to name him in her will though Benét divided with him the $5,000 that constituted her estate.

7. Mary Colum, *Life and the Dream* (New York, 1947), 363.
8. Van Doren, *Three Worlds*, 219.

Her coldness to her only son probably rose from complex emotions: guilt, horror of his connection with his father, and a desire to forget the past. Yet Wylie was never insensitive to what she considered a personal failure: an unmaternal nature. Her confession before death that she thought her childlessness her greatest frustration suggests that she felt remorse toward Philip. Cordial to his mother's friends at her funeral, Philip Hichborn III remarked that he had been taught to hate Elinor Wylie but that, like many others, he had found her "magical"[9] when they met. Like his father, he was to die a suicide only a few years after Wylie's burial; California obituaries called him a talented writer of verse.

To most who mourned her Elinor Wylie seemed an impeccable beauty and a genius of peccable character; few artists of the 1920s provoked so much personal comment. Like the Aesthetic writers she read and resembled, Wylie led a life of histrionic aspect, and in her meticulous attention to her appearance and surroundings as well as her art, she tried, like them, to lend her life artistic dimension. As in the case of aesthetes like her friends the Sitwells, Carl Van Vechten, and Cecil Beaton, her behavior, clothes, and tastes appeared to be additional reflections of her imagination. Thus the notice paid her behavior is intrinsic to an account of her as an artist, for her aura and aspect were in some ways contrived by Elinor Wylie as an index to her art. Jean Starr Untermeyer thought her arrogant but spoke of a cultivated "frosted brilliance" like that of her poems. Edith Olivier considered her the most egotistical person she knew but never forgot the first moment she met Elinor Wylie, "wearing a dress . . . [that] looked like frozen green water."[10] Her elegance in dress and bearing identified her immediately for Olivier as the author of *The Venetian Glass Nephew*.

Some people, of course, responded to Wylie's personality alone, not to the composite figure, artist and beauty, who, aloof in Greek garb, read "Velvet Shoes" for audiences that thought her "the white queen of a white country."[11] Thomas Wolfe pronounced her "horrible"; Sara Teasdale thought her "hysterical"; Kathleen Norris, novelist-sister of Benét's first wife Teresa, said she

9. *Ibid.*, 241.
10. Edith Olivier, "Concerning Elinor Wylie," in Jane D. Wise (ed.), *Last Poems of Elinor Wylie* (New York, 1943), xiii.
11. Van Doren, *Three Worlds*, 222.

was so troublesome and dissatisfied that she was glad to remove Benét's children from her influence.[12] That even friends seemed to feel the need to make judgments about her personality reveals the extent of its power to fascinate, one aspect of the compelling energy—and, perhaps, idealism—that led her to disrupt her life twice and to write eight books in seven years. For recklessness masked a significant quality in Elinor Wylie: a passionate sensibility and with it the passion to live and to write memorably. One perceives an ingenuous cruelty in the manner in which she left two husbands and, before death, entered upon a romance that pained the third. The conduct of her emotional life, however, reveals both a need to free herself from ties that impeded her personal development as a writer and a Shelleyan conception of love. She left Hichborn because her marriage to him was both confining and physically repugnant and because, as she said, it left no room for her mind. Her extraordinary devotion to Wylie was finally compromised by the assertion of her artistic ambition and because she found the marriage no longer passionate. In her last years, she declared herself really in love for the first time, proposing not to divorce but to leave her third husband, William Rose Benét, in order to live in England near the man who inflamed both her heart and her imagination. Her selfishness was in one respect the reflex of a romantic quest for perfection.

This quest resulted in the scholarship that helped form her novels, in her intelligent devotion to the poetry of Shelley, in the shrewd, well-tuned criticism of her poems and essays about Aesthetic art. Her sister Nancy's frivolous and fond biography attributed to this quest minor fancies for Swanage lobsters, greenish-blue typing paper with matching ribbon, and French dresses. Even Elinor Wylie's well-known vanity, thought Rebecca West, was traceable to a desire to be perfect. And of her vanity there are many stories. Carl Van Doren knew she lied about her age, saying she was two years younger than she was. On her tombstone Benét perpetuated the lie, and his memorial poem to her, "Now She Belongs to the Years," bore the legend "Elinor Wylie—1887—1928" though most of its readers were aware that she had been born in 1885. Mary Colum, Van Doren, Kathleen Norris, and others recalled the tears and even lasting hostility that ensued if Wylie was not made

12. Gordan, "Legend Revisited," 463.

the center of any gathering she attended. James Branch Cabell (whom she dropped because he could not praise *The Orphan Angel*) remembered scenes, worthy of Sarah Bernhardt, he thought, if her appearance or talent was slighted by comparison to another's. And Carl Van Vechten confessed that he thought her entire career as a woman and an artist was based on the need for flattery.

In *The Web and the Rock* Thomas Wolfe describes an apparently typical exchange between Wylie and Van Vechten at a New York party. She is styled "the poetess, Rosalind Bailey," "object of [the] idolatry" of "a precious coterie." He appears as Paul Van Vleeck, a novelist whose books were about "tattooed duchesses . . . and negro prize fighters who read Greek." Wolfe pays tribute to Wylie's beauty but, with restrained astonishment, reveals her obsession with it:

> At this moment Rosalind Bailey entered the room. . . . There was no doubt at all who she was. Her cold beauty was celebrated, her picture was well known, and, in justice to her, it must be said that she . . . fully lived up to her photographs. . . . The impression that she gave was virginal and girlish, and it was not contrived. She had the long, straight, lovely legs of a young girl, she was tall, and she carried herself proudly. . . . Anyone who ever saw her would always retain the memory of her . . . quality of . . . passion and of ice.
>
> Immediately, however, she began to behave in a strange manner. Taking no notice of . . . newcomers, she swept through the doorway and then stood there . . . with a proud and outraged look.
>
> "Frank," she said, in a cold, decisive voice, "I will *not*"—her voice rose strongly on the word—"stay here in this room as long as Paul remains.". . .
>
> "Now, Rosalind," said Van Vleeck, . . . speaking petulantly, "I'm not going to talk to you.". . .
>
> "I am *not* going to be insulted [she cried] . . . he said that Eleanora Duse was the most beautiful woman he had ever seen!". . .
>
> She burst into tears, and turning, fell into the comforting arms of her husband . . . , sobbing convulsively like a child.[13]

Thomas Wolfe's vision of Elinor Wylie is of a woman whose vanity was a neurosis. There are other, casual accounts of her that show this quest for

13. Thomas Wolfe, *The Web and the Rock* (New York, 1940), 482–83.

adulation or, perhaps, as she saw it, for recognition. In a memorandum affixed to an unpublished poem of hers in the Wylie Archive, Russel Crouse explained its genesis in her irritation at not being allowed to play a question and answer game at his apartment. Late in joining Crouse, Benét, and Dorothy Parker, Wylie was angered to be asked to be briefly silent. Sitting at a typewriter, she wrote "With a Bare Bodkin," thrust it at Crouse for publication in his *Post* column, then flounced out. Since her vanity did not permit her to wear the spectacles that would correct her myopia, she had made many typing errors. Careful not to afflict what he thought a vulnerable self-esteem, Crouse retyped the poem.

Crouse's perception that she was vulnerable was shared by those who loved Elinor Wylie best, and their accounts modify the less sympathetic memoirs of her acquaintances. Many eulogized the gallantry with which she faced physical pain as well as her wit and civility, her interest in the careers of others, and her good-natured solicitude for the unfortunate. Benét, to whom she was "'a creature of light'" as well as a creature of opposites, saw also in her a sweet timidity:

> you are
> a child of leonine spirit   You have not feathers
> save in your hat yet you alight with a rush
> and then are away on wings   You are precise
> and still and haunted
> . . . a woman ancient
> in grief and knowledge   a pythia   a falcon
> with amber eyes   or just a little girl
> in her first starched dress [14]

Lecturing to college students, he remarked that Elinor Wylie was "spontaneous and baffled [like Shelley] by the matter-of-factness of the world."[15] Edmund Wilson declared that although sophisticated her spirit was essentially alien to the world, and her art was a ritual escape from it. Nancy Hoyt liked writing of a smart, soignée Elinor Wylie but remembered that her sister stammered when frightened, as she usually was before readings at which she appeared perfectly poised. And in letters to Benét, written after Wylie's

14. Benét, *The Dust Which Is God*, 327, 236–37.
15. William Rose Benét, *Prose and Poetry of Elinor Wylie* (Norton, Mass., 1934), 3–4.

funeral, Edna St. Vincent Millay recalled how easily she could be hurt—the result of years of being pointed at in crowds (as Sinclair Lewis remembered happening at a theater in Washington) or harried from various English houses when her connection with Wylie was discovered to be illicit. She remembered, too, that Elinor Wylie saw her own defects ironically, that she was "so gay and splendid about tragic things, so comically serious about silly ones." In an outcry emblematic of many made in December, 1928, Millay—her rival among women poets of the 1920s—lamented the passing of one whose art few except H. L. Mencken did not respect and whose character, repelling some, pleased others surpassingly: "Oh, she was lovely! There was nobody like her at all." [16]

Elinor Morton Hoyt was born on September 7, 1885, in Somerville, New Jersey. She once told Horace Wylie that she expected people would think of Paris or Persepolis as her birthplace; New Jersey was unromantic. Her father's ancestors were English, tracing their lineage to a John Hoyt of Somerset in 1418. They had been Pennsylvanians since the eighteenth century. Wylie was proud of her English blood and once confided to Walter de la Mare that she wished the United States had remained a British colony. Her handsome father, Henry Martyn Hoyt, was a lawyer who graduated from Yale in 1878. Her paternal grandfather was a judge and once governor of Pennsylvania. Her strong-minded mother Nancy (Anne) McMichael came of Irish stock, sufficiently blended over the years to make her a Colonial Dame. Nancy's grandfather had been editor of the *Saturday Evening Post*, and her father Morton McMichael was a successful banker with a taste for books and European travel. The Hoyts chose as Elinor's godfather the Shakespearean scholar Henry Howard Furness, who interested himself in her education. Elinor's mother and father were happily married at first though their lives were troubled by Nancy's ill health (she was hypochondriacal, a tendency reinforced by difficult pregnancies). At his death in 1910 Elinor's father had a mistress; he was the only family member sympathetic to his daughter's alliance with Horace Wylie and, many thought, the only one who understood her.

In childhood Elinor was tutored by European governesses in the nursery

16. Allan Ross Macdougall (ed.), *Letters of Edna St. Vincent Millay*, (New York, 1952), 217.

at Rosemont, Pennsylvania, where the family moved in 1887. With her brother Henry and sister Constance she was taught to recite French and German ballads and to draw. Her interest in art was early and permanent; like William Carlos Williams', her decision to write poetry was a second choice for she had wanted first to be a painter. In 1882 she was enrolled in Miss Baldwin's School in Bryn Mawr. It was a serious and energetic institution, devoted to the preparation of young women for college. In view of her parents' belief that education for girls should be decorative, it is surprising that she was sent there. In 1928, obituaries confused Miss Baldwin's with Bryn Mawr College and attributed to Elinor Wylie the college education she longed for and never had.

When her father became assistant attorney general of the United States in 1897, Elinor moved to Washington, D.C., and was enrolled in another ambitious school, Mrs. Flint's, now Holton Arms. There she worked hard at history, political economy, Shakespeare, and French and was considered an excellent student. She had already had the experience that more than any other vivified her imagination: she had discovered the poetry of Shelley.[17] And she began to seem to others a "blue-stocking," intent upon either an intellectual or artistic career. This choice alarmed her parents. Like most families of their time and class, the Hoyts envisioned for Elinor a suitable marriage and the charitable pursuits of the well-born matron. But their daughter, however convinced in the pursuit of elegance, was also determinedly writing sonnets and taking life classes at the Corcoran Gallery. (Asked if the model wore clothes, she replied, "Oh yes, two blue side-combs."[18] This was a youthful example of the bright wit that animated her light verse and novels and would put her at ease with Dorothy Parker.)

Nancy McMichael urged upon her daughter the importance of a debut. Like Edith Wharton, to whom Edmund Wilson later compared her, Elinor was frightened into the social whirl in 1903, Alice Longworth decreeing that she was radiant. Her grandfather McMichael then took her on a tour of Europe. In England the beauty that won others' interest as well as her own prompted Bram Stoker to dedicate a novel to her. But in 1904 she had an unhappy romance. Devoted to books, inexperienced with heartache, she

---

17. See Wylie's account of this discovery in "Excess of Charity," *Collected Prose* (New York, 1946), 844–45.
18. For this anecdote, see Hoyt, *Elinor Wylie*, 17.

suffered intensely. Throughout her life as a writer, particularly as a novelist, she would return again and again to the image of a kind, silly boy from whom the heroine is forcibly parted; indeed, in some ways, the paradigm of innocent adolescent love was one that Wylie pitted against the prospect of mature but sullied attraction. In confusion and defiance, she rushed into marriage with an acceptable man whom she knew superficially: Philip Simmons Hichborn II, three years older than she and the son of a rear admiral.

Their marriage ceremony was conducted by the Episcopal Bishop Henry Yates Satterlee on December 12, 1906. The president of the United States, Theodore Roosevelt, was present as was William Rose Benét, Elinor's brother's roommate at Yale. Philip Hichborn was handsome; all her life Elinor Wylie was attracted to elegant men. Hichborn was also a sportsman and a socialite with literary ambitions. (His indifferent book *Hoofbeats* was published by the United Hunts Club of America after his death in 1912.) *Town Topics*, the gossip sheet that stigmatized the young and sensitive Edith Wharton, delighted in contrasting what it called his silent studiousness with Elinor Hichborn's fun-loving but difficult manner. The assessment was inappropriate; few knew that Philip Hichborn was given to schizophrenic rages in which he threatened suicide or told Elinor that he hated her.

Their son, Philip Hichborn III, was born on September 22, 1907, awakening jealousy in his father and prompting Elinor to confide her unhappiness to her family. Though Hichborn was once institutionalized for dementia praecox they counseled fidelity. At twenty-two, Elinor Hichborn considered her life over. All that remained to her were tea parties and the marital relations that she found unpleasant and that made her long for the kindness of her lost suitor or for the imagined tenderness of Shelley. In *The Dust Which Is God*, William Rose Benét described what Wylie had told him of this life:

> at last it came to her
> that nothing lay beyond   who of long time
> had given her heart forever to the deathless
> beat of verbal music   and through it to one
> loved too greatly of God   his royal language
> around her glittered like ocean as she lay
> numb from the fevered clasp and the desperate working
> of possession   and the sobbing aftermath.[19]

19. Benét, *The Dust Which Is God*, 350.

In 1910 Elinor Hichborn met Horace Wylie. Courteous and scholarly, he was a winning conversationalist and a bibliophile, an adventurous man with an interest in poetry, history, astronomy, golf, and beautiful women. To Elinor he had a princely air. Their courtship was necessarily founded on duplicity. Elinor avowed (and even felt) friendship for Katherine Wylie while Horace and she met secretly in their "Arcadia"—Rock Creek Park—to read poems and indulge their mutual yearning. Longing to live permanently with a man who wrote notes about her hair but loved her cleverness, Elinor was haunted by the cruelty of leaving her child. She claimed later that her feelings for Horace, like her feelings for Benét, were never sensual but dictated by a need for intellectual completion and romantic escape; and, of course, a major theme of her mature poems is the embarrassed wonder and surprised anxiety of a woman who arouses sensuality in others but cannot requite it. Still, her determination to disclaim sensuality may have been the result of her breeding and also of her awareness that her life made her seem to onlookers such as Virginia Woolf a "femme fatale." [20] She saw herself, however, merely as a woman in search of congenial security.

Shortly after her father died (and perhaps impelled by the loss of his protection), Elinor Hichborn left Washington with Horace Wylie on December 16, 1910. They traveled through Europe, leaving no address, though letters sent Poste Restante followed them with family rebukes and newspaper clippings full of the distress of Philip Hichborn and Katherine Wylie. In 1911 Elinor permitted Horace to return to his wife for the sake of their children; but after a brief reconciliation and deeding most of his property to Katherine, Horace rejoined Elinor abroad. Their obsession with each other was deplored by their families and even by President William Howard Taft, who attempted to find and separate them. They assumed the name Waring after Browning's "What's become of Waring / Since he gave them all the slip" and lived quietly in various cottages in Burley, Hampshire, and in Witley, Godalming.

Elinor read constantly. In 1911 she had sixty copies of poems she had been writing brought out by a local printer. This early book was called *Incidental Numbers*, and one of its lyrics, "From Whom No Secrets Are Hid," reveals the extent both of her loyalty to Wylie and her conviction of guilt:

20. Gordan, "Legend Revisited," 460.

> I never shall repent me of
> My sin—the promise stands;
> I never shall deny my love,
> My soul is in [God's] hands.

It is interesting to contrast this poem with another which she wrote in 1922 and for which her friend Leonora Speyer found a title, "From the Wall":

> Woman, be steel against loving, enfold and defend you,
> Turn from the innocent look and the arrogant tongue;
> You shall be coppery dross to the purses that spend you;
> Lock up your years like a necklace of emeralds strung.
> Lock up your heart like a jewel; be cruel and clever;
> Woman, be strong against loving, be iron, be stone;
> Never and never and never and never and never
> Give for the tears of a lover a tear of your own.[21]

Far more articulate and powerful than the 1911 lyric, "From the Wall" says a great deal about the mature Elinor Wylie's feelings toward lovers. Indeed, its angry directness seems to describe a lifetime of disillusionment. By 1922 she had left Horace Wylie and was engaged to William Rose Benét. When she wrote this poem, she was presumably "in love." Yet she emphasizes the risk of love as a war in which the female must defend herself or be "spen[t]"; indeed, the poem declares that a woman cannot avoid being spent—she can only hope to thwart and dissatisfy the spender. It is a poem in which a cynical yet frightened speaker counsels women to use their intelligence—"be cruel and clever"—against a man's appeal to their pity. Surely it would be difficult to find among ostensibly "feminist" poems a more bitter description than this poem's of the male, whose look is "innocent" but whose tongue is "arrogant." Against his will to destroy her by appealing to her affection with tears, the female must pit her sole defense: the ability to "lock [herself] up," to be sexually frigid. By 1922 Elinor Wylie was a different woman from the writer of "From Whom No Secrets Are Hid."

Perhaps no love, even her genuine love for Wylie, could sufficiently atone for the difficulty of their early years together during which the Hoyts were unreconciled to Elinor's unconventional life and Katherine Wylie refused to

---

21. Wise (ed.), *Last Poems of Elinor Wylie*, 46.

accommodate Horace with a divorce. American newspapers openly blamed Elinor for the suicide of Philip Hichborn on March 26, 1912. Her son "Beeyup" was cut off from her and her family as, naïvely, she had not expected. The high blood pressure and acute headaches that troubled her days with Hichborn abruptly returned; they continued throughout her life, reflecting her emotional condition.

In 1914, determined to be a true "wife" to Wylie, Elinor made her first unsuccessful attempt to have his child. She had scarcely recovered from the hysterical blindness it induced when the Aliens Restriction Order enacted at the outset of Britain's entrance into World War I made the "Warings'" pseudonymity impossible. Forced to sell their country house at a great loss, they returned to the United States. Horace Wylie was now in need of money and in poor health. The couple settled first in Boston, then in Somesville, and finally in Bar Harbor, Maine, spending winters at cheap boarding houses in the South. In May, 1916, Elinor's second (actually third) son was born and died one week later. On August 7, after her brother Henry gave evidence for the plaintiff in Katherine Wylie's uncontested suit for divorce, Horace and Elinor were able to marry. But the marriage did not mollify family or friends, most of whom continued to consider them outcasts.

By 1919 they had had a succession of temporary homes from Maine to New York City. Elinor was thirty-four and Horace fifty-one when she suffered the miscarriage that ended their efforts to have children. She had meanwhile begun to write poetry in earnest. On November 28, 1919, "with hesitation," she wrote to Harriet Munroe, editor of *Poetry*, enclosing "Atavism," "Silver Filigree," "Fire and Sleet and Candlelight," and "Velvet Shoes" and asked if her work would be "modern" enough for *Poetry*. Munroe's response was encouraging: "I find your poems quite 'modern' enough for *Poetry*, in fact they interest so much that I would like to see more." [22] The poems were published in April, 1920; the title "Still Colors" emphasized important attributes of Wylie's art—its visual qualities and the formal control and concern with design that suggested a painting. Suddenly Elinor Wylie was no longer merely a notorious woman; she was a recognized writer.

Horace Wylie, on the other hand, was hard-pressed to support them. The former millionaire had at last achieved a clerkship at the Interstate Commerce

22. Olson, *Elinor Wylie*, 153.

Commission for $100 a month. Elinor often left their tiny house on Florida Avenue in Washington, D.C., to visit at her mother's home, 1701 Rhode Island Avenue. There she was frequently in the company of her brother's friend William Rose Benét. Working in New York on the *Literary Review*, Benét was a hearty, impressionable man who fell quickly in love with Mrs. Wylie. Of the subsequent period in her life, Stanley Olson wrote, "Nearly a decade after leaving her first husband, to the year, Elinor turned from her second. Horace was consigned, as Philip Hichborn had been in 1910, to the past. He was tiresome and boring; he was no help to her at all. Just as Horace had been used to help Elinor leave Phil, so now another man was assisting her desertion of Horace."[23]

Many people shared Olson's view when in January, 1921, Elinor Wylie moved to New York and a career—and life—of her own. Is it a fair one? Elinor Wylie's responses were never simple. Perhaps the combination of misfortune, money worries, and ostracism overwhelmed her customary compassion for the confused but courageous man who still loved her. Perhaps she sincerely believed that her new life in New York would help Horace as well as herself. Benét's fictionalized account of this period in Elinor's marriage to Wylie suggests that his continued passion and her lack of it distressed her. Her apartment at 1 University Place, however, did not so much separate her from Wylie or join her to Benét as establish her independence as a professional woman. And Horace Wylie was never "consigned . . . to the past." Until she died he remained for her the handsome, literate aristocrat to whom she had been deeply drawn; her last love affair, many thought, was an effort to recapture—with a man much like Horace—the early days of their love. Only two years after she left him, she was writing to him to request information for *The Venetian Glass Nephew* though he was by then in love with another Eleanor, the third Mrs. Wylie. Then, in 1927, just before her death, Elinor sent him a letter that may be interpreted as honest, self-serving, or both but that was written with the deep feeling characteristic of her last years:

> Dearest Horace, A strange thing is going to happen to you, for that thing is going to come true which undoubtedly you once desired, and for which you will now not care a straw. I am going to admit to you that I wish with all my heart I had never left you. . . . You must not tell this, because the

23. *Ibid.*, 290–91.

knowledge of it would give pain to Bill, who is one of the best people who ever lived and with whom I expect to pass the remainder of my days. But you and I know that the remainder is not long, and the entire past— which is so much longer—makes me wish to tell you the truth.

I love you Horace with an unchanged love which is far more than friendship, and which will persist until my death. . . . You are constantly in my thoughts, and remembered with an affection which is undoubtedly the strongest I shall ever feel. . . .

Well, my dear, do not think I am divorcing Bill or something like that. He is the best boy imaginable. . . . But I loved you first, I loved you more, I loved him afterwards, but now, that I love you both, I love you best. . . . If ever you want me, I will come back openly.

The letter ended with the remarkable comment, "I have never cheated any one, you know."[24]

Horace Wylie, of course, could not have known in 1920 that Elinor Wylie would be able to leave him for a genuine career. But by January 3, 1923, she was literary editor of *Vanity Fair*; she had spent a summer at the MacDowell Colony, working on *Jennifer Lorn*; she had won the Julia Ellsworth Ford prize for her first volume of poems, *Nets to Catch the Wind*; and on September 18, 1922, she had filed for divorce from Horace on grounds of nonsupport. Her marriage to Benét took place on October 5, 1923, four days after the divorce was granted. Colonel James Benét, father of the groom, went abroad to avoid the ceremony. Amy Lowell warned Elinor that one more marriage would finish her in society. Her anguished mother would have to be brought to heel, Elinor said, with "rough kindness." Elinor's own attitude was superficially gay. People noticed that the groom served her least whim and that she—the older and in crucial ways the more experienced partner—treated him with the affection of a superior toward a trusted associate. Edmund Wilson, her colleague at *Vanity Fair*, had taken pains to point out to her the danger of being a famous writer married to a beginner (even though the beginner had helped launch her in New York). Her response was candid: "Yes," she said, "it would be a pity that a first-rate poet should be turned into a second-rate poet by marrying a third-rate poet."[25]

The couple settled in an apartment near Sheridan Square where Elinor

24. Letter in Wylie Archive.
25. Edmund Wilson, *The Twenties*, ed. Leon Edel (New York, 1975), 79.

worked at writing and stepmotherhood with an intensity that often made her ill. (Benét was a widower with a son and two daughters, all young children who were alternately charmed and frightened by her glamour.) A second book of poems, *Black Armour*, appeared in 1924 and was more highly praised than *Nets to Catch the Wind*. *Jennifer Lorn*'s publication had resulted in British as well as American acclaim, in torchlight processions through the streets of Greenwich Village, and in ceremonial dinners with menus from its pages. Elinor Wylie decided that she enjoyed writing novels that provided her scope for an interest in character and in fantasy. Henceforth she would work alternately in poetry and fiction, the fabric of her novels illumining the poems; and though she never enjoyed writing the glib short stories for which *The New Yorker* or *Smart Set* paid her well, her novels were planned with delight and care.

In 1924 she was at work on *The Venetian Glass Nephew*. It was a book, she declared, that had no relation to her life with Benét. But when it appeared, readers who wondered whether *Jennifer Lorn*'s impressive husband Gerald Ponyard were not Horace Wylie began wondering whether the glass man Virginio was Benét. In both novels the husbands are failures. Ponyard insists that the heroine (red-haired and proud like Elinor Wylie) be perfect as an artifact; Virginio is physically and intellectually deficient compared to his wife Rosalba. And in both cases the wife tries to change her nature to meet her husband's need, her sacrifice resulting in real or psychic death. Thus began in her fiction as in her verse that preoccupation with personal frustration that friends noted in Elinor Wylie's conversation.

It was during this period that she became known for a high-strung temperament, for taking risks with her health and finances, and for proclaiming that she wished she could commit suicide. On one occasion she is said to have waked Katharine Anne Porter near dawn to say goodbye to her; reminded of the incident before she died, Miss Porter said, "She was *always* threatening suicide." [26] But her beauty seemed heightened; it intoxicated an

26. Katharine Anne Porter, reminiscing about Elinor Wylie to Professor Thomas Walsh of Georgetown University (October 20, 1977), spoke of her beauty and talent and also of the fact that she seemed frequently unhappy and often threatened suicide. An instance of such a threat, made to Miss Porter, is mentioned in Virginia Spencer Carr, *The Lonely Hunter: A Biography of Carson McCullers* (New York, 1975), 156. Such suicidal wishes suggest a number of responses: the conviction of failure and guilt evident in some Wylie poems; a highly sensitive temperament; and a need for sympathy and for self-dramatization.

already drunk Ernest Hemingway one evening, and he proposed that she accompany him to Europe.

When another miscarriage tried her delicate health, the Benéts bought a cottage in New Canaan, Connecticut, presumably as a retreat. There, however, Elinor's ability to write and care for his three children came seriously into question. Though all her life Elinor Wylie had domestic help—a staff of four when first with Wylie and even, when she lived alone, a cook and maid—she was fastidious about neatness, cuisine, and the personal manners of her household. In New Canaan, her acute headaches and high blood pressure were the results of an old obsession with perfection and of her anxiety to run an elegant ménage while contributing to its support. Her doctors were alarmed. Benét sold the cottage and sent his children (who reportedly disliked Elinor) to live with their aunt Kathleen Norris in California. The Benéts made their last home on West 9th Street in Manhattan. It was 1925, and in three years Elinor Wylie would be dead.

But for a brief time she enjoyed a life that, unlike that of her girlhood, was both productive and successful. Her apartment (with the period furnishings retained from her marriage to Wylie) became the scene of soirées attended by Edmund Wilson, Carl Van Vechten, Edna Millay, Dorothy Parker, and the other writers, painters, and theater people who befriended the Benéts. Some secretly disliked Elinor for controlling her husband or for demanding homage; others were fascinated by the figure in white or silver who treated her own drawing room as a stage or sat, glacial and proud, in those of George Gershwin or Lawrence Langner. In the past Elinor Wylie had liked parties, but by May, 1926, when she was completing *The Orphan Angel*, she developed a need for solitude that increased until her death. *The Orphan Angel*, a fictional celebration of her personal vision of Shelley, was her first lengthy indulgence of a preoccupation that had been hers since childhood. The more famous she became, the more superior to herself she considered Shelley; the more dissatisfied with her marriage, the more certain she should be "companioned by a cloud" (*Collected Poems*, 176), his ghostly presence. Her partiality would produce the eloquent *Mr. Hodge and Mr. Hazard*. But rivals such as Sara Teasdale mocked her devout Shelley worship, tracing it to sexual boredom.[27]

27. Olson, *Elinor Wylie*, 245, quotes Teasdale's malicious jingle: "Elinor Wylie, Elinor Wylie, What do I hear you say? / I wish it were Shelley astride my belly instead of poor Bill Benét."

At the height of her celebrity she declared that she had to leave New York and revisit that country where her life had been tranquil, England. She left Benét in the summer of 1926, leasing an apartment in Chelsea. Afterward they lived together only intermittently. Her husband was increasingly cast off for Elinor Wylie's fantasies of the past and her independent present.

At first she did not court solitude in England but enjoyed the flattery attendant on her fame. She was lionized by Arthur Machen, by the Shelley scholar Roger Ingpen, by Walter de la Mare, and by Mrs. Belloc Lowndes. She was a toast among such Exquisites as Stephen Tennant, son of Lady Grey of Wilsford. She met Osbert and Sacheverell Sitwell and (as she called him) the "chinless poet," Brian Howard. Cecil Beaton, for whose sister Barbara ("Baba") Elinor Wylie probably wrote the poem "Beware," took a photograph of her in a gossamer dress on the lawn at Wilsford where she often visited Tennant. Tennant looked, the diplomat Charles Ritchie recalled, like the youthful Shelley. His apartments with "white velvet sofas, . . . disorder of perfumes . . . orchid satin sheets . . . and scented fires"[28] recalled settings Wylie depicted in *Jennifer Lorn.* And she enjoyed his conversation, which was like that of the characters in novels of Machen or Ronald Firbank which she read with relish. Though some—like the novelist Rosalind Lehmann— thought Wylie's self-absorption sinister, most of her British friends admired her elegance. Virginia Woolf was almost unique in calling her unattractive, describing her to Vita Sackville-West as a "hatchet-minded, cadaverous, acid voiced, bare-boned, spavined, patriotic, nasal, thick legged American" and not at all the "green and sweet voiced nymph"[29] she had expected to meet. Thus began a surprisingly unsuccessful acquaintance in the course of which Woolf irritated Wylie by inquiring whether she could indeed be well-born if she made money by writing and why she did not abandon standard English and "let herself go in her native American [with] something in the line of Ring Lardner."[30]

Wylie spent the next winter and spring in New York, preparing the poems of *Trivial Breath* for publication. She planned to buy a house in Chilmark, England, with monies from the sale of *The Orphan Angel* to the Book-of-the-Month Club. The English countryside had always cheered her;

28. Charles Ritchie, *The Siren Years* (London, 1974), 153.
29. Gordan, "Legend Revisited," 460.
30. Edmund Wilson, "The American Language," *Shores of Light,* 126.

the company of her friends among the English aristocracy suited her, for their tastes were hers and they saw the indiscretions of her past as showing vitality, not want of virtue. In early summer of 1927 she was again in England, where she underwent the experience that troubled her last years and provided the subject of her posthumously published poems, *Angels and Earthly Creatures.*

For decades only intimate friends knew the name of the man with interests in philosophy and gardening who provoked the distressing passion Elinor Wylie could not conceal before death. Benét, who met him at last in the summer of 1928, thought he resembled Horace Wylie:

> bronzed   quick on the uptake   smiling
> like sunlight   then quite grave   an outdoor man
> with a queer love of books [31]

Henry de Clifford Woodhouse, a former RAF flier, of Rockylane Farm, Rotherfield Grays, Oxfordshire, his wife Rebecca, and their two children met Elinor Wylie during the summer of 1926. Their friendship deepened in 1927. Elinor spent weekends at their manor house at Henley-on-Thames from which she wrote Benét letters praising the countryside—"like heaven, precisely"—and the Woodhouse family. At first her friendship with Rebecca, whom she made a confidante, figured in her letters. Then, despite her attempts at normalcy and secrecy, it became clear to Benét that his wife was in love with "Cliff," with whom she took long walks discussing Donne's sermons and who sometimes visited her Chelsea apartment. But it was also clear that Woodhouse intended to be faithful to his wife. Despite a declaration of feeling commemorated in the "One Person" sonnets of *Angels and Earthly Creatures*, the couple vowed to renounce each other. Elinor Wylie could not, however, resign herself to such facile denial. She suffered; poems like "The Loving Cup" and "Beltane" show strain and grief. Obviously, she had expected the old romance with Wylie to be reenacted; but this time the lover was not willing. In July 1927, she contracted influenza; her physical discomfort and emotional depression served as models for the poet Hazard's in the last novel she was beginning to write. By fall she was in New York, apparently happy in a round of entertainments that accompanied the publication of *Trivial Breath.* But

31. Benét, *The Dust Which Is God*, 350.

Peter Arno's sketch of her for *The New Yorker*, which accompanied a verse portrait she did of herself, with some irony showed a woman airy and charming but troubled.

Elinor Wylie was once again in England in May, 1928. During a visit to the Woodhouses she fainted and fell on a stairway, suffering the first of the strokes that would kill her. When she fell, she was alone. Coming to consciousness, she tried to be gay at their garden party, but her pain was apparent—she had fractured two vertebrae—so that Clifford Woodhouse conveyed her to a train for London. Perhaps the stroke occurred because Elinor was tense in the presence of a man she had begun to think of as a sexual provocateur. Edith Olivier nursed her in her house in Salisbury, where Wylie wrote incessantly—often of death—and tried to hide her headaches and dizziness. By September 1, the breach with Woodhouse was such that she could ridicule him in a letter to Benét as a man in "heavy cotton blankets soaked in bilge water." But Benét, loyally responding by calling Cliff, "Woodlice," knew Elinor was seriously in love. "I always hope I shall be one of your very best friends," he wrote sadly.[32]

By mid-October of 1928 Elinor was living alone in a house near Woodhouse, completing the passionate sonnets she would with extraordinary candor present to him and Rebecca as a Christmas gift. A second stroke occurred during her sleep. She awoke with a paralyzed cheek, falsely attributed to Bell's paralysis. She had bought her English cottage and planned to settle there permanently in spring, but despite fatigue she agreed to visit Benét in New York for Christmas.

When she arrived she was haggard and obviously unwell. Yet friends such as Mary Colum who heard her read the sonnets to "One Person" thought her a more assured, if frustrated and even tragic, being. With continual recourse to medicines she assembled her final poems for publication and died just as she had finished. Benét's grief for her outlasted his later marriages, and her image (like the influence of her style on his) persisted in his poetry. In dozens of poems he invoked the vision of an ordinary man enchanted by an otherworldly spirit. The true occupation of that spirit was radiance. Its kindness was the condescension of genius:

32. See Olson, *Elinor Wylie*, 318.

I saw myself go out of a moonlit gate
and turn to the right . . .
I saw myself   a midge on the silver face
of the moon   trudge   up the sky
and through the molten silver and finespun lace
of clouds go by. . . .
I saw myself come to that misty house
on the other side of nowhere   where you are
Discreetly hidden under whispering boughs
it gleams like a star. . . .
The door glowed open   'O it's you!' you said [33]

In one of her last letters to Benét from England Elinor Wylie resolved that she would no longer write bill-paying verse or stories; she intended to become poorer and poorer in order to write with increased application and seriousness. Solitary twelve-mile walks in English fields would replace soirées; seclusion and the bitter renunciation of her love for Woodhouse would, she hoped, make her a richer artist. Her emotional life struck many as an odyssey of almost fictional scintillation. The public persona she developed as a result seemed incomparably arrogant. What is significant at last, however, is the development of her passion for a life in art. She regarded that life as redemptive, as a holy trust.

Her friend Sinclair Lewis' remark at the publication of *Jennifer Lorn*— "America has ceased to be a Colony, has become a Power" [34]—caught the extravagant mood of those who liked to pay tribute to her urbanity, to her informed taste for old silver and the novels of Thomas Love Peacock, to the witty voice of the poems and novels. It was a voice that could be salty, grave, or mordant but proposed with intimate authority the loveliness of the things of this world. She once reproved her brother's sister-in-law Tallulah Bankhead for asking whether she had had many lovers, saying that she was conservative about love and had simply married when she had experienced it. That conservatism, not attributed to her private life, was always remarked in her art. Like the best American writers, Elinor Wylie cared about tradition and, before she died, proved herself its champion.

33. William Rose Benét, "Doppelganger," *Man Possessed* (New York, 1927), 119; quoted also as part of *The Dust Which Is God*, 352.
34. Mark Schorer, *Sinclair Lewis: An American Life* (New York, 1961), 380.

She was, her sister subtitled her biography, "an unknown lady"[35] in many ways. But one of her last poems, "My Best Content Were Death," proclaimed a heroism in dealing with despair and misfortune that even her enemies conceded she possessed. That bravery seemed to mourners her liveliest quality. It had been the theme of poems like "The Eagle and the Mole," so admired by William Butler Yeats that he called it "a lovely heroic song."[36]

35. Hoyt, *Elinor Wylie*.
36. William Butler Yeats, *Letters*, ed. Allan Wade (London, 1954), 836.

CHAPTER II · *JENNIFER LORN*
AN ARGUMENT AGAINST
DECADENCE

She had the style of a little princess. . . . The small,
serious damsel, in her stiff little dress, only looked like an
Infanta of Velasquez. . . . Her anxious eyes, her charming lips, her slip of a figure, were as touching as a childish
prayer.

HENRY JAMES, *The Portrait of a Lady*

This high-spirited girl, who moves, for my mind's eye, in
the stiff brocaded folds of an Infanta, was . . . born with a
silver spoon in her mouth, in a world that Henry James
and Edith Wharton . . . could understand and picture.

ELIZABETH SHEPLEY SERGEANT, "Elinor Wylie," in
Fire Under the Andes

he attractions of Aesthetic art and its dangers and
limitations when it approaches Decadence are a major
theme of Elinor Wylie, enunciated and developed in
her poems and appearing with force and concentration in two of her novels. It was a theme to which her
background, social and literary, suited her and whose
seriousness she set forth decisively in her first novel, *Jennifer Lorn* (1923).
Readers of that volume who already admired the poet of *Nets to Catch the Wind*
(1921) were surprised and pleased to find in her fiction not only a fanciful
lyricism but the ability to weave a narrative of more than one dimension. For
in one way *Jennifer Lorn* is a humorous Gothic romance in the nineteenth-
century tradition, full of escapade and flourish; in another, it is an argument of
some asperity and consequence against the excesses of that sensibility Elinor
Wylie herself possessed and which she had encountered among her contem-

poraries who had common tutors, the late nineteenth-century Aesthetic poets.

Jennifer Lorn—an elegantly bound book, its title page and woodcut decorations suggesting the printing fashions of the eighteenth century as interpreted by Aubrey Beardsley—had been begun at 1 University Place, New York, during Elinor Wylie's second season as a professional writer. She had long wanted to discover a way of demonstrating her preoccupation with character and history. The composition of *Jennifer Lorn* took time, for Wylie had to blend her own life and the lives of the eighteenth-century women she studied and present them in a style convenient to her own erudition. She seems to have acknowledged the efficacy of her efforts for at her death she declared that *Jennifer Lorn* was better than her other novels. As late as 1950, Max Beerbohm was rereading it with a delight that prompted him to write to a friend, praising *Jennifer Lorn* "as a lovely series of soap-bubbles blown in a garden on a sunny day and prismatically floating hither and thither—and not breaking. They float still, and will always do so."[1]

Although Beerbohm and others thought *Jennifer* a tour de force, Wylie seems to have intended that it have several levels of meaning. On one hand it was a parody of Aesthetic novels. On another it was—as some suspected—autobiographical. And it summoned her love of occult learning and old romances to make comments on human nature through literary allusion. To trace its genesis is to discover the serious intention of its author.

In a letter to William Rose Benét, sent from the MacDowell Colony where she completed *Jennifer Lorn*, Wylie said that she was reading William Beckford's *Vathek*. Anyone who examined *Vathek* together with *Jennifer Lorn* would find parallels. The caliph Vathek is as fierce as the antihero of *Jennifer* and just as acquisitive. Three of *Vathek*'s minor characters resemble characters in *Jennifer Lorn*; and Wylie obviously tried to reproduce the qualities of innocence and decay Beckford described. Yet there are differences between *Vathek* and *Jennifer* that reveal Wylie's special gifts. Beckford's novel is a string of absurd, even brutal incidents and is peopled by blind Negresses and qualified by blasphemy and diabolism. But *Jennifer Lorn* includes brutal ele-

---

1. See Katharine Lyon Mix, *Max and the Americans* (Brattleboro, Vt., 1974), 169.

ments as burlesque, and it is a civilized book, subtler than *Vathek*. Most of all, it is a romance with an essential plan. The fascination of Beckford's characters with food, feasting, and jewels is shared by *Jennifer*; yet such desires are depicted there as ridiculous. Elinor Wylie, like others of her class, regretted the excesses of the 1920s: *Jennifer* may have been an attack upon them.

Jennifer Lorn is the story of the seventeen-year-old daughter of the Scottish Earl of Tam-Linn and the Honourable Clarinda Cleverly-Neville who is "the most beautiful girl in Devonshire; indeed, with the possible exception of a few Genoese and Sicilian peasants and a shawled colleen or two in Galway, . . . the most beautiful girl in the world" (*Collected Prose*, 29). Red-haired like Elinor Wylie and like James Abbott McNeill Whistler's Jo[2] and with a porcelain complexion, she is "thin and clear as green leaves in April" (30) but languid and, in her white muslin dresses, always on the verge of pretty indisposition. It might be foolish to imagine the terrible Gerald Ponyard, with his poniardlike intelligence, his "cold and deadly skill at gaming" for money and power, wishing to marry her (12). But when Gerald, heir to an old but impoverished barony, returns with wealth and polish from France and the Indian service, a suitable marriage to a compliant girl whose beauty suggests the gloss of artifice is his chief ambition. He regards a wife, like the cream-colored horses, palace, and sapphire he has picked up in India, as an acquisition. For him, a true aesthete, white currants are best when "delicate as fruit blown in Venetian glass" (25). His first glimpse of Jennifer, leaning negligently "over a sundial on a summer's day," looking like one of the more tranquil

2. Whistler's mistress during his London years in the 1860s was an Irish girl, Johanna Heffernan, who served as his model in many early pictures, including *Wapping* and *Symphony in White No. 1: The White Girl*. Her red hair, suggestive of the bold temperament she actually possessed, makes a vivid contrast with the poses of enervation or startled arrest in which Whistler depicts her. By giving Jennifer Lorn red hair—Wylie's own hair color—Wylie may have sought to describe the same contrast between her essentially emotional nature and the "cage" in which her husband Gerald places her. Certainly Gerald's orders that Jennifer dress in white or black recall the preferences of Whistler for a sobriety of costume that heightened the natural character of his subjects. As this book means to suggest, Elinor Wylie, who originally wished to be a painter and who grew up in Washington, D.C., where the Freer Gallery exhibited many Whistlers, seems to have known Whistler's style well. In many instances in her work she seems to be quoting it. Red hair was not fashionable in the 1920s; Wylie's choice of that color for Jennifer Lorn suggests not only a knowledge of Whistler but other impulses. In Islam (where Book III of *Jennifer Lorn* takes place) red hair is considered alluring; and since it was her own color she may have had an autobiographical motive: to connect the repressed Jennifer Lorn and the repressed wife of Philip Hichborn.

portraits of Fragonard, evokes an uncharacteristically dramatic response: "He utter[s] a choking cry and [springs] violently to his feet" (32). Jennifer's relatives cannot understand his infatuation; they prefer plump and vital women to this "half-animate" girl, "a pink marble nymph . . . among cypresses" (36).

Elinor Wylie's subtle alternatives do not at first explain his fancy: "Whether Gerald now fell under the disturbing influence of a true passion for Jennifer's fine-spun flesh, or whether he merely wished to possess her as he might have possessed a Chelsea figurine or a delicate piece of Meissen, is a question which . . . may not improbably remain forever shrouded in mystery" (36). The rest of the book clarifies the nature of his attraction. It is not physical. For Jennifer is forced to realize on her wedding night that "her own proximity" cannot "accelerate the measured pulses of her husband's blood; he was above fear, and though love might move him to tenderness it could never submerge him in folly"; so that, preposterously on one hand, sadly on the other, we watch this "doll . . . cold as wax" being read to from Bernardin de St. Pierre on her honeymoon, her husband gazing at her intermittently "to lick up the cream of her beauty and swallow it with quiet satisfaction" (49, 48, 50).

Gerald's true interest in Jennifer is that of the connoisseur in an artifact that can be improved. He is devotedly attached to "precious lacquer cabinets, consoles and tables in marquetry, columns and vases in porphyry" (75). Indeed, the one "tragedy" that affects Gerald in a course of adventures that include Jennifer's death is the forced auction of "bits of porcelain and ormulu; . . . transparent clays of China and Japan" which he attends at the house of a ruined banker (74–75). As the novel develops, he devotes himself to transforming Jennifer into a transcendent *objet d'art*. She must frequent *coiffeurs* and couturiers until her hair shines like "well-polished Sheffield" and her figure resembles "a copy of Venus Anadyomene in gold and ivory" (67, 46). When at Gerald's post in India, Jennifer is expected to pose against the Taj Mahal, hair powdered in the fashion of the Rue St. Denis. There, she will be, he says, "an exquisite impertinence against the background of mortal grief conjured into still solemnities of marble" (130). What fascinates Gerald in Jennifer is her quality of artifice arrested in life. Yet he never loves her as he does a jasper bowl, bid at nine hundred livres, at the banker's auction: "He would never give it to his wife so long as he lived; . . . he could almost have sworn that if it had come to a choice between them, he would have selected his newer acquisition to have and to hold forever" (75–76).

Jennifer is gentle, sentimental, childlike. Given to missing her parents, warbling ballads, and dining on "three young lettuce leaves" to keep up courage in a difficult life, she attracts romantic affection and reciprocates it with terrified reluctance (64). Her marriage to Gerald results in a devotion to William Collins' "Ode to Evening" with its invocation of the "gradual dusky veil" of death. Yet one is not allowed to take her depression seriously. Beneath the surface of Wylie's tale are cruelty, deprivation, and lust. On its charming surface, the characters, as if in ceremonial masks, act out a story of petty greed, artistic pretension, love, and delicate suffering. Thus on her honeymoon in France, Jennifer is met by a young relative of the French ambassador who overtakes her in a conservatory full of rosebushes. Distantly, the boy perceives her emotional starvation and that fear of Gerald which makes her solicit the protection of other men. He embodies innocent desire (and is founded on the figure of the suitor Wylie lost in youth). But his romantic fervor and comical self-absorption make his wish to rescue her full of furbelow and funny: "'At last I have found you!' cried the young man in accents vibrant with joy; I have even had the supreme good fortune to find you when you were evidently in want of assistance; to speak of beauty in distress were impertinence; to liken you to Ariadne were immediately to suggest the absurd comparison of myself with Perseus; may I venture to recall to your mind the homely proverb that a friend in need is a friend indeed?'" (77–78). Here, Wylie's style, like Beerbohm's during his Duke of Dorset's proposal to Zuleika Dobson, achieves its genial humor by inflating a bubble of elaborate rhetoric which is then incongruously burst. The "'homely proverb'" is ill at ease amid the youth's high-flown sentences, and Jennifer's response to it is equally inane: "'Oh, my dear Sir, . . . what felicity to know that you are English, or at the very worst, Scotch!'" (Likewise, the Duke's chapter-long wooing of Zuleika, an empurpled enumeration of his wealth and honors, is concluded with Zuleika's summary reduction of his character: "'I think you are an awful snob.'")[3]

3. Max Beerbohm, *Zuleika Dobson* (New York, 1926), 71.

Jennifer's timorous romance with the youth is a prefigurement of her love for the Persian Prince Abbas, an attraction of children of the same age, sensibility, and enshacklement to convention. Wylie treats it with a gentle comedy that nevertheless demonstrates the fatuity of obsession with the superficial:

> "I saw you first in a Hackney coach in London, last October . . . I do not recall what you were wearing at the time, but I know that you appeared to me a seraph robed in snow—"
> "That must have been my ermine mantle—"
> "And again in the gardens of the Tuileries; night was falling; you seemed a star in darkness—"
> "And that was my black velvet *pelisse*, without doubt," cried Jennifer with warm interest. "Was I not wearing at the same time a white veil?"
> "Veil?" exclaimed the youth. "O lovely sound—sweet augury, ecstatic hope—what visions are conjured up by that one word!" (81)

Ponyard, of course, is proof against romance. When the boy sends Jennifer a basket of white roses, he stamps them to shreds, vengeful as he never would have been toward the gift of an artifact she inspired. "For a whole week Jennifer [is] inconsolable" (87).

The Ponyards reach India and the "miniature palace" filled with "indigo hangings and silver arabesques," fragrant with "sandalwood, aloes, musk, cassia and sweet calamus" that Jennifer hoped would make her happy but did not, away from her favorite Devon (99, 100, 101). Child of the pastoral pretense of the late eighteenth century, she is terrified by genuine exoticism. She is, the novel tells us, the descendant of the fell Tamburlaine the Great. Yet the Indian climate results for her in "fears, tears, fainting fits, smelling-salts, cambric handkerchiefs steeped in lavender water, sleeping potions and chincona pills" (124).

On a trip to Shiraz, Gerald's party is waylaid by "barbarians . . . wearing sheep-skin caps" (166). Though he routs them temporarily, he is overcome by twenty Turcoman arrows and, apparently dead, is buried like a vampire with a stake through his heart. (That Gerald is like a vampire is never said explicitly in the novel, but his demands drain Jennifer of energy.) His wife falls into the hands of the Khan's procuress, the Banou, and is brought to Persia's rightful ruler, Abbas, to be fattened for the Khan's harem.

Abbas is "a slim and languid youth of perhaps nineteen or twenty indolent Persian summers," whom we first encounter lying on "trampled rose leaves," toying with a desire to become a Roman Catholic (135, 136). He is an expert at cuisine. His mentor, the rough, kind priest Father O'Donnell, deplores his instinctive sensuality, a parody of the Wildean sensuality of Dorian Gray. Even as Ponyard, who respects only objects, is a mild reflection of Dorian's corrupter, Lord Henry Wotton, Father O'Donnell is a good genius, like Dorian's friend, the artist Basil Hallward. Though he constantly reminds Abbas of the superiority of soul to body, the priest cannot change the boy's temperament. Not seduced to sin like Dorian, only decoratively slothful and congenitally epicene, Abbas has become a great cook because his father forbade him to be that dangerous being, an artist. Thus Oscar Wilde's dictum in his Preface to *Dorian Gray*—"All art is quite useless"—is parodied in Abbas' denial that his food should be eaten: " 'In cooking, to create a masterpiece for the nose alone—that is exquisite, that is Art!' " (148). In this connection, one remembers that in Wilde's early play *Vera* there is a Prince Paul who declares that "to make a good salad is to be a brilliant diplomatist" and "the only immortality I desire is to invent a new sauce."[4]

Elinor Wylie's analysis in *Jennifer Lorn* of the limitations of the Aesthetic sensibility is intensified with the introduction of the figure of the prince. Ponyard, of course, is a dandy, the Aesthete in dress personally represented by writers from Théophile Gautier and Jules Barbey d'Aurevilly to Wilde and his disciple, Ronald Firbank, and such Americans as Carl Van Vechten. Like Beau Brummel, whom Beerbohm respectfully lampoons, Ponyard is a master of the philosophy of clothes. He is horrified as the Beau would have been when Jennifer once urges him to abandon his severe (and Whistlerian) blacks and whites for the blue and silver of a *"petit maître"* (64). Prince Abbas is also "a dandy"; but he is "a troubadour, a silken sprig of extravagant royalty," not, as he claims, a "conqueror" like the austere and tyrannical Ponyard but "an artist" (136, 137). Gerald had fallen in love with Jennifer because she looked like a painting. Abbas falls in love with her because, to him, she resembles "the pure gravity of an antique cameo" of the Virgin promised him by Father O'Donnell (140). Gerald prefers his jasper bowl to his wife; Abbas, who

4. Oscar Wilde, *Works*, ed. E. F. Maine (London, 1954), 17, 648.

worships the "spiritual exhaltation" emanating from the red earthen bowl that inspires him to cookery, wants to marry Jennifer so that he can serve and befriend her (146). Yet despite his youthful adoration, there is a Ponyard-like avidity in his temperament. Having offended the priest by saying that the Virgin of the cameo is "'a woman who smiles into the face of her beloved!'" he is denied that image; he chooses Jennifer instead (151). In this way, Gerald, the aesthete-critic, and Abbas, the decadent artist, are one.

Yet Abbas offers the frightened girl what Gerald does not: amorousness. Promised a "hideous future" by the Khan's procuress—less hideous because it involves rape than because it means swallowing mutton fat!—Jennifer decides to elope with the prince (174). What ensues is an extravagant pastorale, typical of Wylie's discreet celebrations of nature in the sensuousness of children whom "innocence had not left . . . nor human love approached too near" (188). Determined to reach Devonshire by donkey, they are "as bright-eyed and agile as the hares and slim gazelles which [frolick] in the deeper forests" (189). Formerly a "porcelain treasure" when she is not envisioned as "'the Clytie of Annibale Caracci engraved by Signor Bartolozzi,'" Jennifer briefly becomes a real girl under the influences of fresh air, love, and freedom (200, 131). Abbas, who prefigures the glass mannequin Virginio of *The Venetian Glass Nephew*, had been described as "a little glass tube" in which "Life's . . . strong fluid" might "crack" (138). Now he, too, becomes hearty and active, neither artificial nor given to pose.

The idyll ends, however, when Jennifer observes Gerald Ponyard at a distance, realizes he is not dead, and demands, for propriety's sake, to return to Shiraz and join him. Abbas, deeply offended, conveys and leaves her there, where the Banou's servants immediately intercept her. Finally, she is treated as an object for the last use of decadence. Scented, stained, and coral-colored, she is installed in the harem under a silken bowstring which she thinks will kill her if she stirs. Moving at the far-off sounds of Abbas' voice, she dies not of strangulation but fright with an outcry to Gerald on her lips. Thus "in death" "he possesse[s] her"—his artifact—"completely" (201).

The novel concludes with a last suppressed contest between Jennifer's two admirers. In a gorgeously improbable scene, Father O'Donnell says mass above the girl's grave in a grove of cypresses. Abbas lies prostrate on the ground, his hand relaxed around the ivory cameo that resembles Jennifer.

When Gerald strides into view, he contemplates killing Abbas with "a small but deadly weapon of beautiful workmanship" (210). Instead, in a sudden wave of pity and insouciance, he merely steals the Byzantine image, "'an exquisite work of art . . . procured . . . at the cost of . . . little expense or pain.'" Critic to the end, he complacently leaves the grave through gardens whose beauty strikes his relentless eye as "redundant" (211).

Jennifer Lorn, like many eighteenth-century novels, is divided into three parts or "books." As a story that ostensibly concerns itself with the hero's acquisition of a fortune and a wife and with their travels and adventures in foreign or exotic lands, it mimes certain traditions of the eighteenth-century picaresque novel while Jennifer's wanton excursions into realms of pure feeling ask us to recall the sentimental novels of the close of that century. At times one hears in the cadences of Wylie's prose faint evocations of the balanced sentences of Jane Austen, on whose Darcy of *Pride and Prejudice* she claimed to have patterned Gerald:[5]

> It is a truth universally acknowledged that a single man in possession of a good fortune must be in want of a wife.
>
> However little known the feelings or views of such a man may be on his first entering a neighbourhood, this truth is so well fixed in the minds of the surrounding families, that he is considered as the rightful property of some or other of their daughters.

> The Honourable Gerald Ponyard was the heir to a barony whose extreme antiquity was the only satisfactory thing about it, and at an early age he made up his mind finally and firmly that the other satisfactory things of life were so essential to his happiness that he could even bring himself to work . . . in order to obtain them. In his day and generation, this was an idea so original and surprising that Gerald, at one time, came very near to being regarded as the black sheep of an otherwise respectable family, but his almost immediate acquisition of vast sums of money did much to remove this prejudice from the minds of his more critical aunts and cousins.
>
> The natural question raised by these gentry was, "Why doesn't Gerald make a good match?" (11–12)

More distinctly, however, her efforts to reproduce an accurate eighteenth-century world led Elinor Wylie to paraphrase the language of that

5. Carl Van Doren, *Three Worlds* (New York, 1936), 218.

Ponyard-like adventurer William Hickey—like Gerald, an originally impoverished sybarite and gamester who enriched himself in the Indian service.
Hickey's *Memoirs* were obviously one of her sources for *Jennifer* since Hickey
and the Ponyards take the same route to India, meet the same storms and
similar potentates, and reach land in nearly the same words:

> On the 30th, a light breeze from the south-west luckily sprang up, which
> carried us into Balasore Roads, where we came to an anchor.[6]

> At the end of another week a light breeze from the southwest carried
> them into Balasore Roads; they anchored off the Island of Sangor. (98)

The amiable, witty good humor associated with much eighteenth-century
fiction, its elements of burlesque and sorties into fantasia, perhaps prompted
Wylie to choose an eighteenth-century setting for her mock-heroic "extrava-
ganza." But her fascination with eighteenth-century decor, colloquialisms,
customs, and costume in general is, in quality, that of Aesthetes such as Austin
Dobson, who fostered the late nineteenth-century taste for eighteenth-
century life and letters by writing, editing, or introducing about fifty books on
eighteenth-century literature as well as composing a series called *Eighteenth-
Century Vignettes*. To Dobson and other Aesthetes, eighteenth-century England
and France before 1789 meant elegance, urbanity, the fine art of the cabinet-
maker and cameo-painter, and the high tone of the *haut monde*. On the two
occasions—in *Jennifer Lorn* and *The Venetian Glass Nephew*—when she argues in
fictional form against the excesses of Aestheticism, Elinor Wylie designs a
landscape, characters, and circumstances that, in their solicitation of superficial characteristics of eighteenth-century novels, would have appealed to
many Aesthetes. In that way she composed a climate of attitudes that hypoth-
esized the Aesthetic preference for elegance, particularly historic elegance,
and then employed it to rehearse foibles that were specifically to be found not
in the eighteenth century but in the *fin de siécle* or, by inheritance, in the
"mauve" novels of the 1920s. Thus *Jennifer Lorn* is filled with the polite rhetoric

---

6. Peter Quennell (ed.), *The Prodigal Rake: Memoirs of William Hickey* (New York, 1962), 229.
Besides the internal evidence furnished by *Jennifer*, there is additional proof that Wylie read
Hickey's journal. The Wylie Archive preserves a list of her projected titles for short stories.
Among them is "Surly Nabob," a phrase of Hickey's (288). An unpublished Wylie letter also
mentions Hickey's journal.

and well-made objects the Aesthetes admired in the abstract and also associated with the eighteenth century. But the novel is not fundamentally concerned with that century or with its literary or mannerly conventions. Its truer subject is the folly of art loved for its own sake. And insofar as it presents this folly both disapprovingly and comically, *Jennifer Lorn* reminds us that the superb form of the eighteenth century was the satire.

The chapter headings of the novel point up its Aesthetic theme: "Excesses in Veneer," "Phoenixes and Pomander Boxes," "The Italian Vinaigrette," "The Shagreen Slippers," "The Rajah's Ruby," "The Byzantine Image," "Rose-Water of Fahjum," and "The Heron's Feather." The titles at first suggest preciousness and the cult of the small object. Finally, as the Persian setting of the last book is devised, they indicate an opulence verging on enervation and decay. If the characters (including Jennifer) recall those of Wilde's *Picture of Dorian Gray*, so does the central conceit of the book wherein all that is left of a human life is its image.

The cameo resembling Jennifer in Wylie's novel and the portrait of Dorian in Wilde's survive the deaths of their subjects. Both Dorian and Jennifer are manipulated by others because their physical beauty appears to transcend nature and to become a paradigm of the continuance of art. That betrayal of natural sympathy is seen as pitiless in each book. Wilde's, of course, with its conviction of the evil which vanity and experimental sensuality can produce, is a moralistic as well as lurid redaction of the corruption of an innocent. In Wylie's novel, however, the silly Jennifer is never corrupted, only exploited, and Gerald Ponyard, though ominous and even brutal in his quest for possessions, remains a figure of fun, Dorian's corrupter, Wotton, being truly sinister.

There are echoes of *Dorian Gray* throughout *Jennifer Lorn*. Some summon remembrance of Wilde's wit, others of his caressive habit of noticing, even at the height of action, a beautiful object. Thus when Gerald Ponyard couches a vision of death and suffering in ironic reduction, "he further regaled [Jennifer] with the story of the suicide of Vatel. . . . 'Over-conscientiousness, my dear, has wrecked many a promising career" (60), and "'Ulagh Bey was himself a poet and a patron of literature; his son had the bad taste to murder him'" (69), we are again reminded of Dorian's patron, for whom acting is more real than life; "morbid" emotions like "suffering" are "ugly" and out of date and violent acts lack decorum. Wilde's Lord Henry would like "to write a novel . . . lovely as a Persian carpet, and as unreal,"[7] and the third book of *Jennifer*, set in Persia, opens with sentences reminiscent of the opening lines of *Dorian*:

> On a summer's afternoon of the most exquisite and entranced loveliness, two men sat upon a pink marble bench in the back garden of Kerim Kahn's palace at Shiraz; the moveless atmosphere about them was saturated with the scent of roses; rose-petals, yellow or delicately flushed with the colours of a shell, lay unregarded at their feet." (133)

> The studio was filled with the rich odour of roses, and when the light summer wind stirred amidst the trees of the garden, there came through the open door the heavy scent of the lilac, or the more delicate perfume of the pink-flowering thorn.[8]

Elinor Wylie's creation of an atmosphere of roses and her depiction of the sulky prince who plucks and crushes a rose so that "its sharp sweetness might revive his soul" evokes the decadent climate of *Dorian Gray*, whose hero "looks as if he were made out of ivory and rose-leaves" and, like Jennifer, "could be made a . . . toy"[9] by a heartless lover (140). Prince Abbas' interest in the elaborate ritual of Roman Catholicism comments on a similar fascination in such poets as Ernest Dowson, Lionel Johnson, and Wilde. His world-weariness, psychic equivalent of Jennifer's languor, also reflects the decadent sensibility, like the larger context of the novel, wherein the "inhuman" Ponyard seeks pleasurable sensations in maneuvering his wife into artistic poses (48).

In *Dorian Gray*, however, celebration of artifice occurs, despite the book's humor, with a gravity that shows Wilde's basic attraction to objects and the life of taste. In *Jennifer Lorn* that celebration is thrown into comic relief. After murdering Basil Hallward, for example, Dorian pauses to retrieve a lamp "of Moorish workmanship, made of dull silver inlaid with arabesques of burnished steel, and studded with coarse turquoises."[10] Presumably he does so because the lamp might be missed in its usual place; but clearly Wilde cannot refrain from depicting the exotic aspect of the lamp and enumerating its

7. Wilde, *Works*, ed. Maine, 44, 45.
8. *Ibid.*, 18.
9. *Ibid.*
10. *Ibid.*

47

attractions for their own sakes. When such distraction occurs in *Jennifer Lorn* it is seen to be absurd, even as the characters' participation in a comedy of traditional Aesthetic roles is also absurd. Thus Gerald's reflection that the pistol with which he wishes to shoot Abbas is well-made, like Jennifer's recollection of what she was wearing when the youth of the conservatory falls in love with her, is shown to be incongruous. Even on her honeymoon Jennifer notes that the book from which Gerald reads is "bound in morocco, and that its pages were propped open with a richly chased nut-cracker" (50).

If one contrasts the pleasant, secure erudition of *Jennifer Lorn* with the occult catalogs of marvels in Joris Karl Huysmans' *A Rebours* (or in those catalogs modeled upon it in *Dorian Gray*) one recognizes the distinction between scholarship that serves higher artistic purposes like delineation of character, and learning whose function it is to place distance between artist and reader, suggesting realms of knowledge that promise sensual revelations or names that conjure up strange or dangerous experiences. Wylie's novel concerns itself with Aesthetic faults but exists also as an independent work in which a sophisticated humor exposes the shortcomings of characters it has created with the intention to please through amusement.

The character of "Jenny Forlorn" recalls, besides Wilde's Sibyl Vane, Jenny Mere, the creation of that satirist of Aesthetic fashions, Max Beerbohm. Beerbohm's Jenny is also an innocent, given to a fondness for bread, honey, and little strawberries consumed in a pastoral setting. She appears in Beerbohm's fairy tale "The Happy Hypocrite" wherein the decadent Lord George Hell, having fallen in love with her and wishing to hide his face with its telltale marks of corruption, commissions of a magician the mask of a good face in order to win Jenny. He does; and he, who "used to boast that he had not seen a buttercup for twenty years,"[11] takes up residence with her in a woodman's cottage which he comes to prefer to palaces. At the end of the tale his real and his false face become one under Jenny's influence. Whereas in *Zuleika Dobson* or "Enoch Soames" or the splendidly tongue-in-cheek "Defense of Cosmetics," Beerbohm lampoons Aesthetic reverence for fancy dress, smart surroundings, French phrases, and all artifices opposed to nature, "The Happy Hypocrite" quietly undertakes to commend simplicity. It is at all times evident that *Jennifer Lorn* may be, in tone, indebted to *Zuleika Dobson*:

11. Max Beerbohm, *The Bodley Head Max Beerbohm*, ed. David Cecil (London, 1970), 23.

"In me you behold a Prince of the Holy Roman Empire, and a Knight of the Most Noble Order of the Garter. Look well at me! I am Hereditary Comber of the Queen's Lap-Dogs. I am young. I am handsome. My temper is sweet, and my character without blemish. In fine, Miss Dobson, I am a most desirable *parti*."

"But," said Zuleika, "I don't love you."[12]

"I was born in Kent, near Sevenoaks, where my ancestral mansion is prettily situated. . . . I have but lately arrived in Paris after an extended stay in Rome and a tour of the more important Italian towns. I hope you do not find my manner of speaking distasteful to you; if so I will hasten to alter it to the best of my ability; I will intone to you the sonorous chants of the priests of Baal or the songs of the ancient Chaldean shepherds if it will but please you a little; if you will smile I might even be valiant enough to speak French."

"Oh, no, no," entreated Jennifer pitifully, "I never wish to hear that detestable jargon again." (78–79)

If Wylie knew Max Beerbohm's work, which is highly likely, Jenny Mere of "The Happy Hypocrite" may have served her as a literary model for Jennifer. Jennifer Lorn, however, is Beerbohm's Jenny divested of power; for in Wylie's tale, innocence does not triumph over the confidence of cupidity.

Though *Jennifer Lorn* is a fantastic novel, its autobiographical element is telling. Elizabeth Shepley Sergeant, interviewing Wylie, alluded to her (perhaps more aptly than she knew) as "Jenny Forlorn."[13] Various circumstances and descriptions in the novel point to a connection between Wylie and her husbands, and the heroine's essential situation and her response to it seem to summarize the author's repressed vision of her own life. The novel, therefore, serves not only to illustrate Wylie's critical preoccupation with the delinquencies of Aestheticism but many of the personal themes that shape her work as a whole.

Jennifer's affections for Devonshire, for Scots ballads, for white and black are Wylie's. Her appearance—her red hair, slender fragility, and creamy skin—recall Wylie's as well as the heroine of the poems, for instance, with her "polished hair," "limbs fine and narrow," hollow cheeks, and "soft" skin

---

12. Beerbohm, *Zuleika Dobson*, 71.
13. Elizabeth Shepley Sergeant, *Fire Under the Andes* (New York, 1927), 121.

(*Collected Poems*, 176, 63, 277). The heroine of the poems has "a dagger in the heart" and has been "fired" "in coldest crucibles of pain" (63, 51). Hence she is desirable to men. Jennifer lacks her mysterious history but suffers deeply, if comically, in the course of the novel. A chief source of her suffering is her sexual attractiveness. Like Wylie or the woman of the poems, she longs always for escape from the dominant male to whom she is bound. The men who offer escape are either boys or father figures, impotent to help her. Her husband Gerald with his greater age, wealth, learning, and taste seems the counterpart of Horace Wylie, and the foreign exile (as Jennifer regards it) which their marriage necessitates and which plunges her into illness and gloom recalls the "Warings'." There are affection, awe, and a hint of ridicule in Wylie's treatment of Gerald's worldly knowledge, but there are distaste and pity for Jennifer in her notice of his cruelty. That characteristic seems modeled on Hichborn, particularly on Hichborn's willingness to subject his wife to trials of physical endurance and his vision of her as a decorative embellishment of the household. To make a strict series of correspondences is risky; still, the boy prince with whom Jennifer tries to run away at the novel's close is young, sensuous, and artistic—a type of Benét? And he is unsuccessful in breaking Gerald's spell over her as Benét never succeeded in relaxing Horace's hold on Elinor. His love for Jennifer makes him welcome the broken heart which she warns him may be his portion.

The emotional career of Jennifer Lorn may describe Elinor Wylie's as well as that of the persona in the poems. In *Black Armour*, published immediately after *Jennifer*, several poems discuss the actual or psychic death of a woman killed by love. Like Jennifer she has tried to please her arrogant lovers—she has been "brave," stifling her own desires; her reward is the "grave" (51). The escapes she has envisioned, recalling Jennifer's pastoral escapade, are futile; the "hut / In the middle of an alder wood"; the "cold deep death" of drowning; the hermitage beside "a water-brook" are useless to aid her either to live happily or to "tear [Mortality] / From [her] ribs" (51, 50, 49, 54, 47). Jennifer does not wish to die, but throughout her life her contented thoughts are "like a released swallow," and her death is caused by a longing for the pure release of perfect love (*Collected Prose*, 81). Jennifer and her adventures are humorously treated, whereas the fate of the heroine of *Black Armour* is viewed with anger, resentment, and frustration. Nevertheless, in *Jennifer Lorn*, Wylie created the essential story of her own life.

In that story love results in destruction. Men, excepting boys and fathers, vanquish the feminine spirit, and marriage turns the female body into an object. Poetry, the countryside, and *menus plaisirs* are palliatives, but the essential destiny of a sensitive woman is emotional starvation followed by death. It must be said, of course, that the Elinor Wylie who mocked herself in "Portrait in Black Paint," chiding,

> She's always wishing to turn back the page
> And live with children in a golden age
>
> . . . .
> Her mind might bloom, she might reform the world
> In those last hours while her hair is curled
> > > > > > > (*Collected Poems*, 277)

consistently exposes Jennifer's foolishness. She is not the brilliantly mordant heroine of the poems but the trivial-minded and childish other self Wylie always acknowledged. In 1923 Elinor Wylie was perhaps subconsciously attempting to solve the riddle of her own personality: the appetite for passion that made her life restless; the contradictory need for asexual companionship and indulgence; most of all, the quest for no constraints or bonds, especially those of commitment. Having said that she wrote fantasies because life was intolerably bitter, she dared compose a fantasy whose literary trappings did not conceal her self. *Jennifer Lorn* is one version of the "wicked destiny" to which she felt subjected (*Collected Prose*, 172).

In concluding this chapter on *Jennifer Lorn* I should like to insist upon its uniqueness by making a final series of contrasts. When it was published it was praised by three noted writers—Sinclair Lewis, James Branch Cabell, and Carl Van Vechten. Not surprisingly, Van Vechten declared it "a permanent masterpiece."[14] He had just finished *Peter Whiffle*, whose fashionably purposeless hero is constantly aware of the " '*semi-humanité des choses*': Capo di Monte porcelains . . . fantastic Venetian glass girandoles."[15] Cabell's praise was, perhaps, in retrospect, "a reflection of the quest of American literati in the Twenties for sophistication of theme, wit that bordered often upon mockery, and a graceful aestheticism that had nothing but contempt for what 'that old

14. Carl Van Vechten, Introduction to *Jennifer Lorn*, in Elinor Wylie, *Collected Prose* (New York, 1946), 8.

15. Carl Van Vechten, *Peter Whiffle, His Life and Works* (New York, 1922), 121.

lady in Dubuque might think.'"[16] As for Lewis, he was admirably capable of appreciating a style unlike his own.

Still, *Jennifer Lorn*'s critical (and popular) success is not suggested by the extant analyses that deplore it; therefore, I feel that some revisionary remarks are in order. Critics who dismiss *Jennifer Lorn* as, in Alfred Kazin's words, a "feverish and artificial book"[17]—and these include Kazin, Van Wyck Brooks, and Thomas A. Gray (whose critical study of Wylie's writing is the only one to which contemporary readers have access)—do not perceive its parodic intent. Van Wyck Brooks, for instance, groups Wylie with Joseph Hergesheimer and the Cabell of *Jurgen*, seeing in *Jennifer* their perverse escapism, their effort to write "richly and wickedly and idly,"[18] which Kazin attributed to a revolt against provincialism in American letters and philistinism in American life: "Carl Van Vechten, Hergesheimer and Elinor Wylie as a novelist . . . were all in agreement with Cabell that, in the existing world, there was little or nothing that deserved admiration or hope."[19] But Brooks's judgment, like Kazin's, fails to distinguish Elinor Wylie's vision and technique from those of her contemporaries. And the distinction is important to an understanding of her work. The novels of Cabell and Van Vechten are of more interest to scholars and historians today than they are to the general public; and the same may be said of *Jennifer Lorn*. Yet I think that will not always be so; for the novels of Elinor Wylie, despite their historical trappings, describe the difficulties of a complex feminine personality in a way that will be of increasing psychological interest. Furthermore, they are written in a style whose elegance explores the fatuity of elegance when it challenges human feeling. Wylie was eager to avoid professional connection with Cabell, justifying her rejection of a proposed title for *Jennifer*—"The Lady Stuffed with Pistachio Nuts"—on the grounds that it recalled the Cabell of *Jurgen*; and in a letter to Benét, sent from the MacDowell Colony, she implored him to find a different title that would not

16. Frederick J. Hoffman, *The Twenties* (New York, 1962), 110. See Hoffman's discussion of the "behavior and affectations" of the determinedly liberated writers of the 1920s, pp. 108–35. The expression "the old lady from Dubuque" was coined by Wylie's friend and publisher Frank Crowninshield. In managing *Vanity Fair*, he attempted to make the magazine sophisticated yet decorous, thus appealing to both young New York flappers and old ladies from the Middle West.

17. Alfred Kazin, *On Native Grounds* (New York, 1942), 242.

18. Van Wyck Brooks, *The Confident Years, 1885–1915* (New York, 1952), 526.

19. Kazin, *On Native Grounds*, 230.

associate her book with the romance of Jurgen, the pawnbroker: "Every-one—and most of all the Colums—thinks that the pistachio title is too terrible; I hate it myself, with its vague suggestion of jurgenism. Padraic wants me to call it Jennifer in Persepolis, and I would give my eternal thanks if you could think of a really good, delicate and suitably fantastic title. . . . This other I dread like a species of profanation." [20]

Cabell's *Jurgen*, the tale of a disillusioned latter-day Faust, is set in a medieval country, Poictesme, from which the middle-aged Jurgen, given a year of youth, sets forth to investigate Heaven and Hell and to meet seductive, often mythic or predatory women like Helen of Troy. Cabell is interested in the land of man's past loves and hopes and how it is translated by reality into a wasteland of "worm's meat." Jurgen, once a poet, now is committed to a life in trade; and his early love, Dorothy la Desirée, has been, like him, made "offal [by] the years." [21] The novel is replete with images like that of a boy carrying a gilded dung fork which demonstrate the ugly uses to which life presses the loveliest objects. In the contours of the novel and its diction, there is a concentration upon malformation, lubricity, and spectacle which renders it quite unlike *Jennifer Lorn*. For Wylie's delicate ironies indicate but never treat the gross, and her wit, though it can be pointed, tends always to suggest a higher spirituality to which flawed human beings may aspire. Cabell's obser-vation in *Beyond Life* that "man alone of animals plays the ape to his dreams" [22] illustrates as well as any the difference between his vision and Elinor Wylie's. His novels sanction romantic escapism with the understanding that man is ludicrously corrupt but needy; in the necessary act of dreaming he is some-how all the more an "ape." Elinor Wylie's novels are full of dreamers, but their dreams, like her middle-aged poet Mr. Hazard's, ennoble them further; and there are in the worlds she creates experiences sufficiently beautiful to inspire dreams that are not escapist but celebrations of what is actual.

If one contrasts *Jennifer Lorn* with Carl Van Vechten's *Peter Whiffle*, written a year before it, one sees many differences between Wylie's style and concep-tions and those of Van Vechten. *Peter Whiffle* is faithfully patterned on Huys-mans' story of the decadent Des Esseintes in his "novel" *A Rebours*, or *Against*

---

20. Letter in Wylie Archive.
21. James Branch Cabell, *Jurgen* (New York, 1927), 35, 51.
22. James Branch Cabell, *Beyond Life* (New York, 1924), 45.

Nature. Like Des Esseintes, Peter Whiffle is a dandy in continuous search of sensations. With a dog called George Moore, he inhabits various chic dwellings, playing at love and toying with art, delivering himself to Van Vechten—who appears in the novel as his friend—of Aesthetic pronouncements like "All great art is a matter of cataloguing life"; or "I am not trying to imitate Dickens or Dostoevsky. They did not write books. They wrote newspapers." The novel takes Whiffle, who dies at the end, seriously despite his surname and recommends occult fiction like the tales of Arthur Machen, about "the disintegration of a soul through an encounter with the mysteries which we are forbidden to know." Whiffle never writes his book; Van Vechten writes about him instead in "a sort of loose biographical form, a free fantasia in the manner of a Liszt Rhapsody." The "rhapsod[ic]" form, reminiscent of the synaesthetic experiments of the Symbolists and, after them, the Decadents and Whistler; the fascination with evil and debility; the contempt for a life of meaning are all treated with earnest fascination by Van Vechten. Van Vechten's prose is often a tissue of scarcely modified clichés amid uninspired description: "It was Spring in Paris and I was young! The chestnut trees were heavy with white blossoms and the air was laden with their perfume. I gazed down the Champs-Elysées, surely the true Elysian Fields, a myriad of lights shining through the dark green, the black, leaved branches. I do not think I spoke many words and I know that Albert did not. He may have been bored, but I think he derived some slight pleasure from my juvenile enthusiasm for, although Paris was old hat to him, he loved this particular old hat." [23]

In Elinor Wylie's *Jennifer Lorn* attention is paid to exoticism of setting and object; to a modified expression of evil in the acquisitiveness of Gerald; to the idea of sensuality, in the prince and the Banou; and to the preference for minor art and great experiences seen superficially which Peter Whiffle exhibits. But in Wylie's novel, this attention assumes the function of exposure. We may, for instance, be amused by Gerald Ponyard's egotism; but at the conclusion of the book his sadism is apparent. *Jennifer Lorn* lightly treats the Aesthetic biases that Peter Whiffle and his "biographer" indulge. Furthermore, Wylie's prose in its figurative intricacy and respect for compositional form bears no resemblance to the often plodding informality of Van Vechten's.

Elinor Wylie is supposed to have shared with Joseph Hergesheimer a

23. Van Vechten, *Peter Whiffle*, 52, 8, 21.

respect for setting as interior decoration. If one reads his representative *Linda Condon*, published in 1919 with a dedication to Carl Van Vechten, one again encounters a different intention from Elinor Wylie's in *Jennifer*. Like Hergesheimer's other books, *Linda Condon* is a novel devoted far more to a realistic redaction of life than any of Wylie's novels. At first about the young Linda, growing up in hotels with a widowed mother who becomes a *demi-mondaine* to support them, the story eventually concerns itself with her mature disillusionment and understanding that a handsome face is useful in a heartless world. It is true that Hergesheimer's settings in *Linda Condon* are employed to distinguish modes of feeling and differences in social back-ground; hence the ascetic house of the Lowries, Linda's New England rela-tives, is quite unlike the sumptuous mansion of the *parvenu* Feldts in New York City, into whose family Linda's mother marries.

Elinor Wylie, however, unlike Hergesheimer, does not attempt in fiction to comment on the life of contemporary society. Her use of setting is given, different from his, to a contemplation of the ethereal otherworld, to the evanescent flutterings of spiritual aspiration and romantic feeling, which could be prompted by the elegances of this world. A comparison of two descriptive passages from the novels of each writer makes this distinction evident:

> They were at lunch in the Feldt dining-room, an interior of heavy, ornately carved black wood, panels of Chinese embroidery in imperial yellow, and a neutral mauve carpet. The effect, with glittering iridescent pyramids of glass, massive frosted repoussé silver, burnished goldplate, and a wide table decoration of orchids and fern, was tropical and intense.[24]

> The long conservatory was dimly lit; after the scintillant atmosphere of the ball-room, where brilliance was shattered into prismatic confusion by countless tinkling icicles of glass in sconce and chandelier, it was a lane of blue dusk, a tropic night striped with stupendous fronds; it was vaulted with palms and hung with ropes of fragrance. High overhead three incredible moons floated in space; the yellow Chinese tissue of which they were fashioned bore a thin tracery of wave. (77)

Hergesheimer's writing serves his purpose of expressing the opulence of the Feldts' taste and their ability to support it. Elinor Wylie's paragraph

---

24. Joseph Hergesheimer, *Linda Condon* (New York, 1919), 87–88.

strives intead after the affinity between things and nature, the emotional and spiritual effects things may ideally produce. Her description moves toward the ethereal: the conservatory becomes "a lane of blue dusk"; the balloons above it are "three incredible moons." Here artificial objects are dignified by their resemblance to the natural world; the poetry of each is improved by association.

One is reminded in reading such a passage, not of the works of Cabell, Van Vechten, or Hergesheimer but, more particularly, of the lyrical relationship between fine things and tender dreams posed in a novel like *The Great Gatsby.* For although Elinor Wylie's intention in *Jennifer Lorn* is to demonstrate, as the eighteenth-century novel liked to do, that any mania is deadly; and although it is clear that she finds the Aesthetic excesses of her characters worthy of comic reproach, she never fails to suggest the loveliness of created things and those ways in which they may inspire in the beholder a spiritual imagination. When such an imagination renders the beholder vulnerable, as it (realistically) does in *Gatsby*, as it does in the fanciful case of Abbas or the richer one of Rosalba of *The Venetian Glass Nephew*, then the pathos of human aspiration toward beauty triumphs as a bitter and inevitable theme.

Edgar Allan Poe's pronouncement in *The Poetic Principle*, that "inspired by an ecstatic prescience of the glories beyond the grave, we struggle, by multiform combinations among the things and thoughts of Time, to attain a portion of that Loveliness whose very elements, perhaps, appertain to eternity alone"[25] bears relation to the art of Elinor Wylie, even in her humorous novel, *Jennifer Lorn*. In it, two men see one girl's beauty as paradigmatic of a superior reality (and for Poe, a beautiful woman, especially a weak or dead one, was such a paradigm). *Jennifer Lorn* burlesques the characteristic failure of broad human sympathy that is the brittle failing of Aestheticism. Elinor Wylie probably chose such a theme because she was herself instinctively, if not contentedly, prone to the symbolic affection for porcelain instead of human beings; because she had noted the same predilection in some of her colleagues; because novels like Van Vechten's aped the surface (rather than the moral resonances) of the Wildean mode, with little sense of its inherent solecisms and injustice. Max Beerbohm, too, had been admitted to a company of Aesthetes, seeing past their postures to a more general truth about life.

25. Edgar Allan Poe, "The Poetic Principle," *Works*, ed. John H. Ingram (4 vols., Edinburgh, 1874–75), III, 205.

In *The Venetian Glass Nephew* Elinor Wylie was to draw a finer net about the habits of mind she undertakes to define in *Jennifer Lorn*. Still, her first novel shows that she had found a subject in Aestheticism—and, particularly, at that extreme at which it became Decadence. Her life and her reading well acquainted her with it. And she could amuse the innocent reader, while warning the more knowledgeable one that Aestheticism in America, as in the England of the 1890s, deserved the recognition of criticism.

CHAPTER III · DEBUT AS AESTHETE
THE EARLY POEMS

As bright white drops upon a leaden sea
Grant so my songs to this grey folk may be:
EZRA POUND, "Grace Before Song,"
A Lume Spento

*ncidental Numbers*, a small collection of verses composed between 1902 and 1911, was Elinor Wylie's first book of poems. Privately printed in England, in an edition of only about sixty copies, the book's pale blue binding and navy lettering imitated an edition of Blake's *Songs of Innocence*. Copies were presented as gifts to Elinor's family and acquaintances. Her mother paid the publication costs.[1] When *Incidental Numbers* appeared, Elinor was twenty-seven years old and living out of wedlock with Horace Wylie in Burley, England. The scandal created by her elopement had cost her her social position in America; her former friends were "convinced that she was done for, socially, and . . . that she had not the courage to form herself into a writer or painter."[2] The slender

---

1. Nancy Hoyt, *Elinor Wylie: The Portrait of an Unknown Lady* (New York, 1935), 36. John D. Gordan, however, says that Horace Wylie paid the publication costs of *Incidental Numbers* ("A Legend Revisited: Elinor Wylie," *American Scholar*, XXXVII [Summer, 1969], 26).
2. Hoyt, *Elinor Wylie*, 26.

volume was testimony to the author's determination to discipline her energies despite the ambiguity and turmoil of her life.

The poetic style is experimental, and there is no single poem worthy of inclusion in Elinor Wylie's second volume, *Nets to Catch the Wind*. Nevertheless, there are continuities between *Incidental Numbers* and her later work. The poems exhibit the interest in technical refinement—metrical variations, inventive rhyming patterns, subtle changes of measure or sound within apparently simple poetic frames—developed in her later volumes. Its themes —magic and enchantment, distress in love, the beauties of nocturnal landscape or of the pastoral in general, pleasure in certain colors, particularly white and silver—consistently reappear later. Even the book's title, *Incidental*, suggesting the author's diffidence (and a nuance of the proud self-deprecation also evident, for example, in *Trivial Breath*), and *Numbers*, directing attention to the poems as exercises in verbal music, establishes a discreet and formal note typical of the later poems.

The volume is eclectic. Both the prose and the poetry of Elinor Wylie always exhibit influences, even borrowings. Most of these are deliberately courted or included for artistic purposes and subsumed into her own style. In *Incidental Numbers*, however, rather than the mature Wylie's characteristic voice, one hears the voice of a poet who has herself heard several voices.

Despite Wylie's lifelong interest in Shelley, his poetry does not instruct her juvenilia. Despite her conscious femininity she does not take significant lessons from such women poets as Emily Dickinson,[3] Christina Rossetti, or

3. There is no evidence that Elinor Wylie ever read the poetry of Emily Dickinson. First published in 1891 when Wylie was eight years old, Dickinson's poetry did not achieve full critical recognition in the United States until the 1930s, after Elinor Wylie's death. It was for the most part disparaged in England, Wylie's adopted country, during her lifetime. Nevertheless, certain similarities between Dickinson's poetry and Wylie's might be pointed out. Each writes frequently in quatrains, though Dickinson's are basically indebted to Isaac Watts and the tradition of Renaissance poetry while Elinor Wylie's have more immediate antecedents in the quatrains of the late nineteenth-century English poets. Both often employ a metaphysical idiom when writing of love. See my article on Dickinson, "'Compound Manner': Emily Dickinson and the Metaphysical Poets," *American Literature*, XXXII (January, 1961), 471–33; and my article, "Elinor Wylie, Edna St. Vincent Millay, and the Elizabethan Sonnet Tradition," in *Poetic Traditions of the English Renaissance*, ed. Maynard Mack and George de Forest Lord (New Haven: 1982), 287–305. One could make other comparisons as to common themes such as the value of solitude, the importance of self-reliance, and the power of others' contumely to prompt one to endurance and survival. But the imagination of each poet is, I think, ultimately different. For a striking—and perhaps coincidental—similarity between the work of each, see below, note 21.

Emily Brontë. (Rossetti's melodious quatrains may have appealed to her, but *Incidental Numbers*, for all its visual qualities, shows none of Rossetti's anguish or Gothic power). Wylie's early poems reflect knowledge of male poets fashionable when she was a girl and doubtless appreciated by Horace Wylie. They were the same poets read by Eliot, Stevens, Pound, and everyone else who began to think about writing poetry in the early 1900s: the poets of the Aesthetic movement.

Wylie's "The Fairy," for instance, which is typical of the collection, exhibits that affection for folklore common to some early poems of Yeats and de la Mare as well as a lush yet artificial and visionary landscape and a concern with traditional metrics and intricate rhyming patterns that these poets, in their youth, shared with the Aesthete Ernest Dowson.

"The Fairy" is the song of a sprite separated from his adventurous and "magical kin." Hearing their wild singing through long nights in valleys mortals love for their safety, he vows someday to escape his enclosure and to join his fellows:

> The folk of the valleys
>   They are not my kin,
> They walk in cool alleys
>   Green gardens within,
> Through closes of roses
>   And orchards within.
>
> Their feet are submitted
>   To pathways secure,
> My footsteps have flitted
>   From lure to bright lure
> Of rillsides' and hillsides'
>   More perilous lure.
>   . . . .
> Some midnight when mortals
>   Are sleeping I'll win
> My way past the portals
>   Of cloud to my kin,
> And meet them, and greet them—
>   My magical kin.
>
> On the moon-whitened meadows,
>   That look to the sky

> Like silvery shadows,
>   We'll dance, they and I,
> With laughter, hereafter,
>   Forever and aye.[4]

"The Fairy" is a slight poem, and it is musical. Its theme of escape prefigures later Wylie poems in which the speaker sets herself apart from the human world. But it is chiefly interesting because its rhyme patterns, ghostly pastoral, and diction call to mind the work of Dowson and Yeats.

Dowson's "Beata Solitudo" describes a "silent valley"

> Where all the voices
>   Of humankind
> Are left behind.[5]

Although the poem's persona does not crave merry company, his imaginary land "where pale stars shine" has much in common with the fairy's. And Wylie's landscape composed of white heather, moonlight, and silver shadows and of green gardens with "closes of roses" recalls the moonlit landscape of Dowson's *The Pierrot of the Minute*, the twilit aura of his love lyrics in "Amor Profanus," and the stayed, artificial greenery of "Coronal." Dowson, too, habitually used "closes of roses"—in "Sapientia Lunae," in "The Garden of Shadow," in "You Would Have Understood Me, Had You Waited," and in "Vitae summa brevis spem nos vetat incohare longam" (They are not long, the weeping and the laughter). It is, of course, an inevitable rhyme; George Herbert rhymes "closes" with "roses" in "Vertue." But the presence in Wylie's "Fairy" of many trappings reminiscent of Dowson—not only the wistful pose of alienation but the setting, theatrically lit in silver, and the languorous language—suggests that his verse served her as one of several models in this early period.

Another model was the early verse of Yeats, whose poems she seems to have known well. *Nets to Catch the Wind* borrows occasional images from Yeats, and Wylie's review of his autobiographical prose shows pronounced interest in his life. (In the only critical review she ever wrote, Edna St. Vincent Millay,

---

4. Elinor Wylie, *Incidental Numbers* (London, 1912), 7–8. Copy in the Berg Collection of English and American Literature, New York Public Library.

5. Mark Longaker (ed.), *The Poems of Ernest Dowson* (Philadelphia, 1962), 71.

later a close friend, scolded Wylie for the abject Yeatsianism of "Madman's Song."[6]) Yeats's poem "The Stolen Child," published in *The Crossways* volume of 1889 which Wylie had probably read by 1909 when she was writing "The Fairy," presents a situation similar to that of her poem. In it a "human child" escapes to the realm of faerie, leaving behind a world "full of weeping" but also of comforting pleasures—a kettle on a hob, calves on warm hillsides, the "oatmeal-chest"—akin to the mortal attractions of Wylie's poem with its "cool alleys," "green gardens," and "pathways secure." Yeats's fairy speaker attracts the child with a description of wild dances under the moon that resembles Wylie's:

> Where the wave of moonlight glosses
> The dim grey sands with light,
> Far off by furthest Rosses
> We foot it all the night,
> Weaving olden dances,
> Mingling hands and mingling glances
> Till the moon has taken flight.

Yeats's vague moonlit landscape is akin to Wylie's "moon-whitened meadows" and fairies that move "like silvery shadows." Each poem depicts human life as unfavorable to transport or happiness and the escapist delights of the fairy world as worth striving for.

"The Fairy"'s theme of alienation from the actual is found, too, in the poetry of Walter de la Mare, who became a friend of Wylie's and shared her interest in porcelain, silver, and small objects. In his first book, *Songs of Childhood* (1902), he created a haunted world of reverie and enchantment, a world of pale moonlight where both trees and people are spectral. The poem "The Fairies Dancing" in that volume depicts "fairies in a ring" who "Sing as they tripped a lilting round / Soft as the moon on wavering wing." The poem's speaker watches day rise, the fairies' "beauty" lie "as a mist," and their singing grow faint under the roar of sunlight. The landscape, waking him "from moonlit dreams," seems somehow diminished, despoiled of the radiance of magic.

If de la Mare's attraction to a gentle landscape, to dream states, and to

6. See Edna St. Vincent Millay, "Elinor Wylie's Poetry," *Saturday Evening Post*, January 28, 1922.

ideas of sterile perfection or uncanny glamour invites comparison to Elinor Wylie's preoccupation with them in *Incidental Numbers*, so also does his fascination with whiteness. The use of the word *white* to create an aura of romantic mystery and an obsession with the conceit of whiteness, seen to represent many states from purity of soul or form to neurosis, were characteristic of the Aesthetic movement, described by Holbrook Jackson in *The Eighteen Nineties.*[7] In *Incidental Numbers* Elinor Wylie demonstrates this Aesthetic interest in the idea of white and its more lustrous counterpart, silver; she retained that interest throughout her writing career. Dorothy Parker remarked in *The New Yorker* (March 21, 1928), only a few months before Wylie's death, "It is impossible, I think, to write of [her] or her work without somewhere using the word 'silver.' It is her word, made for her." "Birches" and other poems in *Incidental Numbers* which describe trees like sylphs "slim in their silver white / Nothing defaces," glimmering "pale in the ardent light," "slender in shining white" present an ideal of Aesthetic perfection founded— as in many poems of Dowson, Johnson, Arthur Symons, Yeats, or in the paintings of the Aesthete James McNeill Whistler—on the conceit of luminous whiteness.

Although her later volumes make the relation of Elinor Wylie to the Aesthetes more imperative, *Incidental Numbers* reveals a sensibility that instinctively chose themes and language reminiscent of theirs. Poems like "Eve in Heaven," which honors the carnal experience of Eve above the innocence of the Virgin Mary; "To Paolo and Francesca in Purgatory," which values passion, not purity; "The Knight Fallen on Evil Days," a tribute to learning, Satan, and solitary endeavor recall the iconoclasm of the Aesthetes; their interest in religion, scholarship, and legend; their whimsy; and their absorption in their craft. Carl Van Doren is correct in saying that Elinor Wylie was not a precocious poet.[8] *Incidental Numbers* marks the debut of a promising amateur whereas *Nets to Catch the Wind*, published ten years later in 1921, is the work of a much more assured writer with a more complex and developed imagination. Nonetheless, *Incidental Numbers* contains distinct Aesthetic patterns of vision and technique that characterized Elinor Wylie's art throughout her career.

7. Holbrook Jackson, *The Eighteen Nineties* (New York, 1966), esp. pp. 140–42.
8. Carl Van Doren, *Three Worlds* (New York, 1936), 220.

By 1921, Elinor Hichborn, then thirty-six, had at last become the legal wife of Horace Wylie. She had suffered a great deal and was shortly to renounce the husband for whose love she had suffered. Whether her bookish seclusion with the literate Wylie had helped her to shape an artistic vision and whether the pain of censure and isolation had hurt her into real poetry, the verse that appeared in *Nets to Catch the Wind* had the technical finish promised by her juvenilia but an intellectual and emotional content that could not have been predicted from it. She appeared on the literary firmament, said the Boston *Transcript* (November 30, 1921), with "amazing suddenness." *Nets to Catch the Wind*, her first professional book, won the Julia Ellsworth Ford prize for the best collection of poems published in 1921, the year Edna Millay brought out *Second April*, Marianne Moore, *Poems*, and H.D., *Hymen*. Edmund Wilson declared that *Nets to Catch the Wind* was not the work of a tyro. Its "style" and "accuracy" "never misse[d]; its colors [were] always right—two qualities exceedingly rare in contemporary American verse."[9]

The title of *Nets to Catch the Wind*, borrowed from a play of John Webster's,[10] draws attention to the idea of art. Wylie's poems were, like fine-spun nets, to trap the wind, identified with reality or, in the Romantic context of Wylie's favorite poets, with the wind, imagination. Babette Deutsch called the volume "almost one uninterrupted cry to escape";[11] and certainly the quest for escape from a hostile, ugly, or commonplace world is the subject of many poems. Yet the subject is variously viewed and treated with complacency, alarm, rejection, sublimation. The reader realizes that what hurt the woman, the "Proud Lady" of the poem that identifies Wylie as the victim of society's "finger of hate" (*Collected Poems*, 32), helped turn the poet to the craft of verse. It is art which begins to suggest itself in *Nets to Catch the Wind* as a mainstay for the author.

Three basic themes are presented in the volume: the scornful indignities

---

9. Edmund Wilson, Jr., "The Bronze Trumpet of Fairyland," *Bookman*, LIV (1922), 579.
10. The phrase appears in Leonora's funeral speech in *The Devil's Law Case*, V.v:

> Vain the ambition of kings,
> Who seek by trophies and dead things
> To leave a living name behind,
> And weave but nets to catch the wind.

11. Babette Deutsch, "Proud Lady," *Virginia Quarterly Review*, VIII (October, 1932), 618.

suffered by the poet-speaker at the hands of a malicious and stupid world; her need to escape the world either by pastoral withdrawal, sleep, or death; and the attractions of a private universe of beautiful sights and objects which so stimulate the persona's imagination that she is able to conquer the world by art.

"Beauty," the first lyric in the volume, expresses the latter theme, its placement in the book implying its dominance. It is a significant poem not only for its technical proficiency—its internal variations show Wylie's skill with quatrains—but because, like others in the volume, it assumes attitudes toward art and its relation to the life of feeling which are Aesthetic:

> Say not of Beauty she is good,
> Or aught but beautiful,
> Or sleek to doves' wings of the wood
> Her wild wings of of a gull.
>
> Call her not wicked; that word's touch
> Consumes her like a curse;
> But love her not too much, too much,
> For that is even worse.
>
> O, she is neither good nor bad,
> But innocent and wild!
> Enshrine her and she dies, who had
> The hard heart of a child. (3)

Beauty, the spirit informing art, is commendable not for those qualities of goodness, generosity, or civility praised in the moral order but for absoluteness and independence. Like Ariel, whom W. H. Auden represents in *The Sea and the Mirror* as an "unfeeling god," Beauty has the "hard heart of a child" and is to be valued for wildness and for her hostility to confinement and idealization alike. Elinor Wylie's Beauty, like Oscar Wilde's in the Preface to *The Picture of Dorian Gray* or Whistler's in the "Ten O'Clock Lecture," is "neither good nor bad." When Wilde wrote, "They are the elect to whom beautiful things mean only Beauty,"[12] he expressed the sentiment of Wylie's opening lines. When Whistler mocked the idea of "Beauty . . . confounded with virtue" and claimed that art is "selfishly occupied with [its] own perfection

12. Oscar Wilde, Preface, *The Picture of Dorian Gray*, in *Works*, ed. G. F. Maine (London, 1954), 17.

only,"[13] he defended the superiority of the creative spirit to partisan claim. Beauty to Elinor Wylie, as to Wilde and Whistler, is its own reason for being; it may not be expected to serve ethical values. Wylie's warning, "love her not too much," however, is significant in light of the poems and prose works she later wrote, many of which teach the enchantment of aesthetic objects and of art yet deplore excessive Aestheticism.

The second poem in *Nets to Catch the Wind*, "The Eagle and the Mole," unites the themes of pain and escapism prominent in the volume. Widely anthologized, it earned the respect of William Butler Yeats, who told Dorothy Wellesley that it was his "sole excitement" in an otherwise bleak period.[14] It might have been expected to capture his fancy, for its Blakean and Words-worthian echoes and its conformity to the hermetic and escapist spirit of *Childe Harold, III*, support a Neo-Romantic attack on society and a preference for proud aloofness and dependency on nature that also inform many of Yeats's poems. The lyric is hortatory, an example of the economic emphasis Wylie managed well:

> Avoid the reeking herd,
> Shun the polluted flock,
> Live like that stoic bird,
> The eagle of the rock.
>
> The huddled warmth of crowds
> Begets and fosters hate;
> He keeps, above the clouds,
> His cliff inviolate.
>
> . . . .
>
> If you would keep your soul
> From spotted sight or sound,
> Live like the velvet mole;
> Go burrow underground.
>
> And there hold intercourse
> With roots of trees and stones,
> With rivers at their source,
> And disembodied bones. (4)

13. James Abbott McNeill Whistler, *The Gentle Art of Making Enemies* (1890; reprint, New York, 1967), 137, 136.

14. William Butler Yeats, *Letters*, ed. Allan Wade (London, 1954), 836.

The poem rejects the contamination of society in favor of secretive contact with the private world of imagination nourished by nature. Its choice of alternatives recalls that of Thel's motto in Blake's *Book of Thel*, a poem which treats the problem of art and reality: "Does the Eagle know what is in the pit? / Or wilt thou go ask the Mole?"[15] The contempt directed at the "reeking herd," "the polluted flock," "the huddled warmth of crowds" which "begets and fosters hate" recalls Childe Harold's conviction that he was "the most unfit / Of men to herd with Man," whose mindless constraints translated him from "a wild-born falcon . . . / To whom the boundless air alone were home" into "a thing / Restless and worn."[16] Wylie recommends the eagle's life, akin to the falcon's. It is a solitary bird, sharp of sight, spectacular in daring, a Romantic metaphor of superb achievement. Yet, Wylie says, not everyone is strong enough to reach its sphere. Some, to avoid "spotted sight or sound," secular distractions that cheapen an artist's gift, must sequester themselves from society in a humbler way. They must "live like the velvet mole; / Go burrow underground." With this requisite detachment, they may then attain to that productive union with nature Wordsworth attributes to Lucy in "A slumber did my spirit seal." For in that elegy, the dead girl, withdrawn from life, finds a more enduring life:

> No motion has she now, no force;
> She neither hears nor sees;
> Rolled round in earth's diurnal course,
> With rocks, and stones, and trees.[17]

Wylie's choice of "trees" and "stones" recalls Wordsworth's, and perhaps his use of "force" and "course" unconsciously suggested itself in her "intercourse" and "source." Her poem, like many Romantic and Neo-Romantic poems, recommends a personal disengagement that results in superior artistic engagement. Emblematic of her own experience in which attraction to a life of scintillation was matched and corrected by commitment to a life of

15. William Blake, *"Thel's Motto," The Book of Thel,* in G. E. Bentley, Jr. (ed.), *William Blake's Writings* (2 vols.; Oxford, 1978), I, 62.

16. Lord Byron, *Childe Harold's Pilgrimage and Other Romantic Poems,* ed. Samuel C. Chew (New York, 1936), 88–89, "Childe Harold's Pilgrimage," Canto the Third, XII, lines 100–101; XV, lines 129–30, 127–28.

17. William Wordsworth, *The Poems,* ed. John O. Hayden (2 vols.; New Haven, 1977), I, 364.

thought, the poem synthesizes the proud passion for isolation that appears elsewhere in *Nets to Catch the Wind*.

"Madman's Song," which immediately follows, for example, enjoins

> Better to see your cheek grown hollow,
> Better to see your temple worn,
> Than to forget to follow, follow,
> After the sound of a silver horn.

However Yeatsian the image of the "silver horn" may be, the advice and antitheses of "Madman's Song" are characteristic of Elinor Wylie. She, who so respected the allure of physical beauty, placed it second to the lure of art. It was better to grow old in the "hunt" for ideal form than "to sleep with your head on a golden pillow": better to be "sallow" and gray early than to abandon the imagination's quest "after the milk-white hounds of the moon" (5). If such advice was a "madman's," counter to that offered by a society interested in the cosmetic and comfortable, it was also Dionysian, hence practical for an artist.

"The Falcon," a later poem in *Nets to Catch the Wind*, poses similar antitheses: the life of the imitative crowd versus the adventurous one of the imaginative artist. Two voices speak, the first wondering and troubled; the second, assertive and explanatory: the two selves, perhaps, of the poet. This poem declares that it is possible to domesticate imagination by the effort of craft and the gift of love. And, though she is a falcon—relative of the fierce eagle—she may be wooed with "a chain of silver twist," "a little hood of scarlet wool": small, exquisite offerings that recall the Aesthetic preoccupation with small objects, a preoccupation Elinor Wylie shared. In "Sunset on the Spire," a poem of seclusion and rapturous involvement with an image of aspiration that suggests the imaginative life, Elinor Wylie clarifies her commitment to art and her conviction that she is an artist. In that poem, food, drink, lover, and friend exist for her in the particularly dramatic, efflorescent moment in which sunset lights a spire. A description of the marriage of nature and artifice—the spire upward-tending like her eagle or falcon—the poem reveals the devotion to art, particularly decorative art ("thin gold mask"), for which she would become famous. Poems like these suggest that *Nets to Catch the Wind* is not a simple "cry to escape" but an effort to embrace a finer life than the ordinary offers. Other poems in the volume clearly describe that world which makes escape appealing or necessary.

"The Church-Bell," for instance, characterizes the mob of men as unable to tolerate a call to self-esteem, valor, or joy. Feet pounding monotonously, their market-carts rumbling, they ignore the bell which has "gone mad" from their indifference, and when its exhortation to freedom of mind becomes too loud and sweet, they tear "its living tongue / Out by the very root" (16–17).

"The Church-Bell" describes spiritual impoverishment in a country setting. In "A Crowded Trolley Car," the setting is urban, but the cowardice and villainy of humanity remain the same. With a use of synecdoche that contrives a nearly surrealistic vision, the poem defines trolley riders in terms of apparently disembodied hands and glances. One rider hangs from his strap like a hanged man. Others resemble Bluebeard's murdered wives, dangling by their hair. In a process of association that grows increasingly nightmarish, the riders become an "Orchard of the strangest fruits / Hanging from the skies." Insensitive, hateful to one another, they are reduced to brutishness by fear; and they repay courage and integrity with death. For the images of murder reach their fulfillment in the last quatrain of the poem in which the hand of Christ is nailed to the cross.

Nets to Catch the Wind finds various antidotes to the pain of living in a hostile world. "Bells in the Rain" contemplates the way in which nature, in this case sleep, heals those whom the world afflicts, "a live man's bloody head." The sleep of the dead, a "deep peace," is contrasted with the "tender[er]" peace afforded to the dreaming living to whom sleep on a rainy evening comes like the rain in "bells of glass / Thinned by the wind, and lightly blown" (11). Droplets of rain, compared to frail glass, and moments of respite from the tortures of life come together in an imagery of artifice that demonstrates Elinor Wylie's Aesthetic response to experience. As the ordered and perishable object—glass, crystal, porcelain—occurred to Théophile Gautier or Oscar Wilde as examples of the beautiful or hopeful, so did they to Wylie. For her in life as in metaphor, the well-wrought artifact implied a tranquility and comeliness to which human nature aspired with difficulty. In "Bells in the Rain," the answer to grief is semi-inanition, depicted in the static shapeliness of artifice.

"Winter Sleep," "Escape," "Sanctuary," and others propose avoidance of a world inimical, particularly to artists, but do so ambivalently. The "little house" (modest counterpart of Yeats "small cabin" in Innisfree) built by the speaker of "Escape" is related to the deadly "sanctuary" which ultimately denies life to the poet-speaker. In the contradictions of her treatment of the theme of withdrawal from the world, Wylie discloses the effects of a sympathetic reading of Yeats.

She handles the theme best in "Wild Peaches." This series of four related, capable sonnets entertains the romantic quest for escape, then rises into acceptance of the world's harshness, symbolically expressed, as elsewhere in the volume, by resignation to the idea of winter.

In the first three sonnets, the speaker and her companion decide, "When the world turns completely upside down," to "emigrate to the Eastern Shore / Aboard a riverboat from Baltimore." In fact, theirs is a retreat to the American past Elinor Wylie would describe in *The Orphan Angel*; for one wears a "coonskin cap" and the other "a gown / Homespun, dyed butternut's dark gold colour." The companion has a "lotus-eating ancestor" to whose euphoria the speaker relates their own: "We'll swim in milk and honey till we drown" (11). Capacious, their images painterly and vivid, the first sonnets concentrate on benign seasons:

> The months between the cherries and the peaches
> Are brimming cornucopias which spill
> Fruits red and purple, sombre-bloomed and black;
> Then, down rich fields and frosty river beaches
> We'll trample bright persimmons, while you kill
> Bronze partridge, speckled quail, and canvasback.

In response to such revelry of feeling and sensuousness of theme, however, the speaker in the concluding sonnet bursts forth in distaste of lush escapism. The companion does not appear in this last sonnet. The speaker, no longer accommodating, defends an asceticism of the inner heart, and the lines are resolute, lively with conviction, even as those of the earlier sonnets seem leisurely and playful.

> Down to the Puritan marrow of my bones
> There's something in this richness that I hate.
> I love the look, austere, immaculate,
> Of landscapes drawn in pearly monotones.

> There's something in my very blood that owns
> Bare hills, cold silver on a sky of slate,
> A thread of water, churned to milky spate
> Streaming through slanted pastures fenced with stones.
>
> I love those skies, thin blue or snowy gray,
> Those fields sparse-planted, rendering meagre sheaves;
> That spring, briefer than apple-blossom's breath,
> Summer, so much too beautiful to stay,
> Swift autumn, like a bonfire of leaves,
> And sleepy winter, like the sleep of death. (12–13)

The landscape at last elected in "Wild Peaches" resembles that of New England, "drawn in pearly monotones"; it is symbolic of an earnest life in which effort and hardship earn a beauty that is more poignant because it is spare and short-lived. In the earlier sonnets of the sequence, the speaker had envisioned a dream life of ease and plenty wherein "the squirrels in their silver fur will fall / Like falling leaves, like fruit, before [the] shot." Coddled by this imaginary nature lavish with strawberries, chestnuts, cider, and plums, she had promised in the octave of the third sonnet, "We shall live well—we shall live very well." Living well, however, is redefined in the last sonnet. There the speaker, declaring herself a "Puritan," abandons idyllic for Spartan pleasures. Now, "thin blue or snowy gray" skies, "bare hills," "meagre sheaves," "a thread of water" (compared with the "ocean swell" of the third sonnet) offer a parsimonious yet more valuable context in which to understand the significance of time and existence. The sestet of the sonnet hastens toward conclusion and the word "death" with a speedy propriety that suggests the brevity of life, like the brevity of spring and summer in New England. The poem entices biographical comment, and one is reminded by the line "There's something in this richness that I hate" of the Elinor Wylie who, however "thriftless of gold and prodigal of love," prided herself on the "strict ascetic habit of control / That industry ha[d] woven for [her] soul": on a life ultimately committed to the labor of art (308).

These essential alternatives—the prospect of escape through death or solitude or the wiser choice of triumphing over a hostile world by valor and by art—repeat themselves consistently in *Nets to Catch the Wind*. The latter alternative assumes higher importance and does so increasingly in Elinor

Wylie's later volumes of verse. Yet the former theme, continually qualified, is never abandoned.

Several poems in *Nets to Catch the Wind* characterize the form of art to which Wylie's personae turn for satisfaction. One lyric, "The Fairy Goldsmith," delights in a litany of rare and special objects wrought with magic craft, objects to which the real world is enemy. The poem attempts a tour de force of the decorative imagination, musically celebrating the charm of artifacts that imitate nature but are in their plasticity more formal and (ironically) in their whimsicality less durable than her products.

"The Fairy Goldsmith" offers "wonderful things" to the admiring observer, all of them miniature, "carven and cut / In intricate ways." Yet though he is aware of their perfection as artifacts, he concedes their uselessness in a real world.

> Touch them and take them,
> But do not break them!
> Beneath your hand
> They will wither like foam
> If you carry them home
> Out of fairy-land.
>
> O, they never can last
> Though you hide them fast
> From moth and from rust;
> In your monstrous day
> They will crumble away
> Into quicksilver dust. (26)

Cherries made of onyx; buds of jade; gilded bees in "amber drops / Which look like honey" but are artificial, not natural; a girl wrought of mother-of-pearl: in each case, jewels crafted by the goldsmith substitute for the living reality. The transitory hence appealing natural phenomena, frost and rain (and sounds: "frail notes lost / From a fairy lute"), are translated into filigree and a chain of turquoises.

The goldsmith's bubble is made of opal. But the glamour of these artifacts is restricted to the world of imagination for in the "monstrous day" of real life they would "crumble away," their loveliness a function of fragility and precious wit.

"The Fairy Goldsmith," a small paradigm of the conceits of *The Venetian Glass Nephew*, reveals that devotion to gems, to colors sensuous or austere, to delicate and intricate small objects found in the literature of the Aesthetes. The charms of the exquisite—all the more charming because they cannot easily survive in the crude arena of ordinary life—are drawn with desire here as they are, for instance, in Wilde's *Picture of Dorian Gray*. In her review of Yeats's autobiographical prose, Elinor Wylie spoke of the "tragedy of [Wilde's] ruin" and appeared to have thought about Wilde—if, as she confessed, ungenerously—for some time.[18] Humorous passages in her novels recall his wit; opulently perfumed phrases in the novels and in some poems evoke his exoticism; and she is of course concerned, like Wilde, with the relationship between life and art. In the gem catalog of *Dorian Gray*—itself, perhaps, influenced by the tortoise episode in Huysmans' *A Rebours*—there appears a fascination with jewels similar to that of "The Fairy Goldsmith" with "the olive-green chrysoberyl that turns red by lamplight, the cymophane with its wire-like line of silver, the pistachio-coloured peridot, rose-pink and wine-yellow topazes, carbuncles of fiery scarlet with tremulous four-rayed stars, flame-red cinnamon-stones. . . . the red-gold of the sunstone, and the moonstone's pearly whiteness, and the broken rainbow of the milky opal."[19]

In Elinor Wylie's poem, objects fashioned from the onyx, chrysoprase, jade (Wilde with his passion for green liked jade, speaking in *Dorian* of vegetables of "jade-green"), pearl, and ivory that decorate the prose of Wilde's novel appear together. The same relation between nature and artifice is also sustained. Wilde's ivy has "green lacquer leaves"; the Goldsmith's "lacquer" is like the "scarlet skin" of an ivory apple. Both ivy and apple are valuable, perversely, because they are not made of natural fibers but cased in hard, glossy veneer. The appeal in such conceits is to a permanence (and strangeness) which artistic objects, unlike nature, can offer. Yet nature's "monstrous day" is there at the end to make the arbitrariness of artifice apparent.

In the Wylie Archive in the Beinecke Library there is a winsome, unpublished poem of Elinor Wylie called "What Did You Buy?" The imagery of this poem resembles that of "The Fairy Goldsmith." But it poses against artifacts,

18. See "Path of the Chameleon," Elinor Wylie, *Collected Prose* (New York, 1946), 866.
19. Wilde, *Works*, 107.

or natural phenomena seen momentarily as static, livelier images that belong
to the hapless world. Like "The Fairy Goldsmith," the poem exhibits Elinor
Wylie's preoccupation with the distinction between nature and artifice:

> O what have you done with your pretty things,
> The shells and bells and humming-birds' wings,
> The buds and berries and gilded bees,
> The little, brittle images?
> One was an ivory Grecian girl,
> One was moonlight and mother o' pearl.
> What have you done with your milk-white hounds?
> What have you done with the silver sounds
> Of lutes and flutes and hunting-horns?
> What have you done with the prickly thorns,
> And the rose, and the snows which are thornless flowers
> The ice, and the spice, and the April showers,
> The cruel jewel of the falcon's look,
> The old cloak tattered, the shepherd's crook,
> The cold dust scattered, the tears that fall?
> What have you done?
>   I have sold them all.
> O what in the world did you buy instead?
> Sea-green slippers embossed with red,
> Bought from the wife of a Mandarin?
> Gloves of velvety chamois-skin
> Mouse-colored, cream-colored, softest fawn?
> Handkerchiefs of linen lawn
> Sweet with blossoms of lavender,
> Or a collar of tawny marten's fur
> Earrings of onyx or jade or gold?
> What did you buy with the things you sold?
> O I bought more beautiful things than these!
> I bought blue doves and cinnamon bees,
> Suns and seasons and thrushes' tunes,
> And moons which never were Reason's moons;
> The glitter of Picture-Show, a mind
> Bitter, chivalrous, brave and kind;
> And O the prettiest Country Toys!
> Dancing girls and prancing boys,
> Rigs and jigs and madrigals

Brighter and lighter than cowslip-balls,
Others as pretty, but pricking the gorse.
I have bought a kicking Kentucky horse,
I have bought a bronze-brown Nightingale,
And a splashing, flashing Golden Whale.
I have bought roses and hawthorne wreaths
Where Beauty lives and moves and breathes:
And a song; and strong to fly over the sea
A ship with sails of cramoisie,
A swift felucca with sails of silk.
I have bought honeydew and milk.

At the left side of the manuscript page, the poets are identified (in a hand that could be Benét's) who would choose the items Wylie enumerates: Ralph Hodgson, the "blue doves and cinnamon bees"; Siegfried Sassoon, the "glitter of Picture-Show"; Robert Graves, the "prettiest Country Toys"; Vachel Lindsay, the "kicking Kentucky horse"; John Masefield, the "ship with sails of cramoisie" which, in the use of the arcane word for crimson, is typical of Wylie. What is interesting in the poem is the conflict between the expectation of the speaker that the listeners will buy objects like "sea-green slippers" or jade earrings and their choice of "thrushes' tunes" or "a . . . Golden Whale." At the last, an unidentified poetic voice declares, "I have bought honeydew and milk." It is that voice which defines Elinor Wylie's understanding of what was primarily important to the poetic mind.

Still, as she was to demonstrate in the often Wildean fancies of Gerald Ponyard in *Jennifer Lorn* or in the fable of *The Venetian Glass Nephew* with its parallels to *Dorian Gray*, the Aesthetic predilection for old brocades, green bronzes, lacquer-work, and carved ivories; the Aesthetic attraction to uncommon words and historic subjects; the interest in achieving "literary expression of that which is most ineffable, and in form the vaguest and most fleeting outlines"[20] were instinctively her own. The most frequently anthologized poem from *Nets to Catch the Wind* is "Velvet Shoes." It is one of Elinor Wylie's virtuoso pieces, uniting that rapt, nearly hermetic elegance of vision and subtlety of technique for which she is known. More than many of her poems it bespeaks her gift. Yet its absorption in the idea of white may be found in the

20. Jackson, *The Eighteen Nineties*, 136.

poetry of the Aesthetes. Louis Untermeyer impressionistically called it "perhaps the whitest poem ever written":[21]

> Let us walk in the white snow
>   In a soundless space;
> With footsteps quiet and slow,
>   At a tranquil pace,
>   Under veils of white lace.
>
> I shall go shod in silk,
>   And you in wool,
> White as a white cow's milk,
>   More beautiful
>   Than the breast of a gull.
>
> We shall walk through the still town
>   In a windless peace;
> We shall step upon white down,
>   Upon silver fleece,
>   Upon softer than these.
>
> We shall walk in velvet shoes:
>   Wherever we go
> Silence will fall like dews
>   On white silence below.
>   We shall walk in the snow. (40)

A controlled lyric, written in fours followed by threes which slow and solemnify its movement, the poem proposes a dignified progress through a dreaming and unreal landscape. The walkers are ceremoniously and inappropriately dressed for winter; but the snow which their rich shoes barely touch is not genuine but illusory. The suggestion in the first line, "Let us walk in the white snow," becomes intention in the last, "We shall walk in the snow." The intervening lines provide winsome images of peace and harmony that intensify and make resolute the speaker's mood. The poem celebrates certain aspects of landscape under fresh snow. But its deeper theme is whiteness itself with its synaesthetic correlative, silence. It is an excursion

21. Louis Untermeyer, "Elinor Wylie," *Modern American Poetry* (New York, 1950), 295. A poem of Emily Dickinson, different in intention, nevertheless contains some similar lines: "We step like Plush, / We stand like snow" (Thomas H. Johnson [ed.], *The Complete Poems of Emily Dickinson* [Boston, 1960], 680).

into an atmosphere of artifice chosen to describe one manifestation of nature. "Silk," "wool," "veils of white lace," "silver fleece," "white down," "velvet shoes": all are materials that suggest a costly and fine remove from discordant life. Natural elements that appear in the poem: "a white cow's milk," "the breast of a gull," "dews," accord with the concepts of colorlessness, soundlessness, and softness fused together in the conceit, *white*.

Here again, as in certain poems of *Incidental Numbers*, are echoes of that literature of whiteness remarked by Holbrook Jackson. In poems of Francis Thompson, Ernest Dowson, Lionel Johnson, Oscar Wilde, Arthur Symons, the early Yeats, and others, Jackson traces an obsession with the idea of whiteness (usually as an emblem of innocence) that found utterance in Aesthetic allusions to silver, moonlight, starlight, ivory, alabaster, and marble. He quotes from Richard Le Gallienne's "White Soul" in *Prose Fancies*; Le Gallienne explains that, in order to praise a girl's virginal innocence, he must use "snow-white words, lily-white words, words of ivory and pearl, words of silver and alabaster, words white as hawthorn and daisy, words white as morning milk, words 'whiter than Venus' doves, and softer than the down beneath their wings.'" [22] Elinor Wylie, who declared, "I love words opalescent, cool, and pearly," and who described "lazy words" as "white cattle under trees" (*Collected Poems*, 240), was also given to envisioning implicit character in words; and in "Velvet Shoes" she describes an event innocent of complication in language that recalls Le Gallienne's. His "white as morning milk" is similar to her "white as a white cow's milk"; gulls occur to her instead of doves; but both are white.

What appeals to the author of "Velvet Shoes," as well as to Le Gallienne and other poets of the 1890s who wrote of "white silence" (Thompson) or "cloisters" "touched with white" (Johnson) or virginity's "swoon of whiteness" (Symons), is an immaculateness of experience. The white snow, Wylie says, is like "white silence." Those who tread upon it do so in no spirit of disturbance. The town is still; the snow is new-fallen, virgin; it elicits in the walkers an emotion of sensuous tranquillity. Jackson's hypothesis that, for the sophisticated Aesthete, whiteness was a symbol of perfection that is also "frankly sensuous" is supportable in Wylie's poem. For it describes a moment

22. Jackson, *The Eighteen Nineties*, 140.

of pure sensuousness—stepping on silver fleece in velvet shoes—which, like the "fleeting outlines" of experience recorded by many Aesthetes, is more effective because it is transitory.

Elinor Wylie, once described by Carl Van Doren as looking like the "white queen of a white country," "white-faced in white satin," and who liked to be told she resembled "iced chalk,"[23] preserved throughout her life a fondness for white and silver dresses and, in art, for images of white, silver, crystal, and glass which helps to define the Aesthetic quality of her imagination. There were psychological reasons for her attraction to Aestheticism and to these images as, doubtless, there were for her preferences in dress and for the iconography of her novels.

Sandra M. Gilbert and Susan Gubar have written persuasively in *The Madwoman in the Attic* about the psychological significance of the wearing of white clothes by women, particularly women artists and in the nineteenth century. White gowns, alternately (and sometimes comprehensively) symbolizing purity/frigidity and vulnerability/magical power, appeared in literature and on the living bodies of those who read and wrote it as indications of a deep-seated response to art and life. Wylie's choice of white or silver dresses (some by Paul Poiret and beaded like armor) probably reflected her desire to advertise sexual aloofness because she had been punished for sexual ardor. Some of her attraction to the conceit *white* in life and in art must have come from a yearning to establish her own virginity. Gilbert and Gubar's psychological theses lend themselves to the interpretation of other aspects of Wylie's work: its fascination with women who attempt "the killing of oneself into an art object"[24] and its preoccupation with thinness, glass, and her own image, all of which they regard as functions of the female artist's self-protective response to social animus. Louis Untermeyer remarked upon the "congealed brilliance" of *Nets to Catch the Wind*;[25] he and others sometimes connected the coldness of Wylie's poetic landscape with what they inferred to be the coldness of her heart. Others realized that her obsession with whiteness was also related to her desire to associate the temper of her poems and the

23. Van Doren, *Three Worlds*, 222, 216.
24. Sandra M. Gilbert and Susan Gubar, *The Madwoman in the Attic* (New Haven, 1980), 34.
25. Louis Untermeyer, "Fire and Ice," *New Republic*, XXIX (December 28, 1921), 133.

topography of her life. These attitudes were, of course, Aesthetic and related her to the Aesthetes, her early tutors.

The subjects and execution of many poems in *Nets to Catch the Wind* imply a design for writing verse identifiable with that of the Aesthetes. The plan Théophile Gautier devised for *Emaux et camées* (the title *Enamels and Cameos* suggests the affinity of his art with Wylie's) includes dicta respected by the English Aesthetes who were Gautier's disciples, dicta sustained in many successful poems of Elinor Wylie. Gautier, disapproving what he thought the sloppy self-indulgence of the Romanticism of Victor Hugo, determined to celebrate art above nature, poetic form above feeling, the miniature and rare above the grand or ordinary. In *Emaux et camées*, he would "treat . . . tiny subjects in a severely formal way . . . like working on gold or copper surfaces with brilliant enamels, or using a graver's wheel on precious stones, agate, cornelian or onyx."[26] Elinor Wylie, who spoke of herself and her contemporaries as "enchanted by a midas-touch or a colder silver madness into workers in metal and glass, in substances hard and brittle, in crisp and sharp-edged forms" (*Collected Prose*, 873), was both to practice this method and to argue its limitations. Convinced that Romantic art was greater in its spiritual aspiration than her own, she translated her formal preoccupation, her passion for "porcelain above humanity," into parables of warning.

Still, in the plan of Gautier as in his poems, there is a temper of mind which Elinor Wylie shared. Writers Elinor Wylie respected were influenced by Gautier's famous poem "L'Art" in which a statue or *médaille austère* outlasts cities and emperors; his "Fantaisies d'hiver" wherein old marbles, snow, and the idea of love unite in one image of still plasticity; and his worship of various images of whiteness in poems like "Symphonie en blanc majeur" in which the woman playing ivory piano keys resembles moonlight on ice, her white breast hiding "frozen secrets." For whether or not she read Gautier, she admired his disciple Austin Dobson's *Proverbs in Porcelain* and the verse of Lionel Johnson from which she took the title of *Black Armour*.

To "The Fairy Goldsmith" and "Velvet Shoes" should be added another

26. Théophile Gautier, *Les progrès de la poésie française depuis 1830*, in *Histoire du romantisme* (3d ed.; Paris, 1874), 322; translated by William K. Wimsatt, Jr., and Cleanth Brooks, *Literary Criticism* (New York, 1957), 489.

lyric that helps define the imagination of Elinor Wylie. "Silver Filigree," one of the first poems she ever published (in *Poetry*, April, 1921), consists of four rhymed quatrains and captures a brief moment in which nature is an artificer:

> The icicles wreathing
>   On trees in festoon
> Swing, swayed to our breathing:
>   They're made of the moon.
>
> She's a pale, waxen taper;
>   And these seem to drip
> Transparent as paper
>   From the flame of her tip.
>
> Molten, smoking a little,
>   Into crystal they pass;
> Falling, freezing, to brittle
>   And delicate glass.
>
> Each a sharp-pointed flower,
>   Each a brief stalactite
> Which hangs for an hour
>   In the blue cave of night.
>   (*Collected Poems*, 36)

The speaker's interest in the icicles is earned by their decorative quality (they are "wreath[ed]" "in festoon"), their fragility and impermanence, their origin, being "made of the moon," in an ethereal world. The poem rehearses the subtle stages by which they "pass" "into crystal" from paper-thin transparencies shed by the pale moon with restrained fire. It is that moment when, having "smok[ed] a little," they freeze into "brittle / And delicate glass," the moment of alteration from a life of animation into one of artifaction that is significant. When not yet formed, the icicles "sway . . . to our breathing," responsive to the life of nature. Once frozen, they achieve the perfection of form and are "sharp-pointed flower[s]," nature hardened into design. Yet the design is fleeting, lasting "an hour," hence precious.

In "Silver Filigree," Wylie shows characteristic attraction to that intense form of white, "silver," and the "filigree" of decoration that also interested the Aesthetes. The poem is not really about icicles but about the shapes they make. If it is contrasted with Coleridge's description in "Frost at Midnight," for example, of "silent icicles / Quietly shining to the quiet Moon," a difference is seen. Coleridge, depicting a soundless landscape under snow, summarizes its silence in the icicles' noiseless shimmer: they are indeed shapes, "h[u]ng up" by the "secret ministry of frost"; but it is their steadfast quietude that interests him. To Elinor Wylie, icicles become "brittle / And delicate glass." She is moved by their resemblance to artifacts and by the distinction between their formality—"Each a sharp-pointed flower"—and nature's fluidity—"the blue cave of night." Furthermore, her observation of one aspect of a wintry scene does not lead her, like Coleridge, to meditate on human concerns. Instead, her poem concentrates on the visual. Its quatrains are carefully carved, like the icicles, their subject.

When reading "Velvet Shoes," "The Fairy Goldsmith," or "Silver Filigree," one is reminded of a pronouncement of the Aesthetic painter James McNeill Whistler: "Art should be independent of all claptrap—and should stand alone and appeal to the artistic sense of eye or ear, without confounding this with emotions entirely foreign to it, as devotion, pity, love, patriotism and the like. All these have no kind of concern with it, and that is why I insist on calling my works "arrangements' and 'harmonies.'" [27] Whistler's was a typical defense of "art for art's sake" and a reaction against the Ruskinian expectation that art should inculcate moral values. Furthermore, his statement, insisting as it does on the visual and formal qualities of artifacts, may be more easily made by the graphic than by the poetic artist. Nevertheless, the Aesthetes as a group attempted a celebration of beauty in design and of the emotional response which that beauty, apart from the spiritual significances it suggested, might provoke. None of Whistler's "arrangements," certainly not his most famous *Arrangement in Gray and Black No. 1*, fails to count on complex human responses to the solitary human form, to rivers at twilight or groups of figures placed together because of mysterious but fraught relationship. Still, their titles call primary attention to the disposition of forms and the tonal harmonies of Whistler's canvases. Similarly, the titles of Elinor Wylie's poems often emphasize their poetic design: "Sea Lullaby," "Song," "Little Sonnet," within a pearly landscape reminiscent of Corot. It appears, too, in the sonnet "August," which studies the distinction between heat and cold in a masterly

27. Whistler, *Gentle Art of Making Enemies*, 127–28.

series of images. The dark, "noiseless" figure of "August"'s Negro in the "red noonday," bearing black-eyed daisies whose copper petals "smoulder" like the sun and seem a "brazier" of burning light, flashes on the eye in the sonnet's octave, relating warm colors to heat and heat to pride and to death: the daisies are "shrivelled." Posed against it is the cry of the sestet for coolness, reserve, and the northern clime, here seen as comfortable and always preferred by Elinor Wylie.

In "August," as in many other poems, she employs figurative speech to suggest aspects of design that comment on life. The burned petals that are brazierlike; the birds of "Winter Sleep" like "bubbles of glass"; the strap-hangers in "A Crowded Trolley Car" who seem an "orchard of the strangest fruits / Hanging from the skies" are viewed in a figurative mode that is painterly yet depicts objects, often artifacts, to make a conceptual point.

The last poem in *Nets to Catch the Wind* is called "Valentine." Its title is gently ironic since the poem declares that the speaker's heart "shall swing" / "Too high, too high to pluck" and the lines promise conservation of feeling rather than its expenditure (41). Here again, in clean accents and cool cadence, are two of the prominent themes of this volume: the need for dignified retreat from a world too often predatory and at the same time a sense of the cost of such retreat. The poet resolves that the heart shall be "A fruit no bee shall suck / No wasp shall sting." Still, in the second quatrain, she recognizes what must be the defeat of all who eschew engagement and suffering. The heart, "on some night of cold," will "fall to ground," for no one living, least of all a "Proud Lady" like herself, sensitive to public censure, can achieve sanctuary. In that instant, the speaker will protect her heart—her self—as she can:

> In apple-leaves of gold
> I'll wrap it round.
>
> And I shall seal it up
> With spice and salt,
> In a carven silver cup,
> In a deep vault.

Gold apple-leaves and the "carven silver cup" suggest the comforting power of aesthetic objects, her private universe, to which this speaker turns from the natural and hostile world. The comfort is fatal, however, "spice," "salt," and "vault" the accoutrements of death. But the poem ends in paradox. The buried heart must be eaten—the speaker must take responsibility for her choice—before she can herself die. It might be expected to be bitter gall:

> But I shall keep it sweet
> By some strange art;
> Wild honey I shall eat
> When I eat my heart.
>
> O honey cool and chaste
> As clover's breath!
> Sweet Heaven I shall taste
> Before my death. (41–42)

The heart preserved from natural discord in an atmosphere of elegant artifice will nonetheless achieve a wild sweetness. This poem, blazoning as it does Elinor Wylie's early sense of her own difference and destiny, proclaims as well what was to her a boon: the loveliness of the world of fine things which could substitute for faithless humanity. This final poem, like others in *Nets to Catch the Wind*, asserts her Aesthetic commitment with an eloquence that did not discount the dangers of its position: dangers increasingly understood as her art matured.

CHAPTER IV · *BLACK ARMOUR*

EMOTIONAL DEFEAT AND

ARTISTIC SUCCESS

As when two men have loved a woman well,
Each hating each, through Love's and Death's deceit;
DANTE GABRIEL ROSSETTI, "Lost on Both Sides,"
The House of Life, XCI

he career of Elinor Wylie is remarkable for what might be called intensity of performance. Scarcely two years after the appearance of *Nets to Catch the Wind* and in the same year as *Jennifer Lorn*, her second volume of poems *Black Armour* was reviewed by the New York *Times* (June 10, 1923). The *Times* discussed attributes that distinguished her lyrics from those of other writers, particularly women. Like Mark Van Doren and Malcolm Cowley, its reviewer found a "cold, terrible emphasis" in *Black Armour*, a hard brightness or restraint.[1] The fluent emotion of the poetry of Edna St. Vincent Millay, for instance, who was Wylie's chief rival (and later her imitator),[2] seemed lacking. Instead, the *Times* decided,

1. See Mark Van Doren's review of *Black Armour* in the *Nation* (June 27, 1923) in which he speaks of Wylie's "cold fire" and "perfect finish" and Malcolm Cowley's in the *Dial* (June, 1923) which calls her verse "hard and bright as a piece of machinery."
2. Edna St. Vincent Millay's friendship with Elinor Wylie is well-documented. Little,

Wylie's poems subdued feeling to chilly introspection. *Black Armour* heightened her reputation for technical brilliance but also for self-possession.

Yet a modern reader must be struck by the frustration expressed in this volume, a frustration that reappears in Wylie's posthumously published poems to "One Person," relieved there by the novel admission of passion. The speaker of *Black Armour* is stifled, thwarted, eager for death; only pride and her commitment to art sustain her. The title of the volume suggests the speaker's fragility. The book is her "armor" against a malicious world. By 1923 Wylie had suffered enough to prompt her to consider the world malicious, and poems like "Heroics" with its near-frantic hatred of "unclean assault" (*Collected Poems*, 61) show that the wounds of her youth never healed. Significantly, however, the poems of *Black Armour* make clear that Wylie's present life was as painful as her past and that, indeed, she had begun to judge personal fulfillment, particularly sexual fulfillment, as forbidden to her.

"Full Moon," the opening poem of *Black Armour*, alludes to the moon's classic ascendancy over poets and lovers; in its usually fecund light the speaker is a mechanical figure, a performing "Harlequin," unable to love or write. The poem introduces a volume whose theme is the failure of accomplishment, artistic and sexual. Its fundamental concerns are the poet's obsession with her ineluctable, disappointed femininity and her longing to be a true artist. The poems cry out for understanding of their author's presumed failure as a woman and her (implausible) suspicion of failure as an artist. Wylie's progressive disenchantment with love is expressed in words that reveal her passion for the discipline of art.

The title *Black Armour* was borrowed from Lionel Johnson, of whom Wylie had written in her review of Yeats's "The Tragic Generation," "I have always loved this lonely and incredibly distinguished creature." She felt "ecstasy," she said, "when I see, through [Yeats's] language transparent as a sheet of crystal,

---

however, has been said of Wylie's influence on Millay's style, which is particularly noticeable in *Fatal Interview* (1931). This collection of sonnets, published three years after Wylie's death and dedicated to her, records the history of an unhappy love affair, like the sonnets to "One Person" in *Angels and Earthly Creatures*. An example of how Millay's sonnets frequently echo Wylie's is her sonnet XI: "Love in the open hand, nothing but that, / . . . / As one should bring you cowslips in a hat"; Wylie's "Love Song" in *Angels* had announced "To Love I have been candid, / Honest, and open-handed" (Elinor Wylie, *Collected Poems* [New York, 1932], 193). See Edna St. Vincent Millay, *Collected Poems*, ed. Norma Millay (New York, 1956), 640.

the proud and touching figure of Lionel Johnson proceed to his doom. I have always loved [him] . . . not only for his delicate and bitter verse, but for his virtues and defects" (*Collected Prose*, 865). Her "ecstasy" was empathetic. Johnson was a poet who hated ordinary life as cordially as Wylie did; who, despite his taste for vice, preserved his personal elegance; who, like her, worshiped the picturesque past. Her "ecstasy" might also have arisen from a sense of narrow escape; Johnson's failure might have been her own. But Johnson's sonnet "The Age of a Dream" with its lament for the medieval era of solemn abbeys and chivalrous love was a nostalgic, post-Romantic celebration of a time of suave adventure: "Imageries of dream reveal a gracious age / Black armour, falling lace, and altar-lights at morn." [3] And a number of poems in *Black Armour*—"Peregrine," "Heroics," "King Honour's Eldest Son"— employed the same nostalgic scenery and knightly figures to conjure up a romance superior to any the present could offer. Ever since Keats's "La Belle Dame" (which itself arose from a poetic tradition of narrative enchantments) knights overwhelmed by evil had been exemplars of the ease with which Satan could overwhelm good. In using Johnson's phrase Wylie acknowledged the persistent influence of the Aesthetic poets. But she was also professing a sense of personal limitation. Despite its Johnsonian title, however, the motif of *Black Armour* was courage. Its author is protected by verse. The intricate "Breastplate" and "Helmet" of the early sections allow her to put her "Beaver Up" for searing confidences yet to display triumphant "Plumes"—adroit lyrics— at the book's close.

The first poem of *Black Armour*, "Full Moon," is revealing. Its agitated speaker walks in a moonlight that symbolizes the possibility of imaginative creativity and the release of love. But she wears "bands"—bonds, really—of silk and miniver: silk, indicating a taste for finery, and miniver, suggesting pride (for the Middle Ages associated "miniver" or ermine with aristocracy). Her clothes are Wylie's oft-described (and oft-worn) Whistlerian white and black. The clothes "muffle mouth and chin." They keep her from imaginative refinement: "I could not suck the moonlight in."

"Harlequin in lozenges / Of love and hate," she is torn between animosity toward the world and forgiveness. And she remembers "loathed" "thoughts"

3. Iain Fletcher (ed.), *The Complete Poems of Lionel Johnson* (London, 1953), 83.

in "corrupt disguises"—interpretations of her past that confuse her. What she desires most is fulfillment as an artist yet she expresses the desire as a wish for death:

> Mortality I could not tear
> From my ribs, to leave them bare
> Ivory in silver air.
> There I walked, and there I raged;
>
> The spiritual savage caged
> Within my skeleton, raged afresh
> To feel, behind a carnal mesh,
> The clean bones crying in the flesh.
>
> (*Collected Poems*, 47)

This is an emblematic poem which articulates Wylie's vision of the problems of her personality. Her womanhood, symbolized by silk and ermine, has led her on a tortuous path. Her flesh itself has been an impediment to the freeing of her better self—the "spiritual savage" unconcerned with vanity and elegance—in the "silver air" of pure imagination. Her craving to "tear" "Mortality" "from [her] ribs" is a desire to rid herself of the physical loveliness that must die so that she may achieve the spiritual luminousness that will last. The "clean bones" are a metaphor of her essential self, the self allied with Shelley's, whose bones were found near the Bay of Lerici.

The theme of "Full Moon" is extended in numerous subsequent poems that describe death by drowning—a death Wylie envisioned continually because of Shelley. Other poems investigate a destruction of self that is not contingent on suicide. And many of the poems of *Black Armour* are self-portraits—not, I think, because Wylie was vain, though she was, but because she was attempting to achieve self-understanding and because like most post-Romantics she valued personal experience. The volume's second section is called "Gauntlet"; it is a reminder that to throw down the gauntlet, a knight's iron and leather glove, was to challenge an adversary. One poem in particular describes Wylie. "Preference" is a hymn to her own appearance, celebrated in the Nicolas Muray portrait:

> These to me are beautiful people;
> Thick hair sliding in a ripple;

A tall throat, round as a column;
A mournful mouth, small and solemn,
Having to confound the mourner
Irony in either corner;
The limbs fine, narrow and strong;
Like the wind they walk along,
Like the whirlwind, bad to follow;
The cheekbones high, the cheeks hollow,
The eyes large and wide apart.
They carry a dagger in the heart
So keen and clean it never rankles. . . .
They wear small bones in wrists and ankles. (63)

Wylie's praise of attributes remarked in herself—as in both the male and female protagonists of her novels—might be embarrassing were it not for the poem's prominent placement in the volume. "Preference" is a challenge. It recognizes that others have not found such people handsome enough to exempt them from hatred; and it sets store by the subject's wounds. The "small bones in wrists and ankles," the hollow cheeks—fragility, thinness— are related not merely to Wylie's own physique but to an ideal physical body which she associated with the ability to feel deeply and consequently to be an artist. She often pointed out that the unhappy Shelley was thin and that Byron dieted constantly to stimulate his imagination. She also makes Byron's connection between being a poet and being dangerous to others: "Like the whirlwind, bad to follow." The speaker of "Preference" declares that "beautiful people" are saved wounds from resentment by intellect and the very depth of their wounds. Yet, one reflects, to wear a dagger that is "keen" and "clean" is to be quintessentially dead, and in later poems Wylie supports that analysis by alluding to the persona as a "skeleton." The poem challenges any who dare pity these unvanquished, vanquished spirits, a challenge repeated in "Let No Charitable Hope."

That poem starkly declares the poet's awareness of the limitations of her own imagination and sexuality:

Now let no charitable hope
Confuse my mind with images
Of eagle and of antelope:
I am in nature none of these.

> I was, being human, born alone;
> I am, being woman, hard beset;
> I live by squeezing from a stone
> The little nourishment I get.

The eagle and the antelope are Romantic self-images; they are not realistic but fantastic, flaunting, dramatic. The poet recognizes that she is "in nature" "human." She refuses to delude herself that she possesses the valor and celerity of the Romantic mind. She cannot soar or run but labors ignominiously—because she is a woman—merely to survive. It is a double avowal of what she would call in a poem to Shelley her own "pitiful" "estate" (157). She is limited by her womanhood and her lack of a pure Romantic gift. Like "Heroics" this poem concludes—one feels less honestly—by striking a dauntless posture and assuming a heroic mask:

> In masks outrageous and austere
> The years go by in single file:
> But none has merited my fear,
> And none has quite escaped my smile. (65)

"Preference" and "Let No Charitable Hope" establish three themes contained in kernel in "Full Moon": the poet's despair of achieving her desire to be a true poet like the Romantics; her knowledge that her own history has provoked a contumely she can withstand only by enlightened patience; and an ambivalent response to her own womanhood whereby she respects and laments the beauty and weakness that afflict yet exalt her.

The last, important lyric of "Gauntlet" is "This Hand." It is a study of a crucial aspect of the theme of womanhood: the poet's sexual frigidity. In other poems of *Black Armour* and in later books Wylie would return to that theme; in "This Hand" it is set forth with fine economy. The "hand" is the poet's who flings the gauntlet; but she considers it in relation to a lover whom she addresses and whose passion she cannot reciprocate. The first quatrain states her awareness that he has been wondering about her—and her coldness—for some time:

> This hand you have observed,
> Impassive and detached,
> With joints adroitly curved,
> And fingers neatly matched:

The speaker, like her hand, is handsome but, filled with contradictory feelings, she is "ambiguous to clasp, / And secret as a fish, / And sudden as an asp." Even in an embrace, the lover cannot be certain of her responses. She is withdrawn, elusive, poisonous when suddenly challenged, and (as the *fish/asp* images convey) not warm-blooded. The speaker acts as she chooses. Her hand will "double to a fist" or "droop," exhibiting aggression or resignation at her "command." The lover's wishes or appeals do not affect her. Her hand, she tells him pitilessly, "lies within your hand / Anatomy of wax." "This Hand" obviously describes the inadequacy of a sexual union. The handclasp of the fourth quatrain is so clearly a metaphor of lovemaking that one hardly need call to mind Freud's symbolic identification of the hand with the phallus or, parenthetically, with the female genitals. Like the "wax doll" Jennifer Lorn on her wedding night, the speaker is nonhuman "wax" in her lover's embrace. She explains, however, that this unhappy situation might have been otherwise:

> If I had seen a thorn
> Broken to grape-vine bud;
> If I had ever borne
> Child of our mingled blood;
>
> Elixirs might escape

That is, if misfortunes had not pursued her so relentlessly, if the thorns she wore had turned to flowers, or if she had been able to bear the lover's child, she might have been able to respond to him with passion. (The line "Elixirs might escape," one of many allusions in the volume to magic, is also a metaphor of feminine arousal.) But, the speaker continues, her destiny is to be unfeeling "stone": "My hand preserves a shape / Too utterly its own" (66).

"This Hand" is explanation, apology, and in its way a challenge to the lover to break the spell of self-absorption that keeps the speaker from achieving human responsiveness. It is a sad and emblematic poem, disclosing Wylie's habitual association of the bearing of children with goodness and womanhood, hinting at the obsession of her later life with the need to bear a child to excuse her marital relations and conversely the subconscious knowledge that her nature was not maternal and consequently, in her view, not truly feminine.

The frigidity of the speaker of "This Hand" is the result of her damaged personality: she conserves her own "shape" and regrets it. The poem fittingly concludes this section of *Black Armour* in which other unfit spirits are considered: "Peregrine," the wanderer, who declares, "I'm a good hater, / But a bad lover"; Lucifer, who calls himself God's "broken arrow" and craves death; "Simon Gerty," the traitor with whose misanthropy Wylie partly sympathizes. Read together, the poems of "Gauntlet" describe a woman troubled by personal failure but defiantly determined to remain brave.

Bravery, however, is inadequate to keep her from the sexual resentment she attempts to eschew, and as a function of pride it is subject to distrust in many poems. Various poems in the volume relate the history of a speaker who has bravely tried to serve the sexual need of others, either as "bondwoman" ("Little Sonnet," 84), or lover. In "Epitaph" such fortitude results in death. It is an impatient, angry poem despite the precision and ease of its quatrains:

> For this she starred her eyes with salt
> And scooped her temples thin,
> Until her face shone pure of fault
> From the forehead to the chin.
>
> In coldest crucibles of pain
> Her shrinking flesh was fired
> And smoothed into a finer grain
> To make it more desired.
>
> Pain left her lips more clear than glass;
> It coloured and cooled her hand.
> She lay a field of scented grass
> Yielded as pasture land.
>
> For this her loveliness was curved
> And carved as silver is:
> For this she was brave: but she deserved
> A better grave than this. (51)

The repeated accents of "for this" are effective for we are not told what "this" is—though the title is prophetic—until the last line. Like the heroine of *The Venetian Glass Nephew* who is fired into porcelain to please a glass husband, the speaker of "Epitaph" has willingly altered herself in "coldest crucibles of pain" so that she can be "pure of fault": physically beautiful and emotionally null. Her cold temperament and her slenderness make her desirable; but by denying her own "flesh"—her inner emotions, her idiosyncrasy—she has become a subject victim, "yielded as pasture land." The metaphors of this poem, too, invite Freudian interpretation since land was, for him, sexually symbolic of the female. And as in "This Hand" the speaker's sexual nature is unfulfilled. The "pasture," the last line bitterly tells us, becomes a "grave." Remarkable in "Epitaph" is the abrupt shift from images of metal and glass to land. The rhymes *glass* and *grass* are so neat that they allay surprise. A charge of mixed metaphor is also disarmed by the underlying psychological and empirical connections between passivity of these materials and of the earth from which they come. The speaker of "Epitaph" has made herself passive, cold, "scented," and frigid because others find those qualities desirable. Such yielding, the persona warns, can result in death.

The most intense and apparently autobiographical presentation of this theme of bravery, sex, and death is "Sequence," a series of three lyrics that appropriately appear toward the close of *Black Armour* in the section "Beaver Up." "Sequence" relates the history of a speaker determined to be fair and giving to two rival men whose destructive passions for her leave her nothing but the will to endure. Because *Black Armour* was written in 1923 when Wylie had recently divorced Horace Wylie to marry William Rose Benét and at that time she was known to complain of the failings of both husbands, it is not unreasonable to hypothesize that these lyrics are a literary record of her personal ambivalence. In the first poem the Freudian imagery of land reappears, associated once again with the grave; and a more dramatic Freudian symbol—the act of descending into a darkness that is not benign but an "unlighted kennel"—is used to denote sexual intercourse:

> This is the end of all, and yet I strive
> To fight for nothing, having nothing kept
> Of loveliness and saved myself alive
> Before this killing distillation crept
> Numbing my limbs, and stiffening my tongue
> To clay, less vital than the salted thorn
> Whereon a tyrant's banneret is hung
> As scarecrow for a harvesting still-born:
> And I am barren in a barren land,
> But who so breaks me, I shall pierce his hand.

This much is true, that there were certain times,
Measured by minutes, with a blank between,
When our two courages could meet, and climb
Into the blue above the blowing green;
But now the lifted pasture is too high,
The shoal too deep, for such were noble graves;
In this unlighted kennel, where to die
Will not awaken hounds, nor anger slaves,
I shall advise me to prepare my couch;
Here it is dark; for more I may not vouch. (81)

The speaker of this poem confronts and welcomes oblivion, having saved herself from it earlier. Her cryptic speech with its array of different images seems deliberately mysterious and alternately reticent and pointed. She appears to describe being poisoned in lines four through six, a fate related to the victory of an opponent who hangs his "tyrant's banneret" to serve as "scarecrow" over the land—herself—which he has ruined but which could only have yielded him a "still-born" harvest. The proliferation of images is grotesque, somewhat confused, and seems to arise from the poet's own rigor of feeling. The couplet of lines nine and ten, however, is powerfully distinct and full of resentment. There the female assumes what is represented as the destructive power of the phallus and, as in "This Hand," her sterility is cited, this time as a weapon. Before, the niggardly speaker concedes, the lovers who are now enemies were occasionally equal in a fellowship of love and able to climb together—for Freud, another metaphor of sex—to serene heights. Now, love is beyond their reach. The speaker will "prepare [her] couch" of death in a place that symbolizes what love has done to her: a "kennel" fit for animals, not human beings. Despite the sweep and authority of the first two lines, the poem is a rather tangled presentation of key images and themes she had used before. But it makes clear again that, to Wylie, the sexual relation results in a kind of death and that, of course, the male in the encounter is an adversary.

The second poem of "Sequence" defines the difference in nature of the speaker's lovers. Neither is suited to her. She is, again, the passive victim of each; and yet she has caused the agony of one:

One of these men will find my skeleton;
To one it will be delicate and slim,

With stars for eyes, and portent of a sun
Rising between the ribs to frighten him;
Yet, being bold, he might embrace it soon
With quick insensate passion in the night,
And by the holy taper of the moon
Encouraged, and because its bones were light
As of filagree of pearl, he might depart
Bearing my jangled heart-strings on his heart.

And he might bury it in sand or sod,
Stamping it down to circumvent the wolf,
And, being kind, commend it to his God,
Whose Mind was swimming somewhere in the gulf
Above his head; but if that other found
The rotten framework of his servitor,
He'd leave it lying on the cluttered ground
Between a bottle and an apple-core,
And go his way, in agony and sweat,
Because he could not pity nor forget. (82)

Here the speaker understands she is to become a mere "skeleton," permanently unable to offer a woman's love. Nevertheless, one man will desire her because she has genius—"stars for eyes, and portent of a sun" "to frighten him" because she is "delicate and slim." His passion will be unfeeling and he himself "bold"; he is a taker and doer, though kind enough to bury her at the end and say a few prayers. There is a hint of mockery in lines thirteen to fifteen.

Another lover has used the speaker during her life as his "servitor." Yet she has evidently abused him, too, for he would not be able to summon the kindness to bury her but would leave her bones amid trash "because he could not pity nor forget." Here the autobiographical element seems decisive: Benét, the first (and latest) lover, stupidly full of passion and regard, though blind to the speaker's needs; Horace Wylie, the second (and earlier) lover, tortured but aloof. Like many of the confessional poems in *Black Armour* this one does not omit the failings of the speaker; yet she regards herself as destroyed by the forces of passion, and her recriminatory spirit is obvious.

The last lyric of "Sequence" summons Wylie's perennial theme of courage in adversity. The speaker declares, "I have contrived a substituted task / To prove my body is devoid of fear." It concludes with another grouping of

Freudian images and with a mixture of hostility and apology. The speaker has been doubly conquered, but she intends to preserve both herself and her fealty to the conquerors. "For various questions which," she says, "I shall not ask, / And various answers which I cannot hear"

> I shall persist, I shall pursue my way
> Believing that his cruelty was fine
> As tempered steel for chastening of clay,
> Impatient of corrosions that were mine;
> He that despised me shall not be forgot;
> He that disparaged me shall be my lord;
> That was a flambeau, half-consumed and hot,
> This was a running light along a sword;
> And though I warmed my fingers at the one,
> The other is my father and my son. (83)

The lover who "despised" her, leaving her bones unburied, is nonetheless memorable; the other who "disparaged" her shall remain her "lord." Wylie's interest in etymology was pronounced. The arcane meaning of the word "disparage" is to "cause to marry unequally; to degrade or dishonour by marrying to one of inferior rank" (*OED*). The speaker has been "disparaged" by being married to her inferior yet she resolves to continue to allow him to master her. The images of the "flambeau" and the "running light along a sword" are phallic and partially destructive yet the speaker determines to withstand their effects by courage. The older lover may have "warmed" her; her new "lord," however inferior to her in rank, must be the sum of men to her.

The poems of "Sequence" are not wholly successful. They contain too many shifts in attention and emphasis, and their narrative line is dissipated by oscillation between death expected, death intended, and death denied at the end for survival. Despite the poems' fluency there is a quality of contrivance in some lines (for example, "*couch / . . . for more I may not vouch*" [italics mine]). Lines like "I shall submerge my body in the mud" (83) reveal a petulance so violent that it becomes cheap feeling, cheaply expressed. Some of the repetitions: "I shall submit my spirit to the storm; / I shall bend down my bosom to the snake / . . . I shall persist, I shall pursue" (83) do not achieve emphasis but excess. Besides, the speaker of "Sequence" is for the most part so sorry for herself and her "jangled heart-strings" that the reader thinks rebelliously, Enough! (Indeed, if he accepts the probability of autobiographical relevance he may pity Benét, who cannot be held entirely responsible for his wife's frigidity and whose sincerity is scorned as foolishness.) In these poems the emotional crisis that Wylie was clearly beginning to experience did not result in disciplined art.

Nevertheless, "Sequence" is important because it reveals the complex sexual disappointment of the heroine of the poems and novels, Wylie herself. That heroine would prefer to "lie folded like a saint" on a bed "narrow and cold and neat" ("Prophecy," 50). Human love has neither satisfied nor preserved her; hence she longs for death as in "Three Wishes" or "Song"; for lonely places as in "South" or "The Good Birds"; for "Demon Lovers," dead men and spirits who make no physical demands on her; and most of all, for bravery.

Bravery, however, can result from pride. The conviction of her essential superiority to her lovers which is suggested in the use of the word *disparage* appears in many poems; and in turn it is submitted to Wylie's critical scrutiny. The second poem in *Black Armour* is "Nebuchadnezzar." It alludes to the story of that king of Babylon in the Book of Daniel whose pride and whose delight in golden images caused him to be punished until he "learned that the Most High rules the Kingdom of Men." Nebuchadnezzar was "driven from among men, and his mind was made like that of a beast, and his dwelling was with the wild asses; he was fed grass like an ox" and "his body was wet with the dew of heaven till his hair grew long as eagle's feathers, and his nails were like birds' claws."[4] When he acknowledged that pride is sinful and beautiful objects are dust, God restored him to reason and glory.

Elinor Wylie valued pride, especially when it manifested itself as fortitude in adversity. She was raised an Episcopalian, and she had an abiding respect for the *Book of Common Prayer* and (like the poets of the 1890s) a predilection for religious subjects which those who knew the mere lineaments of her life found surprising. Her own pride, however defensive, as well as her attraction to objects, were a source of concern to her. "Nebuchadnezzar" is revealing for it acknowledges the king's delinquency yet it allows him to speak from exile where he has kept the flame of humanity and refuses to lose his sense of the beautiful. "Crouch[ing] on [his] knees" as the relentless God ordains, he nonetheless sees appreciatively that "the cool white rain / Curves the clover

4. Daniel 5:22.

over [his] head like a wave," and though he must eat grass, he declares it "ripe." Like Wylie's other misfits and sinners or the heroine of the love poems, he is courageous, if "weary" of courage. Like the speaker of "Three Wishes," "Song," and "Drowned Woman" he is tired of his own personality, particularly his "jewelled brain" (52): "My body," he says, "is weary to death of my mischievous brain." Nevertheless, the very vices for which he is punished—pride and the worship of things—sustain him. He has "devoured the strength" of his exile and he finds it sweet (48).

Black Armour discloses Wylie's ambivalence about her personal nature, spiritual and sexual; but it also addresses the problem of her art. The theme of art would dominate her next volume of poems, *Trivial Breath*, but in *Black Armour* it begins to assume importance as in a series of lyrics she attempts to formulate an aesthetic. Some of these poems describe the sort of art Wylie herself produced; others consider either its virtues or limitations. While she was writing *Black Armour*, she was also composing her longest and most specific essay on the nature of true art, "Jewelled Bindings," in which she discusses the merits and deficiencies of an artist of "jewelled brain." With similar gravity *Black Armour*'s poems about art rehearse the essay's postulates.

In the poem "Nonchalance" Wylie anatomizes a poet's ability to represent and order inharmonious and formless experience:

> This cool and laughing mind, renewed
> From covert sources like a spring's,
> Is potent to translate the mood
> Of all distraught and twisted things.

The title "Nonchalance" is seen to be appropriate in the first line of the poem; for the French *non chaloir*, not to care, comes from the Latin *non calere*, not to be hot; and, as was natural in a poet who valued strict control, Wylie associates poetic form with "cool[ness]," even irony. The good poet's mind is for her, as for the Romantics, nourished by nature, and the good poem is a shapely arrangement of elements hitherto deformed or unsettled:

> In this clear water shall be cast
> Outrageous shapes of steel and gold,
> And all their hot and clotted past
> Beaded with bubbles silver-cold.

Here, like many poets, Wylie defines good poetry in terms suited to the ambition and quality of her own best poems. "Clear water" implies the formal simplicity her own work sought; "silver-cold," its polish and restraint. Then, in the last quatrain, Wylie explains that the artifact is never the mere sum of its elements but a rival reality achieved by the transforming intelligence of the artist. That reality is capable, like nature, of sustaining the reader:

> The moving power takes their heat
> Into itself, forgetting them;
> And warmth in trickles, slow and sweet
> Comforts a fainting lily-stem. (72)

In "Self-Portrait" Wylie not only defines the activity of the poetic imagination; she claims that she herself possesses it. Such an imagination is

> A lens of crystal whose transparence calms
> Queer stars to clarity, and disentangles
> Fox-fires to form austere refracted angles:

It is an analytic yet synthetic force. "Self-Portrait," however, then shifts to a denigration of her own soul, which she describes as

> This vanity, blown hither and thither
> By trivial breath, over the whole world's length. (72)

The compliments Wylie pays her mind are followed in this sonnet by a mournful consideration of her humanity, which is not like "stone," not of "sculptured strength." This leads in turn to her spiritual inadequacy. In calling her next volume *Trivial Breath* she was recalling the words of "Self-Portrait." Thus "Self-Portrait" records the beginning of a conflict between her adequate wit and her inadequate spirit, one that resulted, she thought, in the diminished art of "jewelled bindings." The harlequin figure of "Full Moon" cannot achieve that oneness with nature which Shelley, for instance, achieved. Her art may be refined but lacks the majesty with which his attempted to contain a universe.

The cryptic poem "Demon Lovers" seems an attempt to explain those qualities in herself which inhibited her art and kept it from Romantic grandeur. The Coleridgean title implies Romantic art, but the poem's subject is a woman in whom two emotions strive for ascendancy: "the peacock and the mocking-bird / Cry forever in her breast." The peacock, a symbol of artistic pride inherited from William Morris and used repeatedly by Beardsley and Wilde, appears to represent excusable satisfaction in artistic performance. But the mocking-bird obviously derides such satisfaction. Elinor Wylie undoubtedly saw the Peacock Room, removed in 1904 from 49 Princes Gate, London, to the Freer Gallery in Washington, D.C., while she was studying art. Whistler's panels depict two fighting birds: one is martial, in full-feather, and the representative of the true artist (Whistler himself) while the other (his delinquent patron Frederick Leyland) scorns him and clutches gold coins in his claws, thus standing for vanity and avarice. Whistler's famous antithesis may underlie her own in "Demon Lovers," whose protagonist cannot reconcile her artistic and venal aspects. Nor can she be helped by a benign spirit—Shelley's—which has gone before since "public libraries have blurred / The pages of his palimpsest." The poem's array of Romantic images and verbal allusions helps to express her problem. She has "clasped and kissed" Mercutio, the spirit of mockery and satire despised by Shelley, and thus her art trivializes the great experiences of life (74).

With the exception of "Nonchalance," Black Armour's lyrics on art betray misgivings about the art, "intricate and crystal," Wylie herself produced (87). It was, as her essay "Jewelled Bindings" declared, an art that was "elaborate, neat, enamelled, elegant, perhaps exquisite" but which nonetheless lacked "the vast suavity of the truly superb." Its bindings were "the spiritual bonds, the sharp and delicately turned shapes and forms which so decoratively constrict the essence of contemporary lyric verse." For she saw herself in "Jewelled Bindings" as one of a group of poets working in this manner. But form itself—"clear small stanzas, brilliant and compact"—did not alone inhibit greatness in her own work or others'; there was the matter of vision, too.

Borrowing the description of the auction catalog from whose pages Wylie took the title, "Jewelled Bindings" compares the passion of a bookbinder for precious decoration to the preciousness of many modern poets:

> Permit me to quote from the picturesque bit of prose whence my title was stolen. "Surrounding it is a large wreath of laurel, tied with a mauve ribbon, and studded with fifty-eight pearls set in gold. . . . The design of the back cover is equally brilliant and contains forty-eight garnets, eight

opals, eight moonstones, twenty-eight turquoises, twelve blue chalcedonies, two hundred and fifty-four amethysts, and nine topazes. . . ."

Surrounding what? you may well ask. At the Anderson Galleries all
this intricacy surrounds Some Poems by John Keats, but in the curious
museum of our own time some, nay many, poems by eminent young
lyricists appear, if not similarly tied with mauve ribbon, at least painstak-
ingly inlaid with seven moonstones and twelve blue chalcedonies. (*Collected Prose*, 872–73)

Wylie's essay is a criticism of Neo-Aestheticism, as is apparent in her use
of the concept of overdecoration and the color mauve. It explains that Wylie
and similar artists resemble "clever goldsmiths" "enchanted by a midas-touch
or colder silver madness into workers in metal and glass, in substances hard
and brittle, in crisp and sharp-edged forms" (873). And the essay compares
the live bird of great art with the "gilded bird" of minor art, singing "from a
small jewelled receptacle of two or three well-polished stanzas" (874). Her
own art, she says—not a bird she dares think live—was born in a snuffbox.

One is reminded, of course, that the Yeats of "Sailing to Byzantium"
would, in 1926, describe art as a gilded bird whose formal song orders time
and chaos. To Wylie, however, Romanticism's engagement with nature con-
stituted the great subject, produced the superb in form. Yeats's bird on its
golden bough was to have such a form as Grecian goldsmiths make of
hammered gold and gold enameling. Thus Yeats would use the very Aesthetic
metaphors Wylie scrutinized for their limitation. She, however, not drawing
Yeats's comparison between art and nature but between kinds of art, speaks of
the bird of great art as proper to a "stone dovecote" or a "bramble bush"
(874). She does not wish to abandon the Aesthetic manner altogether, for it is
"deliberate," "a discipline . . . not to be too impetuously scorned." But a "real
bird" would need more freedom than she can provide. She is a minor poet,
not an "authentic genius" like Keats attuned to the life of nature (874).

"Jewelled Bindings" sets forth the responsible argument with her own
artistry that appears in *Black Armour* and gathers strength in Wylie's later
volumes. At the end of her short life, prompted by timely interest in metaphysical and Elizabethan verse, she was casting about for another way of
writing; and as a woman, she thought she had at last achieved emotional
scope. In *Black Armour* she made poetry, as Yeats once announced grandly, out

of the argument with her own self. Her very dissatisfaction with her art and her womanhood became—as Denys Sutton writes of Whistler—"asset[s]."

Considering the qualities of mind, the nature of the art of this kindred spirit, Sutton says,

> It is the aesthete's disadvantage, and failing even, that he is rarely, if ever, satisfied, and that he is a perfectionist; his is a position which inevitably cuts him off from the warming vigour of life. For an artist, moreover, the wilful pursuit of a conscious aestheticism can prove a dangerous policy; in the end it may engender a certain debility. The very qualities which distinguish Whistler's art—a love of delicacy, an inherent elegance and a delight in a transitory and fragmentary mood—were perilous for a painter like him, who could not summon truly robust artistic resources to his assistance. He could have surrendered more exclusively to the softer and insinuating components in his make-up and given in whole-heartedly to his dandyism; fortunately he did not succumb to this temptation. His very stubbornness and his refusal to compromise provided the sinews for his art and served to support his more delicate fancies; the Puritan . . . in him came to the rescue. Paradoxically, he was saved by another asset and one which, at first sight, might have constituted a weakness. This was the dissatisfaction with his own achievement which may be discerned beneath the carapace of his very complete egotism.[5]

Like Whistler vain of her appearance and dress; interested in "delicacy, inherent elegance" whether in porcelain or human gesture; committed to a description of transient mood, fleeting apparition, and art as the subject of art, Elinor Wylie was also "a perfectionist" and, like him, dissatisfied with her own achievement. She, too, had the "Puritan marrow of [her] bones" (*Collected Poems*, 12), which made her strive, often against the grain of her personality, for an art pure of idiosyncrasy and earned by difficult endeavor. Friends' memoirs insist that she was indeed an egotist. Yet her response to her own "conscious aestheticism" was severe: she chose it as a major subject, fashioned for it a discriminating language.

The book jacket of *Black Armour* was designed by Elinor Wylie herself: black, with the image of a silvery knight at joust. He carries a bright, sharp lance and holds himself erect. His carriage bespeaks skill, cleverness, energy, but not failure—as do the poems of *Black Armour*.

5. Denys Sutton, *James McNeill Whistler* (London, 1966), 6.

CHAPTER V · *THE VENETIAN*
GLASS NEPHEW

"She is very clever, too clever for a woman. She lacks the indefinable charm of weakness. It is the feet of clay that make the gold of the image precious. Her feet are very pretty, but they are not feet of clay. White porcelain feet, if you like. They have been through the fire, and what fire does not destroy, it hardens. She has had experiences."

OSCAR WILDE, *The Picture of Dorian Gray*

"You turn feverish men into cool, quiet marble. What a blessed change for them!"

NATHANIEL HAWTHORNE, *The Marble Faun*

 n his Oxford years during the late 1870s, Oscar Wilde became the subject of an irate sermon at the University Church for having made the " 'heathen[ish]' " remark, " 'Oh, would that I could live up to my blue china!' " [1] Wilde's affection for porcelain was a taste in part informed by contemporary critical theories about the best art being decorative, the best poems like "hard shape[s]": [2] theories derived from French Symbolists such as Théophile Gautier and still vivid in the views of Wilde's teacher, Walter Pater. Such a taste reflected Wilde's essential distrust of nature's crudities and his respect for art as design; for in a figurine from Sèvres or Meissen, the human body with all its vital awkwardness might be fixed in sculptural poise, its fleeting attractions made more lucid by artifice; or in the scenes on a piece of Chinese export porcelain, the

1. Quoted in Hesketh Pearson, *Oscar Wilde* (New York, 1946), 29.
2. William K. Wimsatt and Cleanth Brooks, *Literary Criticism* (New York, 1957), 489.

continually shifting aspects of nature might be reduced to a coherent, miniature landscape, tranquil and emblematic. More trivially, interest in china was
a function of Wilde's dandyism and exhibitionism.

For a number of reasons, china became a craze among the Aesthetes and
"snobs" of the late nineteenth and early twentieth centuries. A revived
interest in the elegance of the eighteenth century in which the rage for
chinoiserie flourished in England and France; the influence of artists like
Whistler, whose "Princess from the Land of Porcelain" adorned the Peacock
Room; the Aesthetic habit of choosing titles such as *Proverbs in Porcelain* and
Ballades in Blue China, implying a carven, bright, minute perfection of poetic
form—all contributed to making fondness for china a function of good taste.
In England in the 1920s those in whom the ideals of the 1890s survived wrote
about and collected porcelain. Cecil Beaton recalled that Lady Diana Cooper,
actress-socialite and daughter of the duke of Rutland, "was to have been part
of a group of Porcelain Figures" at a party in Venice in 1926.[3] At that time, one
year after the publication of *The Venetian Glass Nephew*, porcelain had become a
metaphor for brilliant artifice, for a life glittering and gay and a Neo-Aesthetic
art of the moderne—suave, mannered, and heartless.

When Elinor Wylie wrote *The Venetian Glass Nephew*, in which a beautiful
and lively girl agrees to become a porcelain figure so that she can please a
husband made of glass, she told her friend Carl Van Doren that the book was
"a kind of moral fairy tale."[4] Five years earlier, in 1920, Ezra Pound's protagonist in *Hugh Selwyn Mauberley* had chosen the conceit of porcelain to describe
the failure and limitation of an Aesthetic art of medallions and private
concerns; for in the poet Mauberley's case, "the glow of porcelain" to which
he is attracted teaches him nothing about politics or society, and real life—
"the coral isle, the lion-coloured sand"—"burst[s] in upon his porcelain
revery" to trouble him. Pound described the fault of Neo-Aesthetic art in one
line, "Luini in porcelain."[5] The art of Bernardino Luini (*ca.* 1475−1531/2),
follower of Leonardo da Vinci, was characterized by neutral coloration,
carefully graded modeling, and the mannered smiles and gestures of his

3. Cecil Beaton, *The Wandering Years* (Boston, 1961), 125.
4. Carl Van Doren, Preface to *The Venetian Glass Nephew*, Elinor Wylie, *Collected Prose* (New York, 1946), 215.
5. Ezra Pound, *Personae* (New York, 1926), "Hugh Selwyn Mauberley," 201.

subjects. Already slick and stylized, such an art rendered into porcelain would epitomize preciousness. Pound's phrase isolates Aestheticism as an effort at further and further refinement with an attendant sacrifice of vitality and strength. It is such an effort Elinor Wylie describes in *The Venetian Glass Nephew*; for there, in the several stages by which porcelain is created, an already graceful woman is made translucent, vitrified, and, of course, passionless china.

There are six major characters in this novel, nicely discriminated as to function: Cardinal Peter Innocent Bon, an old, pious, simple prelate (as his name makes clear) who desires a nephew; Angelo Querini, philosopher and friend of Voltaire, who has raised his niece Rosalba to respect the rule of reason; Chastelneuf, chevalier de Langeist, really the famous Casanova de Seingalt who is, as he was historically, a man of taste and necromantic learning but whom Elinor Wylie portrays in his middle years, a softened and refined roué; Count Carlo Gozzi, in the novel as in history the Venetian playwright of fabulous comedies; Rosalba, surnamed Berni after the Cardinal de Bernis of Casanova's *Memoirs*, her reputed father; and Virginio, the nephew made by Chastelneuf's magic and the glassblower's art of Alvise Luna. In the outlines of these characters, fact and fiction merge.[6] For instance, Rosalba is invented; yet, since she is a francophile, an infant prodigy, and a woman of graceful wit, she recalls Rosalba Carriera, the Venetian pastelist (1675–1757) described by Elinor Wylie's esteemed Austin Dobson in *Rosalba's Journal*. The real Rosalba did a portrait of a Mr. Whithead who resembles Virginio in his spangled attire; and the delicacy and archness of her pastels suggest the climate of Wylie's novel.

Wylie is careful throughout the novel to assign suitable aspects and responses to her characters. Thus since Cardinal Innocent Bon's "mind move[s] happily in an atmosphere of miracles," he is unflurried when Chas-

---

6. Edmund Wilson in "A Letter to Elinor Wylie" assumed the severe character of Dr. Samuel Johnson to criticize *The Venetian Glass Nephew*. One of his several objections to the tale was that it "mingled the fictitious with the real in a manner hardly allowable"; his argument is that Elinor Wylie was not to ascribe to Gozzi or Chastelneuf-Casanova any action—such as their involvement in the fictional story of the *Nephew*—which their historical memoirs did not. This seems a particularly tendentious opinion. It is possible, of course, that Wilson was merely imagining that the reasonable Johnson would think Wylie's work licentious. But since his essay purports to be criticism, his views are no doubt his own, despite the mask he adopts. See *The Shores of Light: A Literary Chronicle of the Twenties and Thirties* (New York, 1952), 261.

telneuf's white magic and the skill of the greedy Luna result in an animated glass "nephew" who in his "saintly . . . fastidious[ness]" he christens Virginio (*Collected Prose*, 239, 265). Preferring that Virginio be a priest and not worldly like the "nephews" of his fellow prelates—whose true relation to their "uncles" he is too naïve to suspect—Peter Innocent is merely resigned when Virginio marries Rosalba. When their physical incompatibility ends in grief and a broken arm for the glass boy and grief and frustration for the real girl, he proposes that Rosalba enter a convent. At the end of the tale, it is Chastelneuf, that splendid creation of Elinor Wylie, who tries to disabuse Peter Innocent of his doting optimism. Brusquely the chevalier reminds him that the desperate plan to turn Rosalba into porcelain is a "vehement" and not a "beneficent" act for which Chastelneuf himself will need "the devil's aid" (303, 300). Even then, the Cardinal blesses whatever solution will assist Virginio, with a tranquil absence of feeling for the flesh, particularly feminine flesh, that is entirely suitable to his habit, years, and temperament.

In contrast to the gentle and gullible Cardinal, Rosalba's guardian Querini has "a mind . . . purely rational," if a "naturally impetuous heart" (263). A "liberal cynic," he allows Rosalba to marry Virginio, wishing to please her; and he utters sentiments on their betrothal humorously worthy of the philosophes: "'Oh, excellent Helvetius! Philanthropically bestow upon these infants a ray of your own illumination! May their bodies remain pagan, their minds emancipated, and their moral qualities incorruptibly pure!' In his excitement he had almost pronounced 'Amen,' but caught himself in time to substitute a sentiment from the 'Republic' of Plato" (264–65). Yet he views the romance with "sceptical amusement," calling it reminiscent of the invention of his friend, Count Carlo Gozzi (264).

That "aristocratic dreamer" is Rosalba's favorite author (265). Falling in love with Virginio, she decides that "she care[s] very little whether [the boy] had emerged from an Arabian orange or flown to earth upon the wings of the celebrated Green Bird, so long as he had come to her at last" (264). Gozzi, of course, wrote the *Fable of the Love of the Three Oranges* and *The Green Bird*, tales of magic like his *Monster*. (The latter title may explain Elinor Wylie's decision to call her fourth chapter "Crystal Monsters," describing the fantastic cellar of Luna the glassblower, where golden griffins, stags, and hummingbirds of glass move easily and delicately in air.) Gozzi, like Querini, loves Rosalba and is at first charmed by the prospect of her marriage to Virginio: "'the lad is actually a fantasy in Murano glass instead of vulgar flesh and blood! I myself could not have invented a prettier conceit, or one more gracefully in accordance with the best magical traditions'" (271). Yet, when the marriage proves disastrous, he, like Querini, is hotly opposed to Rosalba's incarceration in a convent. Like any philosophe, he rallies to the cause of nature, not "fairy drama": "'Is it a crime on this unlucky infant's part that we have incontinently wedded her to a glass mannikin instead of decent blood and bone? God pardon us for our unholy meddling, for we have hurt the loveliest thing alive!'" (292). In the characters of Querini and Gozzi, Elinor Wylie enlists reason and imagination in the support of the true course of nature. In the character of Chastelneuf-Casanova, nature pleads for its own fulfillment.

The adventurer M. de Chastelneuf, who "had at one time or another attracted the attention of almost every court of Europe" with his "courtly, if a little antiquated and florid" manners, his "falcon look" and his "impassioned fervour," needs money and thus uses his knowledge of Paracelsus to create Virginio—appropriately on a Friday sacred to Venus (237, 295). Having empowered the glass boy to be a husband, he comes to understand that he has not prepared him to be a playfellow. When the young Rosalba attempts suicide because her liveliness distresses her husband, Chastelneuf speaks to her in a style that reminds us that, though of a certain age, he is still Casanova, lover of women:

> "My child, my child, you have observed that I love you, but have you comprehended the quality of my love? It is such as you will never discover in the hollow veins of Virginio or among the noble ganglions of Querini's intellect; it is love, lust, passion, humility, and wonder; it is human, not divine, not animal, but the love of mortal for mortal; it is at your service. I love you; I have loved many times and in many fashions, but this love is all your own. Use it as you will; I have no expectation that you can return it in kind." (294–95)

> "Why did you not tell me that you wished to die? Do you understand that I am always here to give you whatever you want? Yes, even if it is death, I will give it to you; but sweetly flavoured and in a golden box." (294)

Elinor Wylie weaves a subtle relationship between Rosalba and Chastelneuf-Casanova. She is the daughter of Louis XV's ambassador to Venice and

Caterina Campana, the famous "C–C–" of Casanova's *Memoirs*, translated by Arthur Machen, whom Elinor Wylie, like Carl Van Vechten, admired. Chastelneuf tells Gozzi and Peter Innocent what Casanova relates to his readers: that he seduced Caterina, intending to marry her, but instead conceived a passion for "M–M–" (Maria Magdalena Pisani), the nun who befriends Caterina in the Murano convent to which she is exiled. Chastelneuf-Casanova conducts a long affair with the nun in a sumptuous casino provided by the Cardinal de Bernis. Eventually he repays the Cardinal's generosity by permitting him to seduce Caterina. When Chastelneuf recalls running races with Caterina in St. Blaise, they are the races run by Casanova and "C–C–" in the Zuecca Gardens at St. Blaze, races Virginio, to Chastelneuf's disgust, cannot run with Caterina's daughter. Elinor Wylie's Chastelneuf, however, is urbane, decorous, kind, lacking Casanova's heated liberality and unctuousness. Indeed, it is his grave intelligence that informs us of the extent of the crime done Rosalba in "shrink[ing]" her into "a china doll": " 'She will be porcelain; fine porcelain, remember, and no longer clay. In a porcelain vessel filled with clear water a rose may live for a little while, but out of clay a rose may rise alive and blooming, set on the roots of elder roses'" (301, 303).

Rosalba is assigned a host of images that suggest vitality: she is a "hummingbird," "a little panther," "a rabbit," "a deer," an "impulsive flower nourished on subterranean flame" (263, 258, 291, 295). With the onset of the terror of her marriage, she becomes a doe "transfixed by an arrow," wearing "a wild beast's pelt above a heart more vulnerable than a little lamb's" (291). The novel identifies her with the fluent Venetian world: "Always she seemed to move and waver in the leaping light" (299). In her "cloak of tawny velvet lined with foxes' skins," she is impetuous, but also an "Infant Sappho" whose poems had been published long before Virginio was created (291, 256).[7]

The "celestial prodigy" Virginio "lacks the roughness and the pitifulness

7. Thomas A. Gray in *Elinor Wylie* (New York, 1969) asserts that since Rosalba is described as "in form and elegance of gesture . . . [an] Artemis," her brows "arched forever in delicate amazement," her mouth "curled like a scarlet petal in some early frost of irony," she is not "natural" but "artificial"; and that Elinor Wylie's "contrived descriptions" of her ingenuousness and vitality are canceled by an underlying desire to render her in the style of a "painting of the period" (140). What must be remembered, however, is the weight of description, all of it on the side of nature. Having called Rosalba an "Artemis"—doubtless to suggest the instinctive refinement that accompanies her voluptuousness—Wylie adds, "Yet not the Artemis of ivory or quarried stone, however exquisite. Rosalba was more vital than opening roses or ripened fruit" (256).

of humanity"; yet his "undoubted beauty" is marvelous as is "his perfect self-possession" (270, 251). With his fair skin and hair like spun glass, his white velvet coat and crystal ring, he is the graceful embodiment of crystal or that favorite "color" of the Aesthetes, white. Elinor Wylie grants him a sympathetic nature, yet genuine feeling—indignation or passion—makes him tremble so that "a faint cracking sensation menace[s] his expanded heart" (258). At the last, Chastelneuf understands the difficulty created by Virginio's marriage: "Although, in her brilliance, [Rosalba] was fire to Virginio's crackling ice, the chevalier remembered suddenly that the essential substance of that element is delicate and tender and more malleable than the very air, whereas ice is denser even than water, and often hard as stone. And he reflected truly that it was Rosalba's spirit that must inevitably be wounded in this unnatural warfare, however brittle Virginio's bones might prove" (297).

Elinor Wylie's characters move in a brightly defined ambience. Her customary scholarship delights in this tale, on whose "easy erudition" Walter de la Mare remarked.[8] No slight effort to recreate a milieu, the novel is instructive and amusing with its deft and comprehensive lore of white magic, the history of Venice and the papacy, of the china works at Sèvres and the interlacing details of the lives of Mme de Staël, Clement XIV, Mesmer, Bailly, and others. Besides, it suggests, by means of a historical background, the continuing problem of artifice. The novel's setting may be Venice in 1782, with gondolas afloat on an iridescent Adriatic; or "the ancient Satory quarter of Versailles," skies "dove-coloured" and snowy (310, 311). The problem it allegorizes is the same that afflicted the lives and literary works of the Aesthetes Elinor Wylie, like Pound, knew: respect for the refinement of a Virginio above the sometimes savage vibrancy of a Rosalba: indulgence of an art of muted colors and restricted themes (represented by Virginio's person and his taste for reading about Adriatic flowers); and dismissal of another kind of art, drawn—even like Rosalba's juvenile poems—from multiple sources and emotions. In *The Venetian Glass Nephew*, nature, represented by Rosalba, does indeed "yield" to art, as Carl Van Doren declares in his preface to the novel;[9] but it is a certain kind of art and a nature that is not artless, only too rich for the faculties of the "artist" Elinor Wylie suggests in her glass mannequin. Still,

8. Quoted in Emily Clark, *Innocence Abroad* (New York, 1931), 176.
9. Van Doren, Preface, Wylie, *Collected Prose*, 218.

the true polarities of the tale hypothesize an enmity between art and nature: the composed Virginio is the elegant product of artifice while Rosalba, desperately leaping into a bonfire—prefigurement of her "firing" at Sèvres— suggests the haplessness of human feeling. Elinor Wylie's sympathy in this novel is, like Querini's, Gozzi's, and of course Chastelneuf's, for Rosalba. One remembers once again her sister's phrase: she "quite often valued fine porcelain above humanity." Nevertheless, the novel signifies not only a distrust of literary Aestheticism but of those chilling values that allowed Nancy Mitford, confessedly an "intellectual snob" and aesthete, to lament during World War II "that the portraits [at Chatsworth] are being ruined by the breaths of the evacuee orphans who are occupying the house."[10] In *The Venetian Glass Nephew*, despite the protests of the reasonable Querini, the fanciful Gozzi, and the amorous Chastelneuf, Rosalba Berni gives herself up to be burned, a sacrifice to an artificial world of "millinery" and "whipped cream" (307, 315). The result is the peace of an "Innocent Landscape": charming, passionless, and from Elinor Wylie's point of view, reductive.

The last chapter, "Interior by Longhi," epitomizes the art that triumphs in the novel, a pleasant and decorative one, "drawn in the palest colours of pearls." Virginio and the changed Rosalba meet and kiss "in a place profoundly quiet." "Their very garments [are] awed into submission" (314). Only the tranquil surface of a painting can describe the peaceful design which together they contrive. And appropriately, the painting is an interior (the Venetian artist Pietro Longhi, friend of Gozzi's rival, Goldoni, did, on one occasion a "Domestic Scene," now in the National Gallery at London, which resembles the one Elinor Wylie envisions). The subject of Elinor Wylie's scrutiny is the art of Aestheticism: devoted not to "mercurial wildness" or to celebration of the out-of-doors in which Rosalba once sported but to rooms bright with bibelots and "mirrored images." It is a "twilight" world from which the figure of Chastelneuf is conspicuously absent (315).

Jennifer Lorn was in part autobiographical; so is *The Venetian Glass Nephew*. The latter novel is not only an allegory about art and nature but a vision of sexual conflict, rendered in the language of fantasy. Accused of coldness and yet traduced for lust, Elinor Wylie was unhappy in marriage. Like Edith Whar-

10. Charles Ritchie, *The Siren Years* (London, 1974), 164.

ton, whom she resembled in class, education, taste, and frustration, Wylie assumed that men, who were more educated and freer in her day than women, could provide her with the intellectual and emotional satisfaction that she could not seek independently. Her marriage to Horace Wylie proved that assumption wrong; and it was an assumption that was unfair to both partners. When she wrote *The Venetian Glass Nephew*, she was married to William Rose Benét. She had worked ardently—some thought craftily—to achieve that marriage; but, like her earlier marriages, it failed to satisfy her need for sympathy and sexual satisfaction. The marriage seems to have been for her a tender friendship. By her own admission, she came to understand sexual passion only at the close of her life, when she was in love with Clifford Woodhouse. (To Benét, however, who would try the patience of later wives with memories of his marriage to Elinor, theirs had been a passion indeed.)

It is thus interesting, even poignant, that *The Venetian Glass Nephew*, although it is a fantasy, seems to shadow forth real experience. Its heroine Rosalba is, like Elinor Wylie, an aristocrat, a beauty, and a writer, dowered with "marvellous wit and . . . inventive lightness of mind" (256). She is matched with a gentle, handsome man who regards her with "simple reverence and awe" (257). He is flawed, however: "captured in an earthly net so fragile that its meshes could not withstand the violence of a human soul" (270). It is clear that he will require of Rosalba infinite stability and calm, the violation and suppression of her fiery personality. Yearning over him and his desire to be an adequate husband to her, Rosalba, like the other characters in the *Nephew*, is forced to regard him as the "boy, the poor boy" (296), a revealing phrase that echoes Elinor Wylie's description of Benét to Horace Wylie as "the best boy imaginable."[11] Rosalba is determined to achieve the composure—really, the nonentity—that will prove no challenge to her fragile husband. Thus, in a symbolic act, she walks into flames that will make her inhuman. Marriage exacts of her the supreme price a poet could pay: loss of feeling. In order to satisfy her husband's needs, she becomes "fine porcelain . . . and no longer clay" (303).

Yet what is remarkable about this "fairy tale" that probably had its genesis in real life is the fact that Wylie presents herself, in Rosalba, as the representative of passion and Benét, or Virginio, as passionless. To all who knew them,

11. See Elinor Wylie's letter to Horace Wylie, Chapter I, at n. 24, above.

however; to those who observed Benét's exquisite uxoriousness and the tide of emotion that overwhelmed him even years after her death at any mention of Elinor, the truth was just the opposite. It was Benét who was sympathetic and passionate, and Elinor Wylie, who was, like Virginio, "unresponsive and chilly" (289).

Therefore, *The Venetian Glass Nephew* is, I think, not an allegory about life and art alone; nor is it merely an allegory about human passion and its absence. It also bodies forth, rather sadly, the conflict in the woman-artist to be an acceptable, that is, an unchallenging, wife, to a man less talented than she, but for whom she has genuine feeling. That there is real affection between the symbolic protagonists is clear. Rosalba goes off to be burned in the purest spirit of resignation, and Virginio is lyrically grateful:

> "Adieu, Virginio, my darling," whispered Rosalba.
> "Adieu, adieu, my heart's beloved," the boy replied. Their voices were too low for audible trembling, but their hands, clinging together in the final instant, shook like thin petals in a hurricane. (307)

Max Beerbohm, who shared Elinor Wylie's interest in magic and transformations of body that explained conversions of soul, wrote her an eight-page letter, never sent, in praise of *The Venetian Glass Nephew*. It began, according to one of his biographers, with the confession: "I don't often read a book which I feel I should like to have written." He told friends, "Here is a woman who can write." [12] But Wylie herself wrote Carl Van Doren in a different mood, perhaps because she dimly realized that this anti-Aesthetic fable was still very much an Aesthetic performance: "I am heartily disgusted with the—really you must forgive me, it is the only possible term—gutless Virginio now that I have him between dull commonplace blue cloth covers. . . . Thus it is to write a book under bad conditions and when one is tired—the lack of vitality is all too apparent in the tale." [13]

The "bad conditions" to which she alluded were the Benét house in New Canaan and the need to care for her three stepchildren; and perhaps because of her frustration during that period the *Nephew* presents an even more desperate portrait than *Jennifer Lorn* of a woman "fired" in "crucibles of pain" (*Collected Poems*, 51). From one perspective it is a chilling diatribe against men

12. Katharine Lyon Mix, *Max and the Americans* (Brattleboro, Vt., 1974), 169.
13. Van Doren, Preface, Wylie, *Collected Prose*, 230.

and husbands—though since the hero is a fatherly Casanova, Wylie once again excuses men who protect, and do not demand sexual response from, the heroine. She always denied that the "gutless Virginio" was Benét; but it is certain that she intended Rosalba to represent herself.

The Venetian Glass Nephew restates for its own time the myth of life and art Wilde made for his decade in *Dorian Gray*. Its theme of the limitations of porcelain achieves critical dimension while the colors and shapes of the novel, like the elegaic faces of Wylie's lovers, have the wistful loveliness of her own arabesque art.

CHAPTER VI · THE CHOSEN IMAGE
SHELLEY AS BETTER SELF

For in the fields of Immortality
My spirit should at first have worshipped thine,
A divine presence in a place divine;
Or should have moved beside it on this earth,
A shadow of that substance, from its birth.

PERCY BYSSHE SHELLEY, *Epipsychidion*

 hen Elinor Wylie finished *The Venetian Glass Nephew*, she was at the midpoint of a career cut short by death and in a period of emotional turmoil that she largely sublimated in art. In one poem after another she had argued the defects and advantages of her own narcissism, explored what she saw as the limitations of human love, and voiced the ambition and modesty of a writer for whom art was supreme and who knew she was not yet a great artist. Elegant and celebrated, Wylie was in 1925 a woman fearful that her accomplishments were few; a woman not contented as a wife and not altogether confident as a writer.

In that year she began *The Orphan Angel*. It was to be a romance about the life and character of Percy Bysshe Shelley. While writing the book she referred to it as *Mortal Image*, a title British publishers retained but which was unfortunately changed in the United States because Willa Cather's *Mortal*

Enemy appeared at the same time. Wylie's original title was drawn from a letter of Shelley to John Gisborne written on June 18, 1822, less than a month before he died. The letter said much about Shelley's character—and also about Elinor Wylie's: "I think one is always in love with something or other; the error, and I confess it is not easy for spirits cased in flesh and blood to avoid it, consists in seeking in a mortal image the likeness of what is perhaps eternal."[1]

Shelley's lines were written about Emilia Viviani, who inspired *Epipsychidion* and made him loathe the poem later because "the person whom it celebrates was a cloud instead of a Juno."[2] The yearning after perfection, expressed in sexual love, the lines convey was a desire all too familiar to Elinor Wylie and one that governed her life to its close. The phrase "spirits cased in flesh and blood" with its underlying Platonic conviction that the soul is compromised by its residence in the body finds continual parallels in her own work. For her, too, the body was a "tenement of clay," housing an "austere and silver-dark" spirit which endlessly strove toward a higher completion (*Collected Poems*, 205, 160). The unguarded honesty and pathos of Shelley's confession of "error" must have touched her; for in 1925 she, too, felt that human love was an error that could cause the pain, hardship, and disorder it once caused Shelley. And by 1925 she looked for support to her chosen image of Shelley—an image she had carefully fashioned since her seventh year.

It was a more complicated and extensive support than one usually finds oneself tracing in works of literary criticism for it was sought on a level that was personal as well as professional. It concerned Shelley as a man as well as a poet. To many of Wylie's contemporaries and critics it appeared the bizarre proof of her "odd"[3] personality, and it sometimes subjected her to ridicule. Yet, though extravagant, it was understandable, artistically productive, and a

1. Percy Bysshe Shelley, *Letters*, ed. Roger Ingpen (2 vols.; London, 1909), II, 976.
2. *Ibid.*
3. In a study of Shelley, *Flight of the Skylark* (Norman, Okla., 1954), Sylva Norman, who does not appear to know Wylie's work well, nevertheless voiced the opinion of many about her Shelley enthusiasm: "Shelley does trail some odd appendages. In America several young male and female students, one is credibly informed, believe themselves to be reincarnations. Another of these *revenants* may or may not be Elinor Wylie whose curious poetic fiction, *The Orphan Angel*, portrayed the poet rescued from drowning by an American brig, and enjoying divers picaresque adventures in the New World" (284).

function not only of Wylie's emotional intensity but of the scholarly sensibility she had developed by her thirty-eighth year. Her "entire devotion" to Shelley was viewed even by herself as a remarkable phenomenon. She could not explain why "The Cloud" and "The Skylark" were the first poems she had ever loved, or why as a child of eleven she was deeply moved by Edward John Trelawny's account of Shelley's burial. Both his poems and his life entranced her:

> I first read "The Cloud" and "The Skylark" in my Third Reader, and I think I was seven years old. This was the same winter when my innocent young mother read "Christabel" aloud to me. My admiration for it was so nearly pure horror that "The Skylark" was a great consolation after dark. "If we were things born not to shed a tear"; even a child can understand those words. Then when I was eleven we were no longer in that Victorian high-ceiled house in Philadelphia, where "The Skylark" first sang to me. It was September in Washington and the air was warm and sweet as if all the grapes and peaches of Maryland and Virginia had flavored it to my taste. I stood before the smallest bookcase in the library, and from its shelves I drew Trelawny's "Recollections." The window was wide open; there was plenty of light and soft autumnal wind in the room. I did not move except to turn the pages. Even the black leather chair was too far away from the scene within the covers of the book. I stood quite still and turned the pages, and the curtains blew in at the window and a few golden leaves blew in between them.
>
> So I read for the first time of Shelley's death and burial. I can remember what I felt in that moment of past time, but never what I thought. It is therefore impossible to tell of it except to draw the picture of the room full of light and softer air and of the child standing in the center of the room and turning the pages of the book, afraid to move, afraid to cry for fear the scene within the pages of the book might be hidden from her eyes, wondering and wondering why the bright creature who had lived within that scene should have died and fallen into dust no stronger than the golden leaves blowing in at the window. (*Collected Prose*, 844–45)

Wylie's recollection of her first awareness of Shelley suggests a lover recalling his first glimpse of the beloved. She remembers the season, the climate, the place, and her feelings, not her thoughts. To the child Elinor Hoyt, Shelley appeared first in the guise of comforter: his "Skylark" was "a great consolation" by contrast with the magical satanism of "Christabel"; he was a "bright creature" whose recognized excellence deserved immortality. His appeal to her was at the outset personal, and throughout her life her response to him remained and grew even more personal.

At the same time her attraction to him led her to become a considerable scholar of Shelleyan materials. When she wrote *The Orphan Angel* and many lyrics that address or celebrate Shelley she knew *Adonais*, *Alastor*, *Epipsychidion*, and the shorter poems by heart, could quote at random from all his other poems and letters, and was aware in minute detail of what had been said of him by his nineteenth-century biographers. In revivifying Shelley in fiction, she easily summoned that wide knowledge, providing as well an interpretation of his life and character that she formulated more objectively in several essays. The literary establishment was respectful of this masterly knowledge; but when it manifested itself—as it did toward the close of her life—in an identification with Shelley so earnest as to affect her choice of London inns, clothes, food, and way of speaking, they reacted with amusement or impatience. To the reader interested in Elinor Wylie, however (or for that matter, to one interested in the affiliation of modern poets with Romantic art) it seems important to ask a few questions. Why did the life of Shelley so absorb her? Was it of equal attraction to her as the poems themselves? What specific effects did this passion of the mind have on her own writing? And, finally, was it in any way dictated by Wylie's awareness that she, like other modern poets, was the immediate descendant of the Aesthetes and that, as her lyric "Tragic Dialogue" laments, "a hundred years" separated her art from Shelley's? (*Collected Poems*, 166).

Each of these questions is, of course, intimately related so that one involves the rest. To entertain the first question is to speculate widely because no form of love is completely explicable. But, as we have seen, the figure of Shelley appeared to Wylie first as comforter. When she remembered "The Skylark" in her dedication (to Shelley) of *Trivial Breath*, she thanked him for his "courtesy" in providing "an innocent bird, an iridescent music / To be my own for all the rest of living." He had given her to "refresh [her] childhood" a "primer" of innocence expressed in radiant language (111). "Cristabel," which she admired and found horrible, is about a pitiable loss of female sexual innocence accomplished by secular as well as diabolical evil and hence would be dimly threatening to a sheltered little girl. The early impression that

Shelley symbolized innocence she kept all her life and made proof against every rejoinder. Aldous Huxley, for instance, teased her after reading her "angelic orphan" that, though he admired the elegance of her style, she had treated her Shelley "too handsomely";[4] and it is true that Wylie never acknowledged Shelley's appetitive selfishness. The line Benét had carved on her tombstone was the one-hundred-fifteenth of *Epipsychidion*: "An image of some bright Eternity." It represents one aspect of Shelley's regard for Emilia Viviani: his Platonic desire for a marriage of souls. But other lines in *Epipsychidion* extol "Passion's golden purity," "burning," "touch[ing]," and "mingl[ing],"[5] an experience he certainly envisioned and desired. In *The Orphan Angel*, stories, and poems, Wylie chose, however, to make him the shy and mystified recipient of others' devotion, a boy-man discomfited by the recollection of his erotic past.

In one way she was supporting the views of Shelley's contemporaries. His cousin Thomas Medwin, borrowing Thomas Jefferson Hogg's phrase, remarked of him, "In no individual perhaps was the moral sense ever more completely developed."[6] Thomas Love Peacock had said he was like "a great apostle of liberty," a man of good temper with almost an "excess of charity."[7] They were speaking of his altruism, his love of the poor and helpless, his self-sacrificing efforts to rescue friends—virtues Wylie faithfully celebrated. They were not, however, setting aside his natural appetites. Wylie's depiction of him as an angel was in part an effort to combat Victorian views like Aubrey De Vere's that he was "a Fallen Angel . . . with sad limitations"[8] as to sex, and though she was capable of admitting that "he had made some grave and tragic errors of judgment" (*Collected Prose*, 843) she disliked having to include sexual appetite among them. It was important to her to insist on Shelley's purity. Why?

4. See Aldous Huxley, *Letters*, ed. Grover Smith (New York, 1969), 277–78, Letter to Elinor Wylie, Christmas, 1926.

5. Percy Bysshe Shelley, *The Complete Poetical Works*, ed. Thomas Hutchinson (London, 1948), 414, *Epipsychidion*, lines 571, 578, 579. All references to Shelley's poetry are to this edition.

6. Thomas Medwin, *The Life of Percy Bysshe Shelley* (London, 1913), 316.

7. Thomas Love Peacock, *Memoirs of Percy Bysshe Shelley*, in *The Life of Shelley*, ed. Humbert Wolfe (2 vols.; London, 1933), II, 359. Wylie uses the latter phrase as the title of her review of the Julian edition of Roger Ingpen and Walter E. Peck (eds.), *The Complete Works of Shelley* (10 vols.; London, 1926–30). See Elinor Wylie, *Collected Prose* (New York, 1946), 839–45.

8. Norman, *Flight of the Skylark*, 22.

In her own life she had been pilloried for what was regarded as sexual delinquency. Even her professional career was affected by her youthful actions. The League of American Penwomen, for example, denied her membership because she had run from a husband to a lover and left a child. Shelley, she knew, was excoriated in print, notably by the *Gentleman's Magazine*, because he had married, then left, young Harriet Westbrook, seducing (as the public thought most vicious) yet another virgin, Mary Godwin. His efforts to regain his children by Harriet were more unsuccessful and humiliating than Wylie's less sincere early efforts to secure young Philip Hichborn. Shelley was ostracized for sins against what Wylie regarded as convention, what he called "Custom." Indeed, she found similarities between the course of her adult life and Shelley's. Importantly, both had been subjected to the accusation of lust. Wylie was convinced that her own actions were high-minded, the results of a quest for moral and intellectual fulfillment. Certainly Shelley's, as his statements and poems proved to her, were the same, and she was not eager to admit that what she thought his superior Platonic erotism might have an admixture of fleshly desire. Thus in representing Shelley as an "angel" or even "archangel" in her poems she was in part defending herself.

Indeed, her great interest in Shelley was perhaps on a fundamental (and subconscious?) level a function of self-interest. Yet it was ennobled by Wylie's profound belief that as a person, and certainly as a poet, Shelley was her superior. On one hand, he seemed to her a companion spirit, one who, especially in love, had made the same mistakes and suffered the same disappointments and calumny as she; one who, like her, regarded the soul as divine and whose celebrations of intellectual beauty inspired and corroborated her own. On the other hand, he was her patron saint, one who "Need never call the Trinity his betters," a master spirit of which she herself was the mere "inferior copy" (*Collected Poems*, 278, 205). As a person, he possessed virtues she lacked; as a poet, he had achieved grand style and utterance. Her saint, he became the subject of several devotional lyrics and essays and the recipient of homage. Her devotion dictated pilgrimages to places sanctified by his presence and even the wearing of appropriately ethereal garb when venerating his memory. This latter aspect of Wylie's regard for Shelley often provoked laughter. And yet her acute absorption in the life and poetry of Shelley produced two responses of lasting value for her art.

Elinor Wylie made of Shelley's life "a supreme fiction." Wallace Stevens, many of whose sympathies she shared, speaks of the work of an artist as the creation of "supreme fictions" in which mankind could find fulfillment, adding that such creation involves "the interaction between reality and imagination."[9] In her fictions about Shelley's life—particularly in *Mr. Hodge and Mr. Hazard* in which she depicts Shelley at the age of forty and allows him to be sexually as well as intellectually complex—Wylie proposed a life ideal in its intention if not in its government or reward. In exploring the life of Shelley, she attempted to freshen her reader's sense of what life might be if experienced by a higher Romantic sensibility. Her vision of Shelley resulted from a fusion of reality, suggested by those who knew him, and her own perceptions. She was aware that her dream of Shelley was in many respects a fiction, yet it gave her comfort and a spur to accomplishment. To her, his failures were really fulfillments. And in the drama of Shelley's poetic aspiration and personal disappointment she saw an emblem of the difference between Romantic art that risked much and Aesthetic art that thrived on limitation. Shelley's life was to her an explication of the worthwhile, and since he was an artist-saint, the hagiographies Wylie wrote in her fictions were studies of aesthetically as well as morally venerable traits. Shelley's genius for epical grand utterance was to Wylie, who practiced small forms like the sonnet and quatrain, clear proof of his technical mastery and wide-ranging philosophical vision. She knew that in her choice of small forms and her avoidance of more expansive ones, in her restrained and chiseled diction and her preference for discreet subjects, she did not show his genius, his broader moral sympathies.

She made this difference one of her major themes, doing homage to Shelley's art in a series of her own poems. One group is characteristically— and colloquially and mundanely—called "A Red Carpet for Shelley." (Since Elinor Wylie preferred highly formal speech one wonders whether the title recommended itself as a means of half-humorously humbling herself before her saint and heightening the distinction between them.) In these devotional poems in which Wylie celebrates Shelley's "pure and fiery pulse / By true divinity informed," she often uses his characteristic imagery (157). Yet it is used not to imitate but to define and exemplify Shelley's genius and to

9. Wallace Stevens, "The Noble Rider and the Sound of Words," *The Necessary Angel* (New York, 1951), 31.

recreate the "atmosphere" of his poetry even as with her devout scholarship she described the patterns of his speech and behavior in her novels. She liked to ask him to "forgive the complicated brittle coil / Of [her] infirm invention"—certainly an allusion to her method of seeing and writing—and to say, imitating his own imagery, that he deserved better: "crystal hills, the veiled prismatic plain" (159).

Although she acknowledged the disparity between Shelley's genius and her own talent, Elinor Wylie's conception of him as a kindred spirit—or, more properly, a better self—did, I think, affect some of the attitudes assumed in her poems and even their settings on occasion. For example, Wylie's poems speak openly of her own beauty, of her unfortunate past and the scorn it provoked toward her in others, and of a desire to escape the world either by writing well or by dying, usually in the sea. Such openness always attracted critical accusations of egoism or personal weakness. Yet in *Adonais*, his celebration of the genius of Keats, Shelley devotes four powerful stanzas to an anatomy of his own appearance, nature, forebodings, and wasted career (never violating the tone or deflecting the intention of his elegy). He calls himself a "frail Form / A phantom among men," "A pard-like Spirit beautiful and swift—/ A Love in desolation masked;—a Power / Girt round with weakness." [10] These lines were the source of many of Wylie's poetic allusions to him as ghost, phantom, or companionable cloud, and they articulate what she emphasized in him and in the Romantic spirit: beauty, celerity of apprehension, loneliness, pain. They are, and were certainly intended to be, ardently confessional, an expression of the disparity Shelley felt between his ability and what he had done with it and between his true self and skill and how they were misjudged. His "life," he said, "burn[ed] in blood" yet his heart was broken; he was "neglected and apart; / A herd-abandoned deer struck by the hunter's dart." [11] Lines like these doubtless encouraged Matthew Arnold to strike out his famous, (reluctantly) censorious description of the Shelley he admired for his gentlemanliness, as "a beautiful *and ineffectual* angel." [12] Their music is so suasive as perhaps to beguile belief that their

10. Shelley, *Works*, ed. Hutchinson, 438, *Adonais*, lines 271–72, 281, 280, 282.

11. *Ibid.*, 439, lines 288, 296–97.

12. In her essay "Excess of Charity," Wylie declares that she "cannot pardon . . . Matthew Arnold for his blindness toward Shelley" (*Collected Prose*, 842). Actually, in his famous essay

accomplished author was, as he called himself, not only "beautiful" but "weak." Yet their outright admission of beauty, like their admission of failure, not only served Shelley's purpose in *Adonais*—to emphasize Keats's gifts— but also defined a certain quality of spirit: aristocratic, finely strung, perhaps doomed to be or to see itself as "broken."

That spirit Wylie recreated in her fictions about Shelley. And to a lesser degree she regarded that spirit as her own. The example of Shelley's characterization of himself in *Adonais* and other poems, the text (as it were) of his self-inquiry, without doubt encouraged Wylie to study herself in art with that complete absorption some critics considered solipsistic. It was perhaps easier for her to prefer "beautiful people" because he numbered himself among them, easier to say she "carr[ied] a dagger in her heart" when Shelley called himself a "stricken deer" (63).

Then, too, what Wylie knew about Shelley's life affected not only her fictions but her poetry. If she was able in fiction to render the precise rhythms of his speech and to imagine from biographical inference how he would respond to new places and new philosophies, she was also able in verse to allude tellingly to his life and art. Besides, her sympathy with the ideas of Shelley was so delicate that it could embrace an adoption of his symbolic modes of feeling: for example, his vision of the sea, of water, and what it signified of eternity and unchanging change. She had known since she was eleven years old that Shelley had died by drowning, a strange accident of fate by which presentiment and hallucination were verified in actual event. And it is surely no accident that in such of her own poems as "Atavism," "Song," or "Drowned Woman," she envisions her own death by drowning; that in "Sea Lullaby," she dreams of the sea strangling a boy; or that in "The Coast Guard's Cottage" she imagines herself making love to a man newly drowned. "The Coast Guard's Cottage" was published in *Trivial Breath* and written at a time

---

"Shelley" Arnold declares that Shelley "resembled" "an angel of charity"; that "he loved high thoughts [and] was poignantly afflicted at the sight of misery"; and pays him many other compliments. He concludes, however, that Shelley "was extremely inflammable"; that "when the passion of love was aroused in [him] . . . his friends could not trust him"; and that "an inhuman want of humour and a superhuman power of self-deception" caused his "misconduct." What perhaps excited Wylie's animus toward Arnold is his final judgment: "The man Shelley . . . is not entirely sane, and Shelley's poetry is not entirely sane either" (see A. Dwight Culler (ed.), *Poetry and Criticism of Matthew Arnold* [Boston, 1961], 363–80).

when Wylie despaired of human love and had begun to reflect that the only true affection she had sustained was her love for Shelley. In that poem she tells the ghostly "flesh of mortal man, lately [her] fellow" that she does not care if his "eyes be blind," if there is "seaweed in [his] hair," or if he no longer has a mouth: "Have cruel fishes made your kisses dumb?"—a description faithful to Trelawny's account of the remains of Shelley, eaten away by fish almost beyond recognition (149).[13] Because of Shelley, water became her image of surcease but also of terrible denial:

> The element of water has denied
> Its child; it is no more his element;
> It never will relent;
> Its silver harvests are more sparsely given
> Than the rewards of heaven,
>
> . . . .
> The water is too wide: (201)

The Shelley Elinor Wylie revered seemed to her a self superior to her own in great ways and in small. Several critics, speaking of Wylie's devotion to Shelley, declared that before her death she imagined herself Shelley reincarnate.[14] Carl Van Doren helps to clarify that issue, saying that she "not only loved Shelley but identified herself with him." Van Doren continues his memoir by quoting one of Wylie's letters in which she apologizes for "writing out of a purple thundercloud of gloom," adding, "I'm sorry that I'm beginning to imitate Shelley in this melancholy fashion. Poor darling Shelley, I have not his other virtues to make my dejection forgivable!"[15] That statement, like others, reveals Wylie's perception of the differences between her own nature and Shelley's; such a perception would never have permitted her to confuse their separate identities. These differences are appealingly rendered or implied in her essays.

Wylie always indicated the distinction, for instance, between her own

13. Edward John Trelawny, *Recollections of Shelley and Byron* in *The Life of Shelley*, ed. Wolfe, II, 217.

14. See Julia Cluck, for instance, in "Elinor Wylie's Shelley Obsession," *PMLA*, LVI (1941), 842; and Stanley Olson, *Elinor Wylie: A Life Apart* (New York, 1979), 258.

15. Carl Van Doren, *Three Worlds* (New York, 1936), 217.

sophistication and Shelley's naïveté. She liked to spoof his elaborate rhetoric as Peacock did more acerbically in *Nightmare Abbey*. He had acquired his rhetoric from the eighteenth century she admired and transformed it into a decorous instrument for the expression of inflammatory ideas. Peacock's brilliant "Scythrop" who chatters about "unconsentaneous" principles and "respective necessitated volition" and his voluble, open-minded atheist appear together in her essay "Mr. Shelley Speaking." In that essay and others it is Shelley's innocence—never wholly masked by verbal elegance—that once again amuses and attracts her. "Imagine," she writes,

> the solemn comedy of the scene, demurely recounted by Peacock, when Shelley takes a sudden fancy to enter the Church of England and his friend warns him gently of the difficulties inherent in such a plan!
>
> "It is an admirable institution," says Shelley with stubborn meekness, "that admits the possibility of diffusing such men over the surface of the land. And am I to deprive myself of the advantages of this admirable institution because there are certain technicalities to which I cannot give my adhesion, but which I need not bring prominently forward?" (*Collected Prose*, 849)

Like Hogg, Trelawny, and other contemporary biographers of Shelley, Elinor Wylie loved the forgetfulness that made him fail to eat, buy a new coat, or trim a sail while reading Aeschylus or writing poetry. To her he was forever the patient idealist who protected Mary Godwin Shelley from her father's tirades, corrected Byron's verses, and took time to run races with Byron's little Allegra in her Italian convent. He was the boy whose hair silvered early, who grieved for the death of his children, who could not in all humorless goodwill understand why his first wife would not live with his mistress as a sister. In short he seemed to Wylie (who had plenty of it) lacking in secular awareness. He was imbued, she thought, with the generosity of a saint. Her vision of him and the feelings she expresses toward him in poetry accord with Mary Shelley's description of Shelley in the Preface to the first (1839) edition of his poems: "He walked beside [those who knew him intimately] like a spirit of good to comfort and benefit—to enlighten the darkness of life with irradiations of genius, to cheer it with his sympathy and love. Any one, once attached to Shelley, must feel all other affections, however true and fond, as wasted on barren soil in comparison. It is our best consolation to know that such a pure-minded and exalted being was once among us."[16] At the close of Elinor Wylie's life, tormented by a last, unhappy love affair, she took renewed solace in the conviction that Shelley's spirit walked beside her; that, as she declared in her last poems, he might be once again her guardian and comforter, once again her supreme beloved after barren loves.

The little follies Wylie permitted herself in her devotion to Shelley did not abate as she grew older. She exaggerated the unpleasant shrillness of her voice because she knew Shelley's voice had been shrill. When William Rose Benét visited her in England in the late 1920s he was annoyingly teased about his preference for beef and beer; by then Wylie subscribed to Shelley's light diet—bread and raisins, vegetables and tea. She liked to imagine that her wide-set eyes and marcelled hair made her face resemble the large-eyed Shelley's with his cap of curls. She let no one forget that Shelley's great-grandfather had come from Somerville, New Jersey, where she was born. She was known to "dress for Shelley."[17] These were pious acts, and they were efforts to close the distance between herself and him.

In the poem "Tragic Dialogue," however, she acknowledges that distance which in character as in genius she knew was absolute. "Tragic Dialogue" concludes *Trivial Breath*, the volume she dedicated to Shelley. In it the chief speaker is questioned about her ability to maintain relationship with an unnamed spirit:

> "Does not the progressive wheel of years
> Composed of baser metals
> Obscure him from your eyes, whose tears
> Have turned to willow petals?"

The years of "baser metals"—the years of Victorian and Georgian verse?—might be expected to cloud Wylie's vision of this spirit. And he is certainly Shelley, whose death in 1821 antedated by one hundred years Wylie's debut as a poet and whose personal sorrow had, like his flesh, mingled according to Romantic creed with the larger life of nature. The questioner persists in the

---

16. Shelley, *Works*, ed. Hutchinson, xi.
17. Emily Clark, *Innocence Abroad* (New York, 1931), 179–80.

second quatrain and represents, perhaps, those who found Wylie's intense
empathy with the personal Shelley rather singular:

> "A hundred years! This iron bar
> Has beaten you, and hindered?"
>
> . . . .
>
> The poet replies in a rush of warmth,
> "Not so: on no extremest star
> Had he and I been kindred.
>
> . . . .
>
> Then she adopts a realistic, humbler view:
> "Ah no, both happily and alas!
> A clover field, a river,
> A hawthorne hedge, a pane of glass
> Had parted us forever." (166)

The clover field, river, and hawthorne hedge, suggestive both of the landscape
of England and of the Romantic lyric, "part" her from Shelley: "happily"
because a saint must remain himself in order for the worshiper to stay content
in a posture of emulation but "alas," for as the use of the word "had" suggests,
if Shelley knew her and her verse, Wylie imagines he would not admit her to
his fellowship. In this quatrain the image of the "pane of glass" seems to me
poignant and illustrative as well of Wylie's conviction of her distinction from
Shelley. Gazing at each other through the most transparent obstruction,
looking into each other's faces, they would nonetheless be "parted . . .
forever" for the measure of their gifts was disproportionate.

When *The Orphan Angel* became a best seller and a Book-of-the-Month
Club Selection Elinor Wylie was paid handsomely and used a large portion of
her reward to purchase a part of the manuscript of *Prometheus Unbound*,
together with a check Shelley had written to William Godwin. She thought of
her purchases, wrote her sister, as of "a saint's relics."[18] Her ardor seemed
comical to some, though not to Edna St. Vincent Millay who, writing after
Wylie's death, remembered how vividly she had spoken of Shelley: "(I think
that . . . Shelley died with you—) / He live[s] on paper now, another way."[19]

---

18. Nancy Hoyt, *Elinor Wylie: The Portrait of an Unknown Lady* (New York, 1935), 127.

19. Edna St. Vincent Millay, "To Elinor Wylie, IV," "Nobody now throughout the pleasant
day," *Collected Poems*, ed. Norma Millay (New York, 1956), 372.

Wylie's devotion to Shelley enriched her own art and performed a useful function in the history of letters. For it is fitting and generative for lesser writers to celebrate greater ones, ultimate possibilities being then implied in discreet achievements. In Elinor Wylie's devotion to Shelley, she herself found "a likeness of what is . . . eternal" (*cf.* p. 114). In finding in his life and art major subjects, she proposed them to other readers.

CHAPTER VII · *THE ORPHAN ANGEL*

That which most breeds art is art.

WILLIAM MORRIS, *The Beauty of Life*

There are some stories [like Shelley's]
which have to be retold by each
generation . . . because of some queer
quality in them which makes them not
only Shelley's story but our own.

VIRGINIA WOOLF, "Not One of Us"

hen Elinor Wylie died, she left several unfinished manuscripts. Among the longest is three chapters of *April, April*, the beginning of a novel that introduces the figure of Shelley to Greenwich Village in 1927. It opens by reestablishing Godwin's Skinner Street shop on a street that resembles Wylie's own West 9th. There a Claire (Clairmont) who looks like Elinor Wylie of the "small . . . wrists and ankles" (*Collected Poems*, 63) waits daily for a Shelley who has met but not yet loved Mary Godwin. He is the blond, freckle-nosed boy with wild curls, lustrous eyes, and stumbling gait who appears in the memoirs of Thomas Jefferson Hogg. He talks like the biographical Shelley, quotes Milton, and loves music. But he also has some of the tastes Elinor Wylie developed in the late 1920s: for cigarettes, dining at the Brevoort Hotel, and buying fancy cakes at Dean's. With his lean, casual, aristocratic grace, one could—unfortu-

nately—imagine him scribbling an occasional quatrain for *Vanity Fair* as did Elinor Wylie. He chats with Claire on a dimly lit spring afternoon fragrant with Wildean roses. Despite his fashionable, even Gatsbyan air, he remains Shelley: innocent, idealistic. He will certainly be entrapped by the pensive minx Mary because the elegant Claire seems not to need his help. The manuscript ends, having established Wylie's knowledge of the Godwin circle and her admiration for Shelley's chivalry.

April, April repeats earlier themes and images. The contrast between her Shelley and a practical, proletarian poet named Mosher (or at one point Moseley) recalls that between Mr. Hazard and Mr. Hodge in Wylie's last novel. *April, April* would probably not have enlarged the scope of Wylie's achievement. Yet it illustrates her increased desire in middle years to write about the life of Shelley and to relate it ever more nearly to her own. In this unfinished fragment she attempted to create a Shelley who lived in her own time and neighborhood. But she had set him on the voyage toward her four years earlier in *The Orphan Angel*.

This most popular of her books created disharmony among critics and colleagues who could not decide whether it was (as Maxwell Anderson said of *Jennifer Lorn*) "realistic, romantic . . . burlesque . . . fantastic, historical, impressionistic, ironic, satiric, epic [or] lyric" or, as Carl Van Doren finally called it, a "comic romance."[1] It closely resembles Virginia Woolf's *Orlando*, published two years later. It is, for instance, openly celebratory with the vivacity of a tour de force. Like *Orlando* it is a playful fantasia that with gossipy intimacy reveals the details of its subject's life, foibles, and enthusiasms. And like *Orlando* it was doubtless motivated in part by romantic feeling. Unlike *Orlando*'s, of course, this feeling was for a great, dead poet who the author believed had changed the face of literature rather than for a minor, living writer with whom the author had had a brief affair. Nevertheless these novels were similar in method. To pay tribute to the versatile gifts of her lover, Vita Sackville-West, Virginia Woolf depicted her in various settings in time. Wylie, too, placed Shelley in an unfamiliar setting—indeed, an often rugged, semibarbarous one—in which his gentle virtues appear undiminished. By revivifying the drowned Shelley and introducing him to the New World in

---

1. Maxwell Anderson in the New York *World*, November 18, 1923; Carl Van Doren, *Three Worlds* (New York, 1936), 233.

which Wylie herself would be born, she gratified a personal desire to associate their lives. The women of the young America of 1822 think Shelley "the mortal image of an angel" (*Collected Prose*, 511). Thus as in *Orlando*, the artist-lover proves the excellence of the beloved by imagining the lover's conquest in other times, other places.

Few who admire the novels of Virginia Woolf would claim that *Orlando* was more than a high-style literary valentine. And there are readers, past and present, who thoroughly dislike *The Orphan Angel*. James Branch Cabell, bored by Wylie's devotion to the smallest details of Shelley's life, dismissed it as baffling, "one of the most gloomy errors in literary history."[2] Stanley Olson, contemptuous of Wylie's Shelley enthusiasm, declares, "Elinor's interest in Shelley brought out the worst in her."[3] Although *The Orphan Angel* is no less a fantasy than *Jennifer* or *The Venetian Glass Nephew* and exhibits the same fascination with history, it differs in ways that probably alienated others as it did Cabell. *Jennifer* and the *Nephew* mention historic personages, but *The Orphan Angel* is centered on a person from the past who was an artist. Thus it attempts to describe Shelley's life, not out of concern for its interesting detail but for Shelley's conduct as a writer. More than *Orlando* it makes every effort to represent his physique, behavior, speech, and thoughts as they were known to have been. There is a reverent earnestness about the novel which, despite its good humor, distinguishes it from Wylie's other books. And her passion to associate herself with Shelley is revealed so clearly in *The Orphan Angel* that the tone of the novel is sometimes sentimental and lacks the wit or bitter tenderness of the early books or the last, best one, *Mr. Hodge and Mr. Hazard*. Finally, the private jokes and secret understandings that make *Orlando* a limited work find certain parallels in *The Orphan Angel*. It is no accident that most of the characters, male and female, resemble Elinor Wylie in one or many respects; or that the woman her Shelley figure seeks to rescue is called Sylvie or Silver, a word so continually associated with Wylie that her husband named her "Sylvia" in *The Dust Which Is God*. The androgynous quality of her characters is somewhat like *Orlando*'s and may originate in Wylie's desire to *be* Shelley: a great poet, a male, a spirit whose adventurousness was even more

2. See Stanley Olson, *Elinor Wylie: A Life Apart* (New York, 1979), 281. In *As I Remember It* (New York, 1955), Cabell says that Wylie never forgave his indifference to *The Orphan Angel*.
3. Stanley Olson, *Elinor Wylie: A Life Apart* (New York, 1979), 283.

pronounced than her own, while at the same time she subconsciously (and often consciously) wished to be Shelley's mate. The androgynous face of her Shelley figures provides a fictive fulfillment of Woolf's prescription in *A Room of One's Own* that "some collaboration" between the masculine and feminine must "take place in the mind" of a true writer.[4] The "man"-poet Wylie conceived to inhabit herself was like Shelley, and so her characters, resembling her, resembling him, enact romances that may symbolize her creative self as Wylie saw it.

The subjects of *Orlando*—the aristocratic lineage and bisexuality of Vita Sackville-West—are less lofty than Elinor Wylie's subject in *The Orphan Angel*: the greatness of Shelley as person and poet. Readers of this novel were to ponder and admire the sincerity with which his innocent spirit encountered the voyage of life. It is as a voyage, then, that she devises the plot of her novel. Anyone conversant with Shelley's poems would understand the appropriateness of that mode for, like his life, they insist on a heroic Platonic ideal of search and discovery. Wylie devises for her Shelley, too, a chivalric dream, a quest, with which Shelley himself might have sympathized, for he must rescue an unfortunate girl—a composite of all the unfortunate girls from Harriet and Mary to Emilia Viviani—with whom the real Shelley concerned himself in his pursuit of "'Vision and Love.'"

Shelley's contrapuntal desires to escape and triumph and yet to rest (expressed in "Stanzas—April, 1814," for instance, which begin with the injunction "Away" and end asking peace) are embodied in Wylie's narrative. It is a picaresque tale, its two central characters, the aristocratic Shiloh (Shelley) and rustic David Butternut suggesting that pair of antithetical adventurers Don Quixote and Sancho Panza. But for all the comedy occasioned by their differences and by the difference between Shiloh's upbringing and assumptions and those of the early Americans he meets, *The Orphan Angel* never loses sight of the sad disquietude of the Shelley who wrote *Alastor*.

Alastor describes "a Poet," "a lovely youth," "Gentle, and brave, and generous," whose "untimely tomb" is made "in the waste wilderness" and who "lived . . . died . . . sung, in solitude."[5] Wylie's Shiloh has had Shelley's

---

4. Virginia Woolf, *A Room of One's Own* (New York, 1929), 181.
5. Percy Bysshe Shelley, *The Complete Poetical Works*, ed. Thomas Hutchinson (London, 1948), *Alastor*, 16, lines 50, 55, 58, 54, 60.

experiences, believes as Shelley declares in *Prometheus Unbound* that "Peace is in the grave," and longs to embark on the journey of death. Failing that, however, he is pleased to embark for America, which he considers a noble wilderness. Byron had nicknamed Shelley "Shiloh" after that biblical sanctuary for the Ark of the Covenant, home of Eli and Samuel, which implied his otherworldly goodness. In a witty and comfortable imaginative gesture Wylie has her Americans in the *Angel* misunderstand Shelley's name, thus looking ahead to the Civil War battle of Shiloh and associating Shelley with a significant American event. In the wilderness his otherworldliness shines with peculiar intensity. He does not, like Alastor, live solitary and die, but, like him, he is surrounded by "strangers [who weep] to hear his passionate notes" and "virgins" who pine and waste "for fond love of his wild eyes."[6] The Shelley who wrote in *Julian and Maddalo*, "I love all waste and solitary places," is represented in *The Orphan Angel* as is the Shelley who served the unfortunate, idealized women, liked politics, and was devoted to social change.

Another Shelley, however, is unrepresented: the man capable of hallucinations, not merely of distracting thoughts; the profoundly tortured personality of the last poems and letters who was, as Wylie herself said in essays, no longer boyish or buoyant but deeply anguished. That Shelley she attempts to commemorate in *Mr. Hodge and Mr. Hazard*; for despite his sensitive and frequent melancholy, Elinor Wylie's Shiloh is still unbroken by life and *The Orphan Angel* is a lighthearted tribute to a Shelley of diverse responses.

When the novel opens it is "the eighth of July, 1822, at half past six in the evening." Readers of Trelawny's *Last Days of Shelley and Byron* will recall that when Shelley's boat disappeared from view on that day, taking him to his death, "it was almost dark" in Leghorn Harbor "although only half-past six o'clock." The sea was "smooth as a sheet of lead," "gusts of wind swept over without ruffling it," and "there was a commotion in the air . . . the crashing voice of a thunder squall."[7] In *The Orphan Angel* the sea is smooth as "glass," the sails of the American vessel *Witch of the West*, pulling out of Leghorn Harbor, are "naked and singing shrouds against the force and violence of the

---

6. *Ibid.*, lines 61–63.

7. Edward John Trelawny, *Recollections of Shelley and Byron*, in *The Life of Shelley*, ed. Humbert Wolfe (2 vols.; London, 1933), II, 215–16.

summer hurricane," and her captain, gazing at "a descending veil of darkness," sees "suddenly, with the amazement of a thunderclap . . . a human countenance emerg[ing] from this sinister obscurity to float upon the dark like a drowning star, without mortality or substance" (329, 331).

The face disturbs Captain Ffoulkastle because it closely resembles that of Jasper Cross, one of his sailors, newly murdered and still lying on deck: "'Strike my timbers,'" he cries (in a colloquial American supposed to recall the bracing idiom of the American seaman Shelley meets in Trelawny's memoirs), "'if I didn't think it was that sarpent Jasper, . . . I'll stake my soul it's Jasper's ghost I seen'" (331). Shelley had visited a Yankee ship in Leghorn Harbor whose mate spoke of it as "a brass sarpent." The mate asked Shelley aboard and invited him to ship to Boston with him. Captain Ffoulkastle, voyaging to Boston, orders the drowning figure taken aboard by David Butternut, a young seaman from Maine who had killed Jasper in self-defense. David becomes for the rest of the novel a symbolic figure, however provincial and young. He represents the unformed United States, respecting Shelley's superior culture and thereby voicing the worshipful thoughts of Wylie herself.

When David sees that the near-drowned youth is Jasper's purer image—"brighter, clearer, fairer, as if from the blessing of another planet" (332)—he concludes that the stranger has been sent to redeem him from sin. Pledging a lasting friendship, he tries to resuscitate him with peach brandy. As the stranger awakes, "slim and strange and foreign to the scene, with his preposterous elegance, his romantic grace, and the aristocratic attenuation of his frame," we know even more clearly what the captain takes months to believe: that he is Shelley (347). He asks for "Edward"—Edward Williams, with whom Shelley drowned—and Charles Vivian, their mate on the ill-fated *Don Juan*; in his pockets are Shelley's volumes of Keats and Sophocles; and in his mouth is Wylie's equivalent of Shelley's rhetoric. To David's solicitous "'Are you all right?'" he replies, "'I am exceedingly sorry to constitute myself a nuisance, and I would not for the world have you distress yourself upon my poor account, but I believe, my dear David, that I am about to solve the great mystery of dissolution'" (335).

These are the comically solemn cadences of Trelawny's Shelley who mourned that he could not swim. Invited to try, he sank straight to the bottom and was "fished out" to announce, "I always find the bottom of the

well, and they say Truth lies there. In another minute I should have found
it. . . . [I]n another minute I might have been in another planet."[8] Trelawny's,
Hogg's, and Peacock's Shelley—the man who, as a simple Italian sailor later
told Shelley's son, was like Jesus Christ—is everywhere present in the aspect
and attitudes of Elinor Wylie's, lying "with quiet eyelids" and the "dark hair"
of the biographies, the locks "folded about his forehead like a spiked and
ghostly crown," to David Butternut, a crown like Christ's (337).

Captain Ffoulkastle urges the stranger, whose name is incorrectly heard as
"Shiloh,"[9] to travel to Boston in Jasper's place in order to save David from
prosecution. His eyes are "wild and stag-like," the "wild eyes" of the poet in
Alastor. He agrees to go, though his spirit "'sinks to desolation'" (343) with
worry about his wife and child left in Lerici. At first it is agreed that he will
work for passage money and ship back as soon as he reaches Boston. Then
David Butternut confides that Jasper Cross had a sister, Sylvie or Silver, and
asks him to travel to St. Louis with him to explain Jasper's death and give her,
an orphan, what help they can. It is precisely the sort of pilgrimage that might
have appealed to Shelley; and since Shiloh is no more certain of his wife's love
than Shelley was before he died, he agrees to accompany David, first dispatch-
ing a letter to Lerici to inquire whether she wants him back.

As the story unfolds, the context in which Wylie has placed her Shiloh
grows more and more apt. Shelley loved boats. "The water," his cousin
Medwin ironically recalled, "was his fatal element";[10] his keenest delight was
either in sailing real boats like the skiff Byron remembered him using on the
flooded Arno or the paper boats with which he amused children (as Shiloh
will amuse the frontier children in *The Orphan Angel*). Shelley's poet in *Alastor*
conducts his search for ideal beauty by sailing upon lonely seas "to seek
strange truths in undiscovered lands."[11] Again and again in the Shelley canon,
revelation—even the ultimate revelation of death as peace—is acquired by
voyaging on water. Depressed, Shelley had once written his wife Mary, "My

8. *Ibid.*, 190.
9. Thus enabling Wylie to use Byron's nickname for Shelley. See Byron's letter to Richard
Belgrave Hoppner on September 10, 1820, in which he says, "I regret you have such a bad
opinion of Shiloh. . . . His *Islam* had much poetry" (Rowland E. Prothero [ed.], *The Works of
Lord Byron* [7 vols.; London, 1898–1901], Vol. V, *Letters and Journals*, 73–74).
10. Thomas Medwin, *The Life of Percy Bysshe Shelley* (London, 1913), 905.
11. *Alastor*, 17, line 77.

great . . . content would be to desert all human society—I would retire with you and our child, to a solitary isle in the sea,—would build a boat, and shut upon my retreat the flood-gates of the world."[12] Wylie's Shiloh closely paraphrases these lines when he says, "My greatest content would be to retire with my wife and child, to some cabin in the wilderness or solitary island in the sea" (364); and Shelley's complex associations with boats as means of escape and of discovery and communication with the visionary ideal he linked with wilderness and solitude are summarized in Shiloh's passage on *The Witch of the West*.

The ship's name recalls the theme of sorcery frequently connected as in *Alastor* or *The Witch of Atlas* with revelation. It will carry Shiloh to the America Shelley praised in *The Revolt of Islam* and lead him upon a search for the woman he dreams about as "a silver sister in a valley alone" (356): Silver Cross, or Sylvie La Croix, or Maria Solidad de Silva—Mary Solitude. The last name implies the dual quest of Shelley's life for the perfect woman he thought he had found in Mary Godwin and for the solitude his wife hated and for which he longed increasingly before his death. Even the nickname "Silver" evokes the "bright silver dream" of *Alastor*'s poet or the vision related in "Two Spirits: An Allegory" in which the beholder glimpses "a silver shape like his early love" which passes "upborne by her wild and glittering hair."[13]

This thematic appropriateness appeals most of all in the exposition of Wylie's novel; but one is pleased again and again by the number and variety of Shelley correspondences which it seems effortlessly to include. Julia Cluck in her article "Elinor Wylie's Shelley Obsession" points out several of these, from the book's chapter headings to events and descriptions. I will not try to list all of them but merely to indicate their scope and quality. Captain Ffoulkastle, for instance, notices that although Shiloh is "very slim and graceful," his "deceptive air of delicacy" veils "an uncommonly strong and active body" (345). Hogg notes that Shelley was slender with a complexion that was delicate and almost feminine; but all his biographers bore witness, as did Hogg, to Shelley's athleticism and to the great pace with which he could walk thirty miles a day if necessary. The search for Silver which Shiloh, despite his "preposterous elegance" and "romantic grace" (346), undertakes almost

---

12. Percy Bysshe Shelley, *Letters*, ed. Roger Ingpen (2 vols.; London, 1909), II, 905.
13. Shelley, *Works*, ed. Hutchinson, "The Two Spirits: An Allegory," 616, line 46.

entirely on foot is Shelley's swift clip, and it persists from New England to California. Shiloh's encounters, remarks, and habits are those of the biographical Shelley. When he refuses to take a stagecoach in West Virginia, he tells David that "stage-coaches are for old women suffering from elephantiasis and a plague of bandboxes" (380), thus telescoping two of Hogg's memoirs: the tale of Shelley's irritation with a heavy old woman sitting between two baskets of apples and onions, whom he expelled from their stagecoach by reciting *Richard II* in lunatic fashion, and the story of his melancholy conviction that an old woman with thick legs, seated opposite him on another coach, had given him elephantiasis. When Shiloh eats "a well-peppered mutton-chop" (378) in New England, we remember that Peacock told him to eat three mutton chops well-peppered as remedy for a physical weakness. Shiloh's writing is indecipherable, like the notes that Trelawny's Shelley scrawled. Like Shelley in his last days, Shiloh reads Aeschylus and Milton, Calderón and Condorcet. Shiloh's fondness for light fare—penny buns, tea, raisins—is that of Hogg's Shelley. When Shiloh composes poetry, it is of course Shelley's poetry.

More important for the purposes of her novel, Elinor Wylie's Shiloh has Shelley's convictions. Hogg wrote that Shelley's creed could be "comprised in a few words": "Above all things, Liberty!"[14] In *The Orphan Angel* Shiloh, who values independence, imagines himself freeing the lonely Silver from hostile forces. As Shelley had done in the cases of Harriet Westbrook and Mary Godwin, as he once longed to do for Emilia Viviani, Shiloh consecrates himself Silver's knight who must answer her "poignant and burning cry" for freedom (358). In the course of the novel he encounters various claims upon his own liberty. He is tempted, for example, to rescue young Melissa Daingerfield of Virginia from a drunken father. Recalling the Shelley of the *Letters* who married Harriet Westbrook to save her from the persecution of being sent to school, Shiloh recoils with indignation at Melissa's "recital of unprecedented suffering" at the hands of Pappy Daingerfield and suggests that David marry her or at the very least that they take her away to be "place[d] . . . under the protection of [an] excellent female" (385, 389). Melissa, like all the other women in the novel (or like the "virgins" in *Alastor*), falls in love with Shiloh's delicacy and flashing eyes but is persuaded to remain in Virginia at a proper seminary. Shiloh's protective affection for her, a type of Shelley's commitment

14. Thomas Jefferson Hogg, *Life of Percy Bysshe Shelley*, in *Life of Shelley*, ed. Wolfe, I, 128.

to Harriet, is echoed in his feeling for frail Mrs. Lillie of Kentucky. But Mrs. Lillie's pert, shallow daughter Rosalie falls in love with him on the eve of her marriage, terrifying him sufficiently to force him from the Lillie house into the wilderness. David Butternut remarks that coquettes alarm Shiloh, and we are reminded of Trelawny's anecdote about Shelley's "dislike of fine ladies"[15] and his horror of the imprisonment of the drawing room. In the face of Rosalie's attraction, as in the teeth of the slavish devotion of Anne, adopted daughter of a Cheyenne chief, Shiloh characteristically escapes into nature:

> Shiloh turned and ran; if he had been running for his life he could not have achieved so passionate an energy as now possessed him in the pursuit of liberty.
> Liberty eluded him among the delicate tawny grasses of the field; it flew visibly, a slender streak of light like a running hare; it fled before his longing, incurably nimble and divine. Its silver scut flashed between the furrows of the next field and was gone. . . . The lovely thing had escaped him for the moment; it had vanished along the narrowing meadows of the distance, but its trace would be phosphorescent in the moonlight, and he would follow it in an hour or two. (472)

Among the Comanches of New Mexico, Shiloh encounters a more ultimate peril to freedom, the prospect of being burned at the stake. Calmly uttering lines from *Prometheus Unbound*, telling the Comanches to " 'Go to the devil' " (570), he narrowly escapes death. David Butternut bitterly declares that Shiloh, like the Shelley of the last letters, always wanted death. Rescued by the bronze-haired Anne, he is saved from her attentions by her chieftain father and goes on to Santa Fe, eluding death again by recovering from a fever. These two threats—death and the ill-assorted needs and passions of women—attend Shiloh throughout his pilgrimage.

There are still other perils to the austere personal freedom he desires. Some are ordinary bodily needs for comfort—needs that conflict with his Shelleyan appetite to escape from the world of the flesh into the sphere of thought. Another, akin to the metaphysical sense of chivalry that prompts his search for Silver, is his more general altruism. Loving hot climates as Shelley did, Shiloh persuades David to travel by the desert route to California, where

15. Trelawny, *Recollections*, II, 188.

Silver has been taken by her wicked Spanish cousin. His suffering in that heat turns his eyes to "consuming fires in their sockets" (617), Wylie's description evoking that of *Alastor*'s poet in whom "Life, and the lustre that consumed it, shone / As in a furnace burning secretly / From his dark eyes alone."[16] Both he and David yearn for the pleasures they had known earlier on the journey: the boat on which they sailed the Mississippi, eating duck and pudding; the mansion of M. Saint-Ange of New Orleans where Shiloh could read the classics and sip the white wine Medwin said Shelley preferred to whisky; even the Lillies' log house in which Shiloh wrote down Shelley's lyric "Buona Notte," downed a sherry cobbler that reminds the reader of the negus Shelley drank with Hogg, and graciously listened to a ditty about heartsease, Shelley's favorite flower.

Like Shelley, who could never tolerate the suffering of animals, Shiloh pities the thirsty mules to whom he has been reciting Calderón's *Autos*, one of Shelley's last enthusiasms. He releases them. When he and David finally stumble on a fountain—which Shiloh calls "Arethusa" after Shelley's poem —his high-mindedness has nearly cost them their lives. Thus, though sometimes moved to postpone the quest for Silver in order to read or write poetry, Shiloh is much more often seduced by philanthropy. Like the Shelley who set out to reform the Irish, he wonders if he and David should not go to New York and nurse its inhabitants, then suffering from yellow fever: "'I question whether we are morally justified in avoiding the plague-stricken city,' said Shiloh with stubborn meekness. 'My own best content would be rather to venture boldly among its cankered multitude, in an attempt to alleviate somewhat the rigour of their agonies. . . . Can we hesitate, when expiring voices call?'" (376). Shiloh is opposed in this instance as in many others by the ever-practical, plain-spoken David Butternut, whose tastes for corn whisky and carousing, safety and sea chanties are much tried in the company of a Platonic poet. In the contrast between them, Elinor Wylie may be contrasting two aspects of herself, the Shelleyan and the homely sides; two kinds of art, the visionary and grand and the ordinary and easy; and two cultures, that of the Old World and that of the New. But Shiloh perseveres in his journey, justifying a remark of Shelley's which he later paraphrases: "I go on until I am

16. Shelley, *Works*, ed. Hutchinson, *Alastor*, 20, lines 252–54.

stopped, and I am never stopped" (491). At the book's close, he has achieved two kinds of liberty, restoring Silver's control of her life and freeing himself of his own dreams of her.

Emily Clark remembered that Elinor Wylie complained of difficulty in finishing *The Orphan Angel* and resolved never to write another book. "Elinor failed to achieve her customary detachment in its accomplishment," Clark explains, because the book was to her " 'a red carpet for Shelley.' " [17] Not only the depth of her affection but the breadth of information she had gleaned in Shelleyana and the lore of early America may have made the year she took to write the *Angel* difficult.

She had always possessed her Shelley library, but she had to appeal to Carl Van Doren and others for information on American history. Van Doren recalled how deliberately she had plotted details in the *Angel*, eager to make the American scene Shiloh encounters historically accurate:

> No formal scholar, she had a scholar's instinct for exactness. She could not be comfortable imagining steamboats on the Ohio in 1822 unless she knew they had been there. . . . She asked me the minutest questions. Had I ever come across any account of a frontier blue-stocking who might be a model for one of the women who courted Shiloh on his travels? I had, in *A New Home—Who'll Follow?* She was sorry that the book was about Michigan and a time later than 1822, but she used it, transforming what she used. [18]

Stephen Vincent Benét, writing an introduction to *The Orphan Angel* for *Collected Prose*, congratulated her accuracy and effort:

> The whole journey of Shiloh and David, across the continent, from Boston to San Diego, may seem to the reader, at times, like a fantastic fairy tale. But every stage of that journey could be plotted on a map of the period— and each stage would be right and probable, down to the number of days it took to traverse it and the means of locomotion used. The transmutation of the material is magic; but the little details of food and drink and gear that make the past live again were sought for and gathered from a hundred sources by a mind that seemed to know by instinct where its necessary victual lay. (323)

17. Emily Clark, *Innocence Abroad* (New York, 1931), 171.
18. Carl Van Doren, *Three Worlds* (New York, 1936), 233.

The same facility and tact Wylie showed in her use of Shelley materials appears in her treatment of the American landscape and of Americans. She chooses the right detail to evoke period, place, and season—Virginia hoecake and prunella shoes; tulip trees, snapping turtles, and "Hope's Celebrated Whisky" in Louisville; Marseilles faience, cognac, and "O Richard, ô mon roi" in the old monarchist's mansion in New Orleans; the yellow adobe houses of San Diego and the orange groves and gull-filled sunshine of a Pacific coast she had never seen. On their journey from one end of the continent to the other, Shiloh and David meet farmers who cannot read, townsmen who scan the *Missouri Intelligencer*, and gentlemen who know Montaigne and Wordsworth by heart.

For all its historical accuracy, *The Orphan Angel* is still a fairy tale. Like *Mr. Hodge and Mr. Hazard*, it is a "romance of the mind" (643), all of whose characters are predictable literary types, even Shiloh who, though never a caricature, draws his animation from the Shelley of the biographies, largely mirroring the young Shelley rather than the despondent, increasingly prudent but disturbed Shelley of 1821–1822. Shiloh insists on his twenty-nine years, his paternity, and his wide experience of life, astonishing David Butternut and those who study his boyish face. He is highly sensitive, subject to fits of sadness, and alternately improvident and practical. But he never achieves the complexity of personality of the Shelley of the last letters and poems. Wylie's friend Aldous Huxley praised her for the "glassy and translucent beauty" of *The Orphan Angel*, saying it had "something of the quality of Shelley's own poems." But he reminded her—gingerly, knowing her temper—that Shelley's "passions were not invariably ethereal" and that her Shiloh was "young and . . . angelic" and somewhat too "handsomely treated."[19]

For Wylie's purpose of creating an essentially cheerful fantasy in which Shelley is introduced to new pleasures and challenges, the graver elements of his character are not germane. Wylie suggests them; even Shelley's sometimes fatal sexuality is hinted at in Shiloh's discomfort at the patchouli worn by Rosalie Lillie. She engages these elements, however, at a deeper level in *Mr. Hodge and Mr. Hazard*.

David Butternut, too, is a type drawn from literature. He represents the

19. Aldous Huxley , *Letters*, ed. Grover Smith (New York, 1969), 277–78, Letter to Elinor Wylie, Christmas, 1926.

wholesome New England boy, carving peach-stones, exclaiming "by jiminy" and "by cracky," impressed and yet repelled by Shiloh's knowledge of classics and languages, and shocked by his manners, which are more formal than his own yet free of prudery. David's simple but enraptured descriptions of the American landscape are, like his tastes, useful foils to Shiloh's, providing a symbolic encounter between the infant culture of the New World and the informed elegance of the Old. But he lacks independent energy. His function is illustrative, representative, evoking the stock "good boy" figures of early American children's books with none of the mischievous autonomy and vitality of a Tom Sawyer or Huckleberry Finn.

Similarly, Pappy Daingerfield with his educated drawl, "gigantic pistol," and "quantity of raven-black hair," sitting superbly astride his horse and "picking his glittering white teeth with his pocket-knife" (396, 397) resembles the dangerous, vaguely Byronic Virginia gentleman of nineteenth-century pulp fiction. (Mark Twain satirizes this type in his account of the feuding Grangerfords in Chapter XVIII of *Huckleberry Finn*.)

Captain Appleby and Professor Lackland, who invite Shiloh and David aboard their riverboat, *Prairie Flower*, are winning but inevitable types of stout soldier and lean scholar. The professor has a "curiously frigid voice," amuses himself with "metaphysics and the philosophies of the elder civilizations," and is embarrassed by the subtle eroticism of Shiloh's epithalamium for his marriage to Rosalie Lillie (418). Captain Appleby, hale, good-humored, and a member of a Massachusetts regiment in the revolutionary war, prefers apple jelly to theories, but as a literate New Englander has read poetry. It is not quite believable that he already knows Shelley's "Exhortation," written in 1820, to which he alludes; but Elinor Wylie's novel, as a whimsical romance, sometimes sacrifices the probable to the possible.

Other minor types reveal the ease of her scholarship. Her Cheyenne chief who assures Shiloh that he is "endeavouring to correct the deficiencies" of his daughter's temperament is thoroughly fantastic and belongs to the eighteenth- and early nineteenth-century literature of the noble savage (595). Don Narciso, Sylvie's predatory Spanish cousin, has his roots in Milton's portrait of Satan and tells Shiloh, "'Mine was an old name in heaven, and one that you have always admired'" (628). These remarks recall both Shelley's early admiration for Milton's Lucifer and the literature of diabolist incarnation with which both Wylie and Shelley were fascinated. Finally, Silver has literary antecedents in Wylie's earlier fiction. When Shiloh meets her, she is "sitting under a white rose-tree" in a garden even as, when Gerald Ponyard first sees Jennifer Lorn, she is in a garden of roses and, as Virginio salutes Rosalba, she watches him from within a garden (621). Like Jennifer, Silver is tremulous and pliable and even more inconsequential: the ordinary heroine of Shiloh's remarkable dream.

Various passages in *The Orphan Angel* assert its fairy-tale quality, a quality heightened, as in fairy tales, by the expectedness of the stock figures. Shiloh's expedition is described by Silver's French godfather, M. Saint-Ange, as an attempt to free a fair lady from a dungeon. Shiloh tells the old man that he is "no prince of chivalric legend, but a wretched creature without durable virtue, and the slave of an enchantment." And he asks, "How can my own poverty and incompetence hope to serve the lady of this fairy tale?" (530). The fairy tale which is *The Orphan Angel*, the "fairy tale" which has to do with Silver's melancholy detainment, and the fairy tale of Shelley's career as a savior of women begin to merge as Shiloh recalls his past: "Several lovely ladies; seven imprisoned princesses. Melissa of the honey-sounding name, and Silver sitting among the ashes of her California exile, made the seven of the fairy-tale, added to those others out of the past [Harriet Westbrook, Mary Godwin, Claire Clairmont, Emilia Viviani, Jane Williams]. Always he had meant to be so wise and valiant, but all the princesses were still in prison, and he was a wretched creature and the slave of an enchantment" (530–31).

When *The Orphan Angel* concludes, the quest over and the last princess free, Wylie's final portrait is of Shiloh as poet, engaged in the primary adventure of the real Shelley's life, the writing of poetry. Although her American figures and landscape have charm as appropriate decoration, it is Shiloh's odyssey as an image of Shelley that earned her novel attention. Historical romance verges under her hand on literary hagiography.

Elinor Wylie's earlier novels concern the problem of art. *The Orphan Angel*, although primarily about Shelley the man, does not avoid his identity as poet. Furthermore, its depiction of Shiloh's devotion to Silver's painted image once again inflects Wylie's earlier theme of the influence of art on imagination and its power over the real.

Shiloh's interests in mathematics and physics, in Milton and Herodotus, represent Shelley's; but so do his shy withdrawals with pen and paper hastily to transcribe a lyric. Shiloh's companions on his American jaunt only half suspect his true genius, and Wylie attempts to portray its nature as Romantic. So, in the Kentucky log house, weary (as Shelley repeatedly declared himself) of the pressures of living, Shiloh nevertheless hears "falling rhythms" engendered in his brain by nature and cannot sleep until he sets them down. Wylie identifies Shiloh's poetic inspiration with the wind—a habitual Romantic association made in Coleridge's lyric "The Aeolian Harp" as in Shelley's own "Ode to the West Wind." The immediacy of appeal the American continent has for Shiloh is compounded of rugged beauty and lonely breadth, for Shelley always loved "waste and solitary places" (559). For Shiloh as for Shelley, desolation provokes poetry.

At the novel's close, having disdained her corrupt cousin's suggestion that he take Silver as a mistress, Shiloh furthers David Butternut's hope to marry her by himself withdrawing. He sits alone on a cliff overlooking the Pacific. Wylie's description of the scene—the "pale blue sky" under which Shiloh appears "in the centre of a circle of golden rays" like halos, the water below full of sea birds (634)—recalls the setting of Shelley's "Stanzas Written in Dejection, Near Naples." In that poem,

> The sun is warm, the sky is clear,
> The waves are dancing fast and bright,
> . . . .
> The winds, the birds, the ocean floods,
> The City's noise itself, is soft like Solitude's.[20]

Shelley confesses himself without hope, health, peace, or calm in "Stanzas," and the poem voices his wish to "hear the sea / Breathe o'er my dying brain its last monotony." Yet he also declares that "despair itself" appears "mild" to him, "Even as the winds and waters are."[21] Though homeless and sad, Wylie's Shiloh is tranquil at the end of The Orphan Angel, having heard in the sounds of sea and wind the natural music he must translate into art.

His dream of the radiant image carried in his pocket recedes, like Shelley's

20. Works, 561, lines 1–2, 8–9.
21. Ibid., lines 35–36, 28, 29.

dreams of many women, into the realm of poetic fancy: "He knew that the miniature of Sylvie was in his pocket; he called her Silver to his own mind, and he could have made a song to her if he had chosen, but now she was no more to him than Arethusa rising from her couch of snows" (634). The image has always appeared to him the exact opposite of the "glitter of gold" which is life: "Here was no violence or moving glitter of gold; here were colours silvery and pearly, and the shape of peace. The lips were cooler than snow-water, the eyes were softer than the end of sorrow" (589). The image is reminiscent of Wylie's description of Rosalba after she has been turned into porcelain, peace on her lips, her aspect "drawn in the palest colours of pearls," her air one "of perfect calm" (314, 313). It is the apotheosis of one emanation of Whistlerian art; and as is so often the case with Wylie's artifacts, it is a miniature. It affords Shiloh more pleasure than the apparition of Silver herself. Small, able to be kept (as the real Silver cannot be), taken at random from its shagreen case, impressionistic and evocative, the perfection of its finish is beyond life's and accords with the Platonic lineaments of Shiloh's dreams. The real Silver is, unlike her portrait, unexceptional: merely the "mortal image" of the eternal feminine.

Surrendering the irrelevant to the real, Shiloh turns his attention from the treasured image to the task of creating his own images: "He would not take the trouble to draw the miniature of Sylvie from his pocket, but presently he would fumble with his slim brown fingers until he had found a pencil and a bit of paper, and he would catch the syllables that were filling his mind with music; they were wilder than sea-birds, but presently he would catch them quite easily in a little net of pencil-marks" (634). The "rainbows under the cliffs" break into waves, "a thunderous music among crystal flakes," even as in Shelley's "Stanzas" the waves are "like light dissolved in star-showers, thrown." They prompt the music of Shiloh's poetry. Thus The Orphan Angel concludes with an evocation of Shelley as poet. "Orphan" because there is no one related to him in virtue, "angel" for his propensities, Shiloh like Shelley is rarely happy as a man but possesses "a godlike prerogative": the genius to write (634).

CHAPTER VIII · *MR. HODGE AND*

MR. HAZARD

"Think of Shelley" [said Mrs. Dalloway]. "I feel that
there's almost everything one wants in *Adonais*."
"Read *Adonais* by all means," Richard conceded.
"But whenever I hear of Shelley I repeat to myself the
words of Matthew Arnold, 'What a set! What a set!'"

VIRGINIA WOOLF, *The Voyage Out*

Vex not thou the poet's mind
   With thy shallow wit;
Vex not thou the poet's mind,
   For thou canst not fathom it.
Clear and bright it should be ever,
Flowing like a crystal river,
Bright as light, and clear as wind.

ALFRED, LORD TENNYSON, "The Poet's Mind"

he Orphan Angel was an effort to celebrate an artistic
mind that Elinor Wylie revered as holy. *Mr. Hodge and
Mr. Hazard* continued that effort from a different perspective. Max Beerbohm once called Wylie "a born
and made ironist": [1] and critical descriptions of her art
frequently emphasize its cleverness. Yet anger, sexual
passion, and grief are expressed in Wylie's writing, carrying an emotional
content that cannot be denied because of the careful form she imposed upon
it. Her early novels showed that the exercises of the ironist did not preclude
emotional response, particularly to the allurements of art and to the piteous-
ness of human life fraught with illusions.

Her last novel, *Mr. Hodge and Mr. Hazard*, bears a palpable strain of

---

1. Katharine Lyon Mix, *Max and the Americans* (Brattleboro, Vt., 1974), 169.

melancholy, bred of the declining happiness of Wylie's last years, of her sense, when she returned to England in middle age, that she was meeting the ghost of her own disordered past, and of her anxiety that she had achieved little as a woman or an artist. There is in the novel, too, a rare tenderness engendered by her affection for the protagonist, Mr. Hazard, that admirable ghost—part Shelley and Wylie, part Byron, yet wholly himself—who returns to a Victorian England that cannot understand him. In her treatment of Mr. Hazard's visit to a country in which are buried his youthful optimism, his children, and his reputation for both genius and folly, Wylie exhibits her admiration for the intellectual largesse and spiritual bravado of the Romantics. But she creates, as well, a vision of human pain which is comprehensible in the simplest terms. Perhaps it was Aldous Huxley's suggestion that she recreate a Shelley who "survive[s] into the Peck-sniffian epoch," "indulg[ing] his ardently romantic platonisms . . . in the appalling gloom and stuffiness of the mid-nineteenth century environment"[2] that prompted her conception of Mr. Hazard. But in the Dickensian figure of Hodge and in the figures of Lady Clara Hunting and her daughters, Wylie created subtle contrasts to the Romantic spirit as she conceived it. This last novel is a touching as well as witty encomium to the hazardous but generous spirits and enterprises of the Romantics, who were for her images of doomed goodness.

The plot of Wylie's novel is simple. Mr. Hazard, a frail poet of forty, decides to revisit England after an absence of fifteen years. He has left in Spain a fashionable wife and a son who disapproves of him and in Missolonghi, where he fought for Greek independence, most of his physical stamina. When the novel opens, his reasons for return are vague. Upon arrival, he is entertained by old friends, the shabby and sentimental Mr. Hartleigh and his practical wife Annamaria, and finds lodgings near them, where he sets up his rows of Greek and Elizabethan books, eats improperly, and alienates his landlady by contracting influenza. This illness, which is a symbolic reaction to the hostile unfamiliarity of England, brings his body closer to the grave but heightens "the incomparable powers of Mr. Hazard's mind" (*Collected Prose*, 668). He engages these powers in two pursuits, both visionary: the completion of a poetic drama about the Book of Job and a search for the vanished faces of

2. Aldous Huxley, *Letters*, ed. Grover Smith (New York, 1969), 278.

his dead children and his former self, all, he thinks, waiting to be glimpsed again in houses or on streets he once frequented.

By chance, rowing on the Thames above Gravelow in quest of a quiet "backwater" where he can temporarily rest, he is startled by two young girls, the daughters of Lady Clara Hunting (694). Charming and volatile—"girls like trees dancing, like little birches turning the river-bank into a frieze"— they think Mr. Hazard "a tramp," "an admirable scarecrow," as they view him alone in a skiff in a shabby coat looking undernourished and without purpose (695, 698, 697). But he is entranced by them both and especially by Allegra, the music of whose name "confuse[s]" him with "echoes" (695). Interrupted by their beautiful mother who is the poised daughter of *Jennifer Lorn's* Gerald Ponyard, the girls babble that they have forgotten to ask Mr. Hazard his name. He utters it and is suddenly overcome by despair for "he [knows] that the sound of his name [will] break the tranquil surface of the scene, and drown him in humiliation" (702). Lady Clara, however, is a woman of the world. Indifferent both to poetry and to the scandals of Hazard's past, she regards him not as a dangerous "wolf" but merely as the "black sheep" of an aristocratic family, "a fool rather than a fiend" (703, 702). His distracted aspect, arcane manners, and sober linen and his obvious attraction to her and her daughters awake in her composed breast "a moderate pang of pity" (703). Seven years younger than he, she nonetheless feels "a slight maternal interest in the unfortunate Mr. Hazard" and invites him to a series of pretty picnics during spring and early summer (707).

Under the influence of Lady Clara's "calm and distinction" and under the spell of the "delicate irregular radiance of Allegra's face" (714, 710), Mr. Hazard loses his conviction of personal failure and his distrust of the world:

> For the first time in seven years he seemed to possess his soul in patience. Now for the moment he regretted nothing, he demanded nothing even of his own driven and conscripted powers. Beyond the light clear fabric of his thoughts, beyond the tranquillity of his thoughts unravelled from their horrid knots and smoothly braided into order, he perceived Allegra. Clara had untied the knots and soothed the tangles of his mind; she had accomplished this miracle without effort, by the subtle expedient of her smiles. But Allegra could do far more than this; the sharp irregular facets of her little face provided a glass for divination and subliminal wisdom. This emotion was not Platonic, or romantic, or animal; it was not love, but revelation. (715)

He turns himself into an amiable if eccentric oarsman-rhymester for the three enchanting presences who entertain him at their estate of Lyonnesse. Lady Clara, "carelessly flattered by his devotion," offers him enough raspberries and sympathy to deter the course of Hazard's emaciation (717). Her daughter Rosa, whose "heart [is] soft for the unlucky," delights in the little lyrics, "the wasted beauty of his [great] songs," that Hazard writes for her (738, 727). Courteous Allegra, like an alabaster shell which he fills "with the light of his own spirit," tolerates his admiration (715). He slips into a "middle state" between old torment and perfect pleasure, "secluded and absolved from all extremities of the heart" (719).

This pleasant state cannot last. Mr. Hodge, prosperously buttoned, thick-set, self-important tutor of Lady Clara's sons, returns with them to Lyonnesse. Fawningly in love with and jealous of Lady Clara, he is scandalized that his idol should admit Mr. Hazard to her house. He upbraids her for frivolity, raking up the sins of Hazard's youth: his expulsion from university, his elopements, his radicalism. He deplores his present mien: "I see insanity in his eyes, and violence, and a base surrender to despair" (745). Mr. Hodge and Mr. Hazard are precise opposites. Hodge is a materialist, an optimist, an upstart, and, because he is ill-bred, a snob. Mr. Hazard, as Lady Clara perfectly perceives, is by birth a gentleman, a dreamer of dreams impracticable, but in poetry, unselfish, "fanatically honest," and "delightfully self-effacing" (745, 744). She cannot understand his genius but is too "liberal and humane" to allow Hodge's animosity to sway her (736). But a cruel aside of Hodge's makes his perilous position clear to Mr. Hazard. When Rosa asks, "'Have you finished your sonnet to Milton, Mr. Hazard?'" Hodge "lower[s] his eyes as if he had stared at a nameless serpent" and says, "'Poor Milton.'" Mr. Hazard "recognize[s] the crack of doom": "He translated Mr. Hodge's two words with accurate skill: they informed him that he was an appalling person, unfit to associate with the innocent and the noble, that his appearance was odd, his principles outrageous, and his opinions contemptible. Their ten laconic letters told him that he was at all points detestable to Mr. Hodge. The lovely grave which was prepared for him in the valley of Lyonnesse was no longer his own; Mr. Hodge had filled it with the rotten body of the past" (739, 740, 742).

In the hospitality of Lady Clara Hazard had assumed an understanding of the essential decency of his spirit, a decency that has transcended passing enthusiasms, lusts, and causes. He longed for and thought he had found in the misted lawns and quiet towers of Lyonnesse a pleasant escape from the demands of great art. Wylie instructs us that the "dreaming docility" into which Mr. Hazard slips at Lyonnesse has brought him along a "cool and level path of folly" (717, 727). But Mr. Hazard is not a Romantic in his early youth; his peers are dead, and his own wish for death is understandable. What he learns from the brutality of Mr. Hodge is that Lyonnesse can offer him neither rest nor death. He must move on: "Behind the puny shield of his breastbone Mr. Hazard's heart paused in horror, knocked three times like a frantic prisoner, and went forward haltingly, as if its pulse were lamed. . . . [He] realized for the thousandth time that it is difficult to die of that sharp and fugitive pang which is commonly miscalled a broken heart" (740, 741).

He leaves Lyonnesse, returning only once more to invite Lady Clara and her daughters to tea in his flat at Gravelow. Instead—more affected by convention than she may realize—Lady Clara sends Mr. Hodge in her place together with her supercilious sons. None of Mr. Hazard's careful preparations for tea—the fresh flowers (that wilt because he forgets to water them), the cream buns (sold to him stale by a shopkeeper who divines his innocence), the clean but spare room—win the approval of his indifferent guests. But his decision to leave Gravelow for London without seeing Lady Clara earns Hodge's. Amazed by Mr. Hazard's composure and pitying his appearance— thin as a storm-bitten scarecrow and as pale as a rain-washed rag"—Mr. Hodge does him the one service a muscular and self-righteous man might do: he helps him pack (773).

Mr. Hazard gives young Tristram an appropriate intaglio to take to his mother: "It appeared to be a blond and frosted moonstone, bearing upon its surface the figures of a lion and a stag. The lion's teeth were sunk in the stag's flying shoulder." Mr. Hazard is, of course, the stag; Mr. Hodge, the powerful lion. The boy is not convinced of its value; but Mr. Hazard, standing alone, "the intellectual colour of his eyes" "full of laughter," is momentarily happy. For he seems to have newly realized the Platonic superiority of his own artist's gift: "There were five points to a star; these three uneasy presences were in the room, and himself, making four, and a fifth which set a crown upon the whole and was superior to the others and remained a part of heaven" (774).

Although the plot of *Mr. Hodge and Mr. Hazard* is not complex, the symbolic associations and correspondences in the novel weave a rich fabric. Elinor

Wylie, with cryptic insistence on its independence of a specific historic context, called it "an everyday fable" with slight "historic trappings." And insofar as Mr. Hazard is an artist and a good man whom the world scorns while Mr. Hodge is an undistinguished but cunning overreacher whom the world favors, her book is an everyday story indeed. But she admitted that "the central character may . . . be regarded as a composite miniature of the whole generation of early nineteenth century romantics" (647). As a host of parallels proves, that summation is entirely true while the climate of the novel itself— setting, imagery, and atmosphere—describes the wane of Romantic feeling and the rise of Victorianism.

If Mr. Hazard is a composite portrait of the dead Romantics, his component images are chiefly Shelley's and, to a lesser degree, Byron's. Elinor Wylie dexterously combines elements of the personalities and histories of both in Mr. Hazard's; yet the real Shelley and the real Byron are alluded to in the novel as separate persons, and Byron's qualities are suggested in the figure of Lord Alonzo Raven, a melancholy name not unlike that Peacock assigned Byron: Mr. Cypress of *Nightmare Abbey*. When Mr. Hazard returns to England he has been in exile for fifteen years. Since Shelley left England in 1818 and since without enthusiasm Mr. Hazard reads Tennyson's *Poems, Chiefly Lyrical* which were published in 1832, the year of his arrival is probably what Shelley's would have been: 1833. He takes rooms on Poland Street, "where he had lodged when he was first expelled from the university"; so had Shelley. He remembers that there had been a "pattern of trellises and green vine-leaves upon the walls"—the same "trellised paper" Hogg says Shelley loved;[3] but in the new era he is shown a room with "a travesty of roses traced in soot upon the walls"—the fulsome rose of Victorian sentimentality and the soot of industrialism (664, 665). Later in the novel he goes to Half-Moon Street, where he is as Shelley was, happy for a few weeks or months, and spends a Sunday afternoon "among the sarcophagi of [his] dead selves" (666). Since Byron visited his mother on Half-Moon Street when on holiday from Harrow, the use of "selves" may be more inclusive.[4]

Mr. Hazard's friend Hartleigh, complaining of the failure of his literary magazine and willing to accept occasional charity from Mr. Hazard, is cer-

3. Thomas Jefferson Hogg, *Life of Percy Bysshe Shelley*, in *The Life of Shelley*, ed. Humbert Wolfe (2 vols.; London, 1933), I, 178. .
4. See Leslie A. Marchand, *Byron* (3 vols.; New York, 1957), I, 69.

tainly the poet-journalist Leigh Hunt, in whose ill-starred fortunes both Shelley and Byron were frequently entangled. His wife Annamaria is Marianne Hunt. Elinor Wylie has been faithful to Mrs. Hunt's alternately affectionate and querulous treatment of Shelley and particularly Byron; for Annamaria discounts Hazard's reputation for beauty, is envious of his Spanish castle, and hides her impatience with his impracticality by offering him castor oil and flannels. Marianne Hunt "pretended a lofty disdain for rank and titles" when with Lord Byron, took "a middle-class attitude of moral superiority to him and his mistress," and, like Annamaria, so spoiled her children that she nearly let them spoil Byron's villa.[5] When Annamaria declares that it is impossible to record an image of Hazard—"His wife has tried it in her novels, over and over again"—the correspondences are Shelleyan, for Mary Shelley attempted to personify Shelley in *Lodore*, *Falkner*, and, most prominently, in Lord Adrian Windsor in *The Last Man*. Her comment that Hazard's wife, "Baddeley's own daughter," nags him is a direct allusion to Mary Shelley's behavior in the last days; and of course Baddeley is the inverse equivalent of *God-* (or Good-)win (656).

After the notorious authoress Caroline Norton entertains Mr. Hazard, she is besieged by gossips who remember the roué and freethinker of decades past: "'Did he speak of her?' 'Of his wife . . . ?' 'No, I meant his first wife.' 'Does he expect his father to forgive him?' 'What did he say of Alonzo Raven? He knew him well.' 'And the wards in Chancery; did both of them die?' 'And had he not several other children? Are any of them living?' 'But one was Raven's child, to be sure, Caroline.' 'I think him fascinating, though shockingly rude, my love'" (672). The phrase "first wife" may allude to Harriet, whose suicide besmirched Shelley's fame; but the excitement of the query reminds one, too, of the bitter scandal that surrounded Byron's separation from Annabella Milbanke. The unforgiving father recalls Sir Timothy Shelley. In 1817 Shelley and Harriet's children were made wards in Chancery. William and Clara, Shelley's children by Mary, died in infancy. The allusion to "Raven's child" may be to Allegra, daughter of Byron and Claire Clairmont, at whose illegitimate birth the Shelleys were present.

There are other specific correspondences to the life and writings of

5. *Ibid.*, III, 1010, 1020.

Shelley. For instance, Mr. Hodge disparagingly remarks that Mr. Hazard's "scoundrelly old grandfather was born in America" (745), as was Shelley's; Hazard has had interest in the idea of the Wandering Jew, as did Shelley at Oxford; Annamaria remembers Shelley's remark to Peacock about gondolas looking like "moths of which a coffin might have been the chrysalis"[6] when she studies Mr. Hazard's deathly pallor; and he refers to himself as a "herd-neglected deer," recalling Shelley's description of himself in *Adonais* (line 297) as a "herd-abandoned deer" (674). Mr. Hazard's son is called Lionel, a name Shelley used for two characters in "Boat on the Serchio" and "Rosalind and Helen" and the name Mary Shelley chose for Lionel Verney, friend of the fictionalized Shelley of *The Last Man*. Mr. Hazard is accused, as was Shelley, of "repulsive self-pity" (756). As Shelley did in his last days, he has appalling nightmares, and he is careless about his appearance, health, and need for nourishment. Finally, Shelley's friends Peacock and Hogg are represented by Hazard's Bird and Piggott. The name "Piggott" may have offered itself as a pseudonym for "Hogg" because Lionel Johnson's middle name was "Pigot."

Still, Mr. Hazard is not, as was Shiloh, an exclusively Shelleyan prototype. Though it is remarked that "he isn't vain or bad-tempered, like Alonzo Raven" (706), and though Byron's well-known vanity and irascibility are associated with Lord Alonzo's, Mr. Hazard exhibits elements of the personality of Byron as well. Forgetful, timid, never the writer of popular verse, Mr. Hazard does not superficially suggest the Regency dandy whose *Childe Harold* was a best seller. Byron, however, had his vulnerable side. Hearing that his childhood love, Mary Duff, was to marry a Mr. Cockburn, he remembered that the news "nearly threw me into convulsions," and his grief when an even fonder sweetheart, Mary Chaworth, rejected him to marry Mr. Musters remained a painful recollection all his life.[7] Certain of Byron's passions achieved metaphysical proportions, as does Mr. Hazard's devotion to Allegra, a terrible wedding of body and spirit. And Byron was capable of feeling, as Hazard feels, that he was "a lone being" who had "not a friend in the world."[8]

Shelley's ill repute in England probably never assumed so sinister a cast as Byron's before his exile; for, though his ideas were conventional, Byron had

6. Edward Dowden, *The Life of Percy Bysshe Shelley* (2 vols.; London, 1886), II, 77.
7. See Marchand, *Byron*, I, 88.
8. *Ibid.*, 337.

had a notable career as a rake, attended at the close by rumors of incest and sodomy. The perspiring curiosity Lady Caroline Norton's friends display about Mr. Hazard has much in it of the avid fascination Byron prompted in those of Lady Caroline Lamb; and Hodge's disgust and warnings recall the righteous indignation of Lady Liddell seeing Byron at St. Peter's and commanding her daughter to keep her eyes down, for "he is dangerous to look at." Indeed Lady Caroline Lamb's first opinion that Byron was "'mad—bad—and dangerous to know'" might with some modification be Annamaria Hartleigh's view of Hazard, whose eyes, like Byron's, burn too brightly and seem to her "unorthodox and rather appalling" (659). Even Hazard himself feels that he is a dangerous person, again resembling Byron. Perceiving that he has caught influenza, Annamaria sends him from her house lest he infect her children. She "had known quite well that he was the enemy of children: that he cast a blight upon them, that they withered in his presence like murdered flowers" (664). Hazard, thinking her precautions correct in a larger metaphoric sense, avoids the Hartleighs for months. Byron had once lamented that "it is my destiny to ruin all I come near,"[9] and one of Mr. Hazard's terrors is that his fondness for the Huntings might weary, compromise, or taint them.

Like Byron, Mr. Hazard has fought at Missolonghi and like Byron, who, Henri Beyle said, had an "antipathy to a full habit of body," he is very thin. In his last days it was remarked that because of his "skeleton-thinness [Byron] could not stand much strain upon his constitution."[10] And in this novel about the living ghost of the Romantic spirit, Elinor Wylie reminds us that Mr. Hazard has the "skull-face" of a "skeleton" (673, 688).

Unlike *The Orphan Angel, Mr. Hodge and Mr. Hazard* does not marshal its Romantic materials in a spirit of recreation or tribute but in a much subtler mood of elegy and the making of literary contrasts. Correspondences between Mr. Hazard's life and the lives of two Romantic poets serve to indicate the disparity between Romantic aspiration with its characteristic failures and Victorian prudence, represented by Mr. Hodge, with its sins of prudery and materialism. The steadiness of Mr. Hodge's character is not slighted in Elinor Wylie's novel; but in the uncertainties of Mr. Hazard's are implied all the sympathies and sensitivity of the Romantic ego.

9. *Ibid.*, II, 692; I, 328; II, 546.
10. *Ibid.*, II, 663.

When Mr. Hartleigh, "loyal to the past," tells Mr. Hazard that he is "'the tenderest-hearted man alive,'" Mr. Hazard responds, "'What makes you think I am alive?'" (653). He has visited the Hartleighs to find "a coffin . . . in the neighborhood"; only briefly in the course of the novel, during his infatuation with the Huntings, has he any illusions that he is more than a "lively ghost" (654, 675). Leaving his flat in the appropriately named Gravelow, he goes daily to the house in which he once lived in search of his youthful self and dead children. It is the quest of a ghost for its companions:

> He . . . gazed at the green front door through which he had emerged so often into the mornings of a younger spring. He had a small precise picture of himself in his mind's eye, exact and critical, etched in sharp lines and bitten with the acid of irony. He laughed shortly under his breath and dismissed his own ghost to oblivion. The ghost of a living man must be a poor creature at best; a stuffless thing, projected into sunshine by a sick brain. But the ghosts of the dead are different; they are sustained and animated by spirits whole and entire, they possess their proper souls. Mr. Hazard watched the green door. . . . [He] knew it was in vain. (691)

Mr. Hazard's "spectral laughter," his "graveyard elegance," his mouth which is "too passionate and mobile for a mouth that has been stopped with dust," reveal him to be a poet who has outlived his prime and his audience (675, 676). He is the last of the Romantics: a man who had once cherished "a hundred fitful and intemperate schemes" but cannot summon interest in the Reform Bill; who, while all around him are energetic, sedulous, and earnest about social causes, still yearns *not* to "[set] his thin shoulder to some useful revolution of a wheel in the machine" but to trace "a river of air . . . to its source . . . a fountain of light": he is a Plotinian visionary (680, 685).

Elinor Wylie's evocation of two attitudes, Romantic and early Victorian, takes two forms: a comparison of public and private. Mr. Hazard, she ironically says, is "lazy": his energies are dissipated in nostalgia, meditation, and the plan for his biblical drama (683). Around him, everyone else is industrious:

> Mr. Macaulay was writing to his sister from the smoking-room of the House of Commons; in June he would be happy to inform her that in less than a fortnight he would dine with Lord Grey, Mr. Boddington, Mr. Price, Sir Robert Inglis, Lord Ripon, and Lord Morpeth. . . . Young Mr. Whiteley was finishing his pamphlet "Three Months in Jamaica," and the Anti-Slavery Society was awaiting it with eagerness. Wilberforce was

dying, and Haydon was painting the Reform Banquet and hearing plenty of excellent stories while he painted. Sometimes these tales were tragic; Sir Charles Bagot told him that Michelangelo's copy of Dante, with a wide margin and his own designs, fell into the hands of the Bishop of Derry and was lost on the passage to Marseilles. There were quantities of new books to offset such losses; Mr. Tennyson's exquisite lyrics, Mr. Browning's *Pauline*, Hartley Coleridge's poems. (682)

When Mr. Hazard dines at the Hartleighs', the gaseous heat of their cluttered Victorian room, the trifle and port on the table, and the good sense in Annamaria's talk make him long for the freedoms of nature and an earlier era; symbolically, he wants to throw the clock through the window:

> The room was a cube of hot bright air, moored fast among the thinner airs of twilight. It did not float, as the trees' branches floated and waved visibly in the green element above them, a sky like a lake reversed, grained and patterned like the surface of water, crossed by cool streams of radiance from the west. The room lay heavy and immovable like a drowned hulk at the bottom of this pool of ether; it did not hang suspended like the tree-tops, it was hopelessly weighed down by the soft imponderable air. . . . The flame of the lamp and the more gaseous flame of the fire . . . were emanations too difficult to breathe, too hot and dense for the delicate rhythm of breathing. Mr. Hazard thought how pleasant it would be if only he might be allowed to lift the black marble clock from the mantelpiece and hurl it through the shut window. The glittering splinters of glass would be neither so thin nor so sharp as the April air rushing in through the broken pane. Of course even to open the window in the old-fashioned way would be better than nothing, but Annamaria would be sure to shut it again. She would remind Mr. Hazard that he ought to be careful; she would pull the shawl about her shoulders and talk about toothache. (679)

Though his name is associated with failure and his poetic reputation is eccentric, Mr. Hazard attracts some attention from the busy early Victorians; from "young Mr. Browning," for instance, whose "devotion" to him (like Browning's to Shelley) is "both tigerish and mulish in its intensity" and who, during Hazard's influenza, insists on "building fires and boiling kettles." But Mr. Hazard has the Romantic scorn of the provident, prefers rainstorms to snug rooms, and, despite his chivalry to chambermaids, is an aristocrat: he "might occasionally have found [Mr. Browning] a comfort if his boots had ever lost their abominable *parvenu* habit of creaking" (669). With no one to understand the "unquiet sparks of ecstasy" one April day can light "in the capricious twilight of his thoughts," Mr. Hazard falls prey to the Huntings (673). Elinor Wylie had described him as a "hunter," "stalking" the "wild deer" of his past (691). Instead, he becomes in a charmingly insouciant yet deadly chase, the hunted.

Mr. Hazard yearns in part for a "backwater," a coffin, a grave in which he can find rest (694). In Lady Clara's estate of Lyonnesse, he thinks he has found it. But although Lyonnesse was, in Arthurian legend, a pleasant country west of Cornwall from which Arthur came, it is also the scene of his last battle, with Modred. After the battle that, as Tennyson's Arthur says, defeated the "old order" which "changeth, yielding place to new," the dying king was borne away by three grieving queens with crowns of gold, Lyonnesse was sunk forty fathoms into the sea, and "noble chance" and "noble knight[s were] no more." [11]

In naming Lady Clara's estate Lyonnesse—a chapter heading calls it "Buried Lyonnesse"—Elinor Wylie evokes this old myth with its tidings of a beautiful lost past and the victory of malice over innocence and implies the faultiness of Hazard's desire to place his hopes in Clara. For Clara's Lyonnesse is ultimately as inimical to Hazard as the fabled one was to Arthur. But the name also conjures up the *Idylls* of Tennyson, a poet who, despite an early history of privation, neurosis, and trial not unlike that of a Romantic Hazard, nevertheless concluded his life, unlike Mr. Hazard, garlanded with his country's honors and faithful in verse to the public values of his time. The Lyonnesse chapters make a delicate contrast between the fortunes (and what, with bias, Elinor Wylie conceives to be the comparative skills) of a poet like Tennyson and a Romantic like Hazard. Lyonnesse seems to Hazard, like certain of Tennyson's minor poems, comforting, musical, charming:

> Mr. Hazard was tired of distances; the small kingdom of Lyonnesse invited him. This valley kingdom, circumscribed and unperilous, gentle in its limitations, was a cure for his soul's vertigo. He surveyed it from the third act of his lyrical drama, and thought it a fit inheritance for his soul. He had no use for larger realms; if he should fall asleep in this valley, if he should fall asleep or die, Lyonnesse was a soft bed and a sweetly scented coffin.

11. Robert Hill, Jr. (ed.), *Tennyson's Poetry* (New York, 1971), 428, "The Passing of Arthur," *Idylls of the King*, lines 408, 398, 399.

Say that from these heights it looked no wider than a grave spangled and plumed with summer grass, and you had said the sum of his desires. (729)

Under its spell, he writes small, contented lyrics and moves "in an elegaic atmosphere" (719).

Yet one remembers that it was Tennyson in "Ulysses" who depicted the glamour, however restrictive, of ceaseless adventure and Tennyson's "The Lotus-Eaters" that studies the danger, however seductive, of repose. Lyonnesse puts Mr. Hazard off his guard: it loosens the "cruel steel" "joints of his armour" (711). Consequently, he does not expect the assault of Mr. Hodge which, though made over a teacup, vanquishes his kingdom of happiness even as Modred's did Arthur's.

By the assiduity with which she draws comparisons between the valley of Lyonnesse and the altitudes to which Mr. Hazard's mind once soared, Elinor Wylie makes a (prejudiced) distinction between Romantic art and what she construes to be the more modest compass of some Victorian poetry. Her novel evokes Tennyson's *The Death of Arthur*: Rosa, Allegra, and Lady Clara are, like the three queens, "ladies in haloes"; and the identification of Lady Clara with Tennyson's Lady Clara Vere de Vere combines with images of Lyonnesse "drenched in light like honey from the broken clouds" to suggest the mellifluous sentiment of Tennyson's popular verse (703, 729). But, as in so much of Tennyson, danger and destruction lie waiting here in an apparent harmony. There can be no room for the Romantic ego of Mr. Hazard in the genteel valley in which he has placed himself. Her novel is Wylie's lament, once again, for what she admired most in the life and art of a poet like Shelley: high-flown conceptions, a reckless generosity of self, an unconformity of genius whose titanism was splendid even in failure.

Peacock relates that Shelley's "favorite heroines" were Nausicaa and Antigone.[12] Neither could be less like Lady Clara Hunting, in whom Elinor Wylie creates an aristocratic figure "cast in [fine] porcelain" who, with "her gliding step, her gown of thin blue muslin, [and] the tinted cameo at her throat, seem[s] emblematical of peace" (701). She has none of Jennifer Lorn's silliness, none of the natural Rosalba's impetuosity and brilliance; but, as Ponyard would have Jennifer appear and as Rosalba is forced to become, Lady Clara

12. Thomas Love Peacock, *Memoirs of Percy Bysshe Shelley*, in *Life of Shelley*, ed. Wolfe, II, 328.

resembles an artifact: graceful, dispassionate, ultimately remote. With "her long throat, her small and arrogant head with its coronet of gilded bronze," she also resembles the persistent antiheroine of Elinor Wylie's self-critical poems. She is lovely; to Hodge, and in a more dangerous way, to Hazard, she is a "Circe," severely limited in moral sympathy (737).

Wylie's detailed descriptions of Lady Clara and her daughters make a further point: if she is like an artifact, it is a certain kind of artifact. "A life-size china [lady]" "cast in a porcelain mould," she is "temperate and well-bred," a woman to whom "the sentimental and the intolerant [are] alike ludicrous" (736). Her equanimity of feeling, like the picturesque costumes she wears, would have appealed to Oscar Wilde. Wondering sincerely but momentarily whether Mr. Hazard is very ill, she dismisses the thought with another: "It's silly to worry about trifles; it spoils the complexion" (738). Her remark, associating mortal sickness with "trifles" and the spoiling of a complexion with compassion, bring to mind Wilde's dictum that "we should treat all the trivial things of life seriously, and all the serious things of life with sincere and studied triviality," an opinion that might seem sage to Lady Clara since it fosters spiritual chic, an artful tranquillity of temperament.[13] Studied nakedly, however, with no bow to its glib and perverse wit, both Wilde's and Lady Clara's remarks lack heart. When Mr. Hazard resigns himself to Clara's care, we are told that he enters "a little silver age, . . . peaceable and hushed, secure against the hurry and violence of an ending"—"an age no longer golden" but seeming "safer for that moderation" (716). "Hurry" and "violence" marked Hazard's life as a Romantic; the golden age was, for him as for Elinor Wylie, the age of Shelley. The "silver age" over which Clara presides is "a paradise of children . . . a middle land, a merciful limbo"—the age of early Tennyson (716). Yet in Lady Clara, with her "cool and thrifty" heart, her artifice of gesture and dress, there are elements expressive of the Aestheticism of Wilde and Whistler (717).

When Mr. Hazard first sees Lady Clara and her daughters, they make a Whistlerian portrait:

> He was bewitched by the fancy that the muslin frocks of Clara and her girls had been accurately matched to the several colours of their eyes. These greys and azures were at home among the willow-trees, between

13. Hesketh Pearson, *Oscar Wilde* (New York, 1946), 226.

heaven and the curve of heaven reflected in the stream. The girls' thin skirts, which were so short as to leave their fragile ankles free, were spattered with river water; there was an engaging plumy disorder in their curls. Even Clara, the veritable looking-glass of grace and freshness, wore along the border of her blue gown a frosty pattern of dandelion feathers; a few of these winged seeds clung like snow-flakes to her soft brown hair. (704)

Impressionistic, decorative, cool in color, this picture of the Huntings is, like Whistler's portraits, an arrangement that proposes an implicit harmony between subject and setting. The grays and azures that Whistler often used, the willow trees reminiscent of his Japanese motifs, the reflections of sky in water that suggest the delicate tonalities of pictures like the famous *Nocturne—Blue and Gold—Old Battersea Bridge* all unite to evoke the mood of his work. There is also a studied, posed quality in Lady Clara's aspect—the dandelion feathers do not casually flake her gown but make a "pattern" upon it; her gown matches her eyes and they match the sky—that reminds one of his portraits of women in which, as in *The White Girl: No. 1*, hair, dress, and background echo each other in color and texture to produce the tonal harmonies Whistler sought to achieve.

By these evocations in Lady Clara's words and attitudes of the Art for Art's Sake movement, Elinor Wylie makes a further contrast between what she considered great art, the art of the Romantics, and the narrower, self-conscious art of Aestheticism. As we have seen, her consistent critical vision of the insularity of Aestheticism, a vision that reached its full expression in the later poems, never kept her from demonstrating Aesthetic characteristics in her own work. Women approaching the aloof perfection of fine porcelain; Rosalba, woman translated into porcelain; the personae of poems such as "Epitaph," in which the woman's "loveliness" is "curved / And carved as silver is" (*Collected Poems*, 51) express her Aesthetic fascination with artifice; china instead of flesh; precious gems and objects to which natural phenomena, like the sea in "Three Wishes," are compared; the exquisite, hermetic, and rare rather than the homely or commonplace. In Lady Clara the artificial and the aristocratic are associated so as to be mutually self-explanatory. It is natural for her to assume decorative poses in chairs shaped like sea shells because in her, breeding has produced a finesse akin to artifice. Elinor Wylie perceives and professes Lady Clara's beauty but also her limitations. Like some self-portraits among Wylie's poems, Lady Clara's image of refined and distant elegance pleases but lacks passion. Next to her, Mr. Hazard—his soul intermittently divided between discord and joy, his projects grand, his carriage headlong—embodies what Elinor Wylie regarded as the higher aspiration of Romantic art. *Mr. Hodge and Mr. Hazard* is a "romance of the mind" in which the distinctions Elinor Wylie liked to make between Romantic art and her own art and between Romantic art and some later nineteenth-century art are made in fictional terms (*Collected Prose*, 647).

Carl Van Doren writes that *Mr. Hodge and Mr. Hazard* sprang directly from a personal experience of Elinor Wylie:

> Returning to England in 1925, ten years after she had left it, she thought of herself as almost Shelley, perhaps a friend of Shelley, returning to England ten or so years after Shelley's death in Italy. From this came *Mr. Hodge and Mr. Hazard*, her fourth novel. It had its origin, she told me, in two words spoken by a stupid man from Oxford, who, hearing she was writing sonnets to Shelley, muttered "'Poor Shelley.'" She heard him. Her revenge was to pillory him as Mr. Hodge, who in the novel hears that Mr. Hazard is writing a sonnet to Milton, and says "'Poor Milton.'—"[14]

Stanley Olson has identified Lady Clara Hunting as Helen Young, the aristocratic wife of an English diplomat at whose home, Formosa Place, Wylie vacationed. Formosa Place was, like Lyonnesse, "towering, massive, and magnificent." Wylie wrote of her admiration for "the old and melancholy house, the river running dark and green beneath green and golden banks, the enchanting breed of blue-eyed [Young] children native to the scene like fauns and dryads,"[15] and she admired Helen Young's ease with life. In the shadow of Young's maternity and self-confidence, Wylie felt ramshackly. She found calm at Formosa, as Hazard does at Lyonnesse. But the Youngs' contentment also threatened her. She was no longer happily married; she had not achieved real motherhood. Indeed, like the scandalous Hazard, father to dead babies and (he thinks) the enemy of children, Wylie alternately yearned toward and shrank from the society of the Youngs' son and daughters. Her characterization of Hazard as an outcast had roots in her concealed but painful timidity

---

14. Carl Van Doren, *Three Worlds* (New York, 1936), 232.
15. Stanley Olson, *Elinor Wylie: A Life Apart* (New York, 1979), 275.

about her own past. Her portrait of Lady Clara with its curious admixture of what Wylie regarded as her own worst traits was tinted with some disapproval, perhaps in self-defense. Helen Young recognized herself in Lady Clara; others, like her sister Nancy, recognized Wylie in Mr. Hazard.

Wylie's phrase, "Mr. Hazard was tired of distances," tellingly expresses her own weariness in the late 1920s (729). There were for Elinor Wylie, as she wrote *Mr. Hodge and Mr. Hazard*, many "distances." There was the long road she had traveled from girlhood in a social ambiance to womanhood as a professional writer. There was the distance between her assumption that she could be a wife and mother and her realization that she was by temperament neither. There was the distance she perceived between her own careful art, epitomized by the small kingdom of Lyonnesse, and the great world of the Romantics, a world whose loss is responsible for Hazard's veritgo and his desire to die. There was also the distance between moderately good health and the dwindling resources that described Wylie's (and Hazard's) condition as she wrote *Mr. Hodge and Mr. Hazard*. Like *Jennifer Lorn*, this is an autobiographical novel, however symbolically conceived. Nancy Hoyt remarks that after *Jennifer*'s success, Wylie planned to continue to write fiction because, unlike poetry, fiction paid.[16] Such a motive would recommend itself to one's family, but it does not explain Elinor Wylie's obvious determination to write fiction nor the clear need she experienced in her short career to express a sense of her own predicament in a form that engaged the plight of character more accessibly than did poetry. Because, like Hazard, she felt herself middle-aged, outcast, cut off from respectability and domesticity, yet was given to yearnings for the visionary and supramundane, she argued their tale in a form that could muster more elements of the casual and scholarly, of the chance accoutrements of reality, than could the lyric voice. She made him one with her, even as Jennifer Lorn had been one, and perhaps she wrote prose to express their misfortunes because prose was to her less finished, more illustrative of breakdown, than verse.

Hazard has more of the qualities she approved in herself than any other character she portrayed. Like the speaker in "A Red Carpet for Shelley, III," Hazard has put himself to "one supreme expense," the use of his energies in

16. Nancy Hoyt, *Elinor Wylie: The Portrait of an Unknown Lady* (New York, 1935), 85.

the cause of art (*Collected Poems*, 158). Like the speaker of "Sonnet," he exercises over his talent "a strict ascetic habit of control" (308). He is painfully responsive to barbs about his past, which like Wylie's is a specter difficult to elude. Both are prone to self-mockery. Both are thin, his thinness associated with beauty as for her it always was. He has her bronze hair though "overlaid with silver," and he is in his fortieth year as she was when the novel was planned (*Collected Prose*, 675). Some of the brilliantly surreal passages devoted to his illness undoubtedly record her own recollections of the hallucinatory feverishness of influenza from which she suffered while the novel was written. His racking headaches and fatigue remind us that Elinor Wylie died of a coronary stroke after a series of such symptoms that began in 1925.

But the aspect of Mr. Hazard's personality that best relates him to Elinor Wylie is pride. The speaker of "Sonnet" is "fanatical in pride, and feather-witted / In the world's business" (*Collected Poems*, 308). Mr. Hazard is constantly at the mercy of shopkeepers and tradesmen, but again and again we are told that he "rejoice[s] to know that he had remained composed and haughty" while suffering a blow; that, however desperate, he is outwardly "glacially composed"; that "his pride scorned his enemies" (*Collected Prose*, 663, 662, 704). Hazard's pride may be "captious," "distrustful," and even ridiculous on occasion but his "frigid demeanour [is] a deliberately contrived effect; [it is] his armour" (725, 731, 711). For an interval Lady Clara's courteous indulgence woos it from him: "It was heavy and cross-grained upon his heart; he looked at Clara and he saw a friend, and little by little the joints of his armour were loosened. It fell away from his breast; it was as though the weight of a millstone had fallen. He laid aside the heaviness of years, and drew his breath lightly and without pain. . . . He wondered how he had ever borne that load of cruel steel over his heart" (711). Mr. Hodge, an efficient and ominous Uriah Heep from Leadenhall Street, strikes his blow while Hazard's breastplate is unlaced; but in the end, we may assume, Hazard's habit of armor will be resumed. Like the speaker's in "Sonnet," that armor has been "patched from desperate fears" (*Collected Poems*, 308).

As we have seen, pride, in Elinor Wylie's poetry, is a means to confront and overcome the world. In Hazard's pride, she describes her own. One of the poems of *Black Armour*, "Self-Portrait," anatomizes other aspects of her mind and spirit that relate Wylie to Hazard. She has an analytic mind like "a lens of crystal whose transparence calms / Queer stars to clarity"; an artistic mind like "A flint, a substance finer-grained than snow, / Graved with the Graces in intaglio." But "for the little rest" there is her body which is meager as Hazard's: "A hollow scooped to blackness in the breast, / The similacrum of a cloud, a feather" (*Collected Poems*, 69). Mr. Hazard's mind, "elegant," "satirical," "disdainful" (*Collected Prose*, 753), is capable of sharp and cosmic perceptions, but when they are turned upon his past illusions he sees himself, as Wylie does, possessing

> Instead of stone, instead of sculptured strength,
> This soul, this vanity, blown hither and thither
> By trivial breath, over the whole world's length.
> (*Collected Poems*, 69)

The world's "arrows and slings" are taken by "A Proud Lady" to fashion into "wings / For the heels of [her] shoes" (32). They are viewed in other moods, however, as inadequate means to flight and self-protection. Just so, the "feathered shoulder-blades" of Mr. Hazard's temporarily beaten spirit do not suggest wings to him. They are instead "goose-feathers from the pillow-case" (*Collected Prose*, 754).

Hazard's portrait is, as Wylie claims in her "Advertisement" to the novel, a "little image of an idealist." Despite the provocative nuances that relate his life to Shelley's and Byron's, he is really neither poet, nor is his story precisely "a disguised biography" of Elinor Wylie. Many characteristics, however—his defiance, his terror and remorse, his asceticism, and his belief in the deathlessness of art and beauty—relate Mr. Hazard to the Elinor Wylie of the verse self-portraits. It is perhaps fitting, because it was her last, that this "symbolic romance" draws more than any other on the life and mind of the author (647).

CHAPTER IX · *TRIVIAL BREATH*

Still one would want more, one would need more,
More than a world of white and snowy scents.
WALLACE STEVENS, "The Poems of Our Climate"

The kingly bard
Must smite the chords rudely and hard,
As with hammer or with mace;
That they may render back
Artful thunder, which conveys
Secrets of the solar track,
Sparks of the supersolar blaze.
RALPH WALDO EMERSON, "Merlin I"

 n one of the poems in *Black Armour* Elinor Wylie spoke of her own spirit: "This soul, this vanity, blown hither and thither / By trivial breath, over the whole world's length" (*Collected Poems*, 69). Five years later those lines provided a modest title for her penultimate volume of poems.

Trivial Breath was published in June, 1928, between covers of striped old rose and gray and with a typeface designed by Lucien Bernhard. Its elegance, praised, for example, in the New York *Post* (June 19), made it seem worthy of Wylie and of the craze in the 1920s for beautiful, sometimes frivolous books. But despite its cheerful resplendence, the book was more severe than any of her earlier volumes in its condemnation of precious art and of egoism. These themes, treated with acerbity, were related in *Trivial Breath* to a governing theme, the greatness of Shelley; and she perhaps turned to them at this time because she had much to say about art and little that was new to say about love.

When *Trivial Breath* appeared Elinor Wylie had already had one heart attack and suffered increasingly from frail health. She was less interested in its reception than in finishing her last volume of poems, *Angels and Earthly Creatures*, whose sonnets to "One Person" celebrated her sorrowful romance with Woodhouse. *Angels* would, for the first time in Wylie's career, express delight in passion and then renounce it, vowing final commitment to a life of the mind which she associated with the figure of Shelley. Most of the poems in that volume would be emotionally charged, remarkable for their expression of elation and hope. Not so the "love" poetry of *Trivial Breath*. Written before Elinor Wylie met Woodhouse, "Confession of Faith," "Where, O Where?" and "Unwilling Admission" are revelations of sexual aversion, fear, and disharmony more chilling than those of *Black Armour*. Lines like the following from "Speed the Parting—" are reminiscent of the magazine verse of Dorothy Parker (and Wylie sometimes wrote in that mode). Their cynicism is blithe, and they have a hard edge that seems easily won:

> The limpid blossom of youth
> Turns into a poison berry;
> Having perceived this truth
> I shall not weep but be merry.
> Therefore die when you please;
> It's not very wise to worry;
> I shall not shiver and freeze;
> I shall not even be sorry. (121)

Others, like the tercets of "Confession of Faith," repeat a pathetic story of frigidity enunciated earlier in *Black Armour*. The story accords with the personal feelings Wylie confided to friends:

> I lack the braver mind
> That dares to find
> The lover friend, and kind.
>
> I fear him to the bone;
> I lie alone
> By the beloved one.

> And, breathless for suspense,
> Erect defense
> Against love's violence
>
> Whose silences portend
> A bloody end
> For lover never friend.
>
> But in default of faith,
> In futile breath,
> I dream no ill of Death. (116)

"Confession of Faith" makes clear that the speaker does not dislike her lover; indeed, he is "the beloved one." But she cannot relate carnal passion, so vivid and—in her experience—violent in the male, to kindness.

Distressed by her own failure to be gracefully yielding, hence truly feminine, anguished not to have achieved a love in which desire and affection fuse, she dreams of death. These feelings of unworthiness and revulsion conspire in "Where, O Where?" to produce an escapist poem akin to those in *Black Armour*. "Where, O Where?" effectively discloses the unhappy speaker's ability to shut off her lover with a completion wrought of desperate need ("blood"):

> I need not die to go
> So far you cannot know
> My escape, my retreat,
> And the prints of my feet
> Written in blood or dew;
> They shall be hid from you,
> In fern-seed lost
> Or the soft flakes of frost.
> . . . .
> You shall see me no more
> Though each night I hide
> In your bed, at your side. (153)

Though able in his company to deny the lover her inner self, her fugitive essence, still she is dependent on him; for she "hide[s]" from her own anxiety each night "at [his] side." And, as she shows in "Unwilling Admission," she is aware of his pain, the "uncounted piercing of [his] side" for which her dissatisfaction is responsible (154). With the exception of the ballad "A Strange Story" and its delightful last quatrain,

> When I died in Bloomsbury
> In the bend of your arm,
> At the end I died merry
> And comforted and warm (137)

there are no poems in *Trivial Breath* that see love as a solace. Even the charming, frequently anthologized "Puritan's Ballad" with its clever, neat antitheses and mischievous rhymes is a revelation of distrust in love.

Indeed, the mood of this volume, in its consideration of most human appetites, is somber. When she wrote it, Wylie was much interested in the ballad form, and in her ballads "Peter and John," "The Devil in Seven Shires," and "The Innocents," she uses the repetitions and metric emphases of that form to explore the relentlessness of evil. Such dark realities of life as infidelity and betrayal, sudden death and "planetary war" owe their malicious power to what Wylie construed to be the spirit of evil in the universe; to combat it the soul must be "glassed in translucent dream" and, though a "dissolving star," brave, courageous, and occupied with the work God intended it to do (160, 161):

> The small soul's dissolving ghost
> Must leave a heart-shape in the dust
> Before it is inspired and lost
> In God: I hope it must. (124)

Wylie's quasi-religious contemplation of the duties of the wise soul in a decadent world harmonizes in *Trivial Breath* with the prominent theme of good as opposed to limited art. In none of her volumes is this theme treated more trenchantly. "Miranda's Supper," "Minotaur," "True Vine," and "Innocent Landscape" weave her distinctive aesthetic in verse form. She had been accused as a person and an artist of the sin of pride—pride in birth and taste, in the beauty of her face, and in the decorum of her art. She had also accused herself of pride, openly and in fiction. Others had related that pride to a limiting choice of subject and to a style whose refinement was solipsistic. Now, in a series of witty poems she herself pointed out the moral insufficiency of an art of mere decor and a life of empty forms.

The barbed heroic couplets of "Miranda's Supper" present a heroine not unlike Elinor Wylie's several self-reflecting personae. Miranda is reminiscent of "A Proud Lady": "pale, elegant, at point to vanish," her breeding implicit in her slimness as in her French shoes and Spanish shawl and the "webbed enchantment" of "her meanest petticoat." It is 1866, and she has survived being "a gentlewoman" whose "lips like beads of coral" "never made her anger oral" when the Yankees invaded her house (127). The house and her "seven thousand lovely acres" at the appropriately named Peacock's Landing are now emptied of Yankee "barbarian hordes" (129, 127). She is alone as her clocks cry out the hour, clocks that signify the richness of rare workmanship and the satisfactions of rank and wealth:

> Seven! Seven! cry all the clocks;
> Five old clocks that chime in chorus,
> One the gift of the Grand Duke Boris,
> Malachite, with Peter in bronze
> Setting his horse at the Persian guns;
> The clock with a print of the Flying Castle;
> The singing-bird clock that came from Basel;
> Bonaparte's clock, with the bees worn shabby;
> And the clock with the voice of an English abbey.
> Wound at the word of a raw top sergeant;
> Wound by the paw of a brutal sentry,
> To toll the obsequies of gentry . . . (128)

It is difficult not to rejoice with Miranda that such exquisite timepieces, having survived time, are no longer subject to the "paw of a brutal sentry." Yet Miranda's vision of the disparity in breeding between Yankee and Southern "gentry" momentarily disposes response and is in the next moment subject to another response: the suspicion of instinctive prejudice in Miranda. And though the possessions she joyfully reclaims are indeed remarkable, her love for them is excessive and her attitude toward the suffering and dying in the world around her is insular and unperceiving. For her the precious clocks have failed to measure time.

Walking into the garden in the cool of a "conventual evening," Miranda looks at its "velvet" lawns and decides, "Nothing is lost! Nothing is lost!" (129, 131, 133). The vague hysteria of the repeated line demonstrates her ability to create illusion. Alone on an estate where emptiness "stream[s]" "like a pennant," (130) she conserves the selfish notion that the turmoil of war has never occurred. Her garden "like sea-green satin" is still "fenced" and she is safe in an atmosphere of immaculate "peace" and withdrawal (130, 129). Briefly, despite the moonlit magnolias "Whose cups contain the Holy Ghost" (129) of her own religion—Southern elegance and ceremony—she wonders about the dead:

> Who has killed them? Who has killed them?
> For a moment's space the lady
> Feels her pulse's beat unsteady,
> Hammering and helter-skelter.

But she is protected from concern by her own narcissism, expressed in an image that recalls the heavy Poiret gowns of silver thread Elinor Wylie liked to wear:

> her heart is safe in shelter
> Willow-vaulted, verdant-pastured,
> Secure in silver mail envestured. (130)

Taking a trowel, she digs for the precious things she has buried in the garden. They are valuable, uncommon; yet the poem, having puckishly lavished some irony on Miranda's vanity—"Three novices went blind at Brussels / To weave the enigma of her scarf" (127)—expends more on the unearthed treasure that excites her enthusiasm:

> Is it horror, or beautiful?
> Is it a mandrake, is it a skull?
> Is it a crucifix, is it a pistol?
> The thing is a cup of Chinese Bristol. (131)

The cup has none of the associations of magic, mortality, sacredness, or danger posed against it in the couplets by *mandrake*, *skull*, *crucifix*, and *pistol*. It is "Pure in color, correct in shape," artistically commendable. Yet it depicts faces "Small as Miranda's finger-nail," marvelously exact but without complication, terror, or ecstasy; they are suave and representative of emotion in miniature. In its china world, the barbaric is subdued and prettified: "Mongol faces, demure and pale" (131). Miranda is grateful to retrieve the cup because the "willow patterns" of the china she has been forced to use "make a lady's soul a slattern's!" (132). Her confusion of morality with aesthetic taste is the result of inflated pride and excessive fondness for the beautiful in the material rather than the spiritual order. Elinor Wylie's antitheses, "willow patterns" and "Chinese Bristol," are well chosen, for the humble willowware was a nineteenth-century household commonplace whereas Chinese Bristol was porcelain made in Bristol, England, in the eighteenth century in careful imitation of expensive Oriental porcelain.

Next, Miranda unearths her silver, and the poem, as might be expected, remembering Elinor Wylie's extraordinary fondness for silver, voluptuously acknowledges its beauty:

> Behold Miranda now uncover,
> With lingering gestures of a lover,
> A grave that brims with twenty moons
> Filling the bowls of the silver spoons.

Yet the poet mischievously describes the hyperbole of Miranda's response to the silver:

> Her mind grew duller, her mouth grew muter,
> Each time she stirred her tea with pewter,
> Or touched a knife with a black bone handle;
> Now she is lighted like a candle. (132)

One might admire Miranda's ability to sublimate fleshly hungers in aesthetic satisfaction were it not for the excess of her Aestheticism. It is on the one hand praiseworthy that for her

> Gros bleu de Sèvres, Italian faience,
> Hold starvation in abeyance;
> Poverty begins to shine,
> The crust of bread is steeped in wine;

but on the other, the passion of love is too great to be directed at twenty spoons, silver or no. The poem instructs us that Miranda sees no difference between the sacramental and the material, a deadly impartiality of vision that is iniquity, not snobbery:

> All the miracle of Cana
> May be performed by painted china,
> And even the portent of the mass
> Imprisoned in a crystal glass.

The rhymes' equation of *Cana* with *china* and the *mass* with *glass* teaches us the indiscriminateness of Miranda's judgment.

The sight of her cherished objects, more than the war's end, "wakens [Miranda] from the dead," and by "the alchemy of Belfast looms," linen tablecloths, she intends to resurrect others with her.

> Tapers shall enchant the rooms
> And make them populous as once;
> . . . .
> All the Peacocks shall return
> As the sea's uncounted pebbles;
> . . . .
> The devout and ivory ladies,
> Back from heaven, back from Hades,
> Back from other earthier scenes,
> Baltimore and New Orleans:
> Back from exile, back from durance,
> Home again to proud assurance. (132–33)

Here Wylie's humorous, pointed couplets slyly reveal her heroine's fatuity. The poem concludes gravely, with implicit disapproval. When Miranda assembles all her artifacts so that she can dine, her "supper" is compared with the Last Supper of Christ: a devastating comparison that teaches the blasphemy of loving objects more than humanity or God:

> Here, prepared within an upper
> Chamber, is Miranda's supper.
> Now partake; it is her body;
> And the carven cup is bloody
> Where her fingers drew it forth
> From mortality of earth.
> Every broken crust and crumb
> Savours of your coming home,
> And the berries she has gathered
> By divinity are fathered.

Eat the bread she is adoring,
Drink the water she is pouring;

Now approach, both man and ghost;
Nothing is lost! Nothing is lost! (133)

The poem emphasizes Miranda's narcissism: she feeds on her own person. Her supper is prepared for her own disciples, those whose god is Meissen. The refrain "Nothing is lost! Nothing is lost" expresses her acquisitiveness and moral frivolity. Wylie's poem with its reductive techniques shows her knowledge of Alexander Pope's *Rape of the Lock*. It proves once again her dexterity in choosing historic literary forms for her own purposes; her Miranda is even a type of Pope's Belinda, silly but in some ways appealing. What is most striking, however, about "Miranda's Supper" is its thoroughly confident, witty attack on the very Aestheticism with which Elinor Wylie was familiar, both in the society of those she knew and in what she read.

Contemporary reviewers failed to perceive Wylie's purpose in "Miranda's Supper," considering it the celebration of a sumptuous and gracious life.[1] But Babette Deutsch wrote one of the shrewdest criticisms that exists of Wylie's work when she spoke of the poem "Minotaur." She recognized that a false and limiting Aestheticism was the subject of that poem and commented, "It is in [Wylie's] frank recognition of her fault that she must disarm her severest critic. 'Minotaur' might readily be taken for an indictment of her own style."[2] "Minotaur" is not, of course, a mere confession but a well-realized Aesthetic poem; that is why it disarms. In it, Wylie's fears—not wholly justified—that she lacked robustness in her life as artist and as woman come together in one fear: fear of the beautiful.

The poem is a stately exhortation:

Go study to disdain
The frail, the over-fine
Which tapers to a line
Knotted about the brain.

. . . .

Distrust the exquisite,
The sharpened silver nerve,

1. See Jessica North, for instance, in "Poems in Cloisonné," *Poetry*, XXXIX, no. 2 (1929), 97.
2. Babette Deutsch, "Proud Lady," *Virginia Quarterly Review*, VIII (October, 1932), 618.

> The lacquered, nacred curve
> Wherein a moon is lit. (114)

Recreating the aspect of her own poetic world that observes carven forms, sharp, silvery, or lacquered, and uses words like "nacred," Wylie affirms the responsibility to "disdain" and "distrust" it when it is "over-fine." The true artist, she says, must have appreciative communion not only with the rare, the refined, or the spiritual but also with the gross and deformed, the greedy minotaur with his bull's head and man's body. The poem's speaker, regarding an image of the monster, advises,

> Gaze ever and at length
> Upon the carven head,
> Devouring it as bread
> To thrive upon its strength.
>
> The sword-deflecting scar
> Indented and oblique
> That stripes the savage cheek;
> The throat made columnar
>
> In copper, and up-raised
> To such a trumpet shape
> No clangour can escape,—
> These only must be praised. (115)

The line "These only must be praised" seems uttered in a mood of atonement and would be excessive advice had the poet not made clear that she is addressing artists who prefer the "frail" to the strong, the "over-fine" to the "savage"—throats like those in "Preference" that are "round as a column" but not made, like the minotaur's, of copper (63). The voice of the minotaur is that of brute reality; the artist must heed it. Furthermore, since his refinement is a kind of disease, the artist should embrace this other truth—savagery—in order to become perfect.

Finally, unless artists, in both their persons and perceptions, are able to extend their interest to Caliban as well as Ariel, the god of art will desert them:

> From flesh refined to glass
> A god goes desert-ward,

> Astride a spotted pard,
> Between an ox and ass.

"Flesh refined to glass" is easily linked with the self-modeled persona of "Epitaph" whose lips were "left . . . more clear than glass" (51) and with the figure of Rosalba in *The Venetian Glass Nephew* who refines her human flesh into porcelain in the triumphal allegory of a certain kind of art over nature. Properly, the god who leaves the artist is "Astride a spotted pard," a *pard* or *camelopard* the Shelleyan symbol of loveliness to Elinor Wylie. He is also "between an ox and ass," humble, dogged animals that in legend surrounded the Christ Child at his birth. The poem concludes, too, with an exhortation:

> Let innocence enchant
> The flesh to fiercer grain
> More fitted to retain
> This burning visitant. (115)

Here, "innocence" suggests the wholesome receptivity of the true artist whose "flesh" must be "fiercer" (more vital) "grain" than glass or porcelain, so that the painful visitation of the god can be endured.

Wylie wrote companion pieces to "Minotaur" in "True Vine" and "Innocent Landscape." "True Vine" concerns itself with a refined sensibility whose "pearly fruit" has "ruin for its centre." Such an artistic sensibility produces "delicate immaculate blossoms" which are "fastidious" and "diaphanous" yet leave no "trace upon the durable hereafter." By comparison, "the obdurate and savage lovely / Whose roots are set profoundly upon trouble"—"trouble" implying the complexity and disorder of crude life—becomes, at the hand of a less narcissistic artist, a "flower" that "grows so fiercely and so bravely / It does not even know that it is noble." The poem concludes, like "Minotaur," with a directive:

> This is the vine to love, whose balsams flourish
> Upon a living soil corrupt and faulty,
> Whose leaves have drunk the skies, and stooped to nourish
> The earth again with honey sweet and salty. (120)

Wylie's choice of natural imagery to define true art—the biblical quotation of "true vine," the "living soil," and the "leaves" which, though reaching into air, are linked firmly to earth—recalls Coleridge's statements about the nature of art and artists. Coleridge argued that the greatest art presupposed a bond between nature and man and that a good poem should grow organically, like a tree. He and other Romantic artists Wylie admired believed that art must express the organic variety of nature. By contrast, the theories of Wilde, Whistler, and the Aesthetes averred that "what Art really reveals to us is Nature's lack of design, her curious crudities, her extraordinary monotony, her absolutely unfinished condition." [3] For them decorative art was praiseworthy for its rejection of nature as an ideal of beauty; for "nature [was] usually wrong" and to great extent was the creation of art, fogs, as Wilde teasingly said, being noticed in London after centuries only because the Impressionists "invented them." [4]

Like "Miranda's Supper," "True Vine" is thematically—as Edmund Wilson wrote of "Bronze Trumpets and Sea Water" in *Nets to Catch the Wind*—"nothing more nor less than a piece of literary criticism." [5] It addresses itself to the problem of art as self-obsession. Its opening line, "There is a serpent in perfection tarnished," makes clear that too much concern with formal perfection can result in the tarnish of imperfection. "Form," Wilde declared (influenced by Gustave Flaubert) "is everything. . . . Start with the worship of form, and there is no secret in art that will not be revealed to you." [6] But "True Vine" contends that the formal absorption of the art of arabesque makes it "quick to languish," "brittle," its immaculateness a deficiency. The "flower" that "does not even know that it is noble" is art concerned not with itself or with form alone but with nature, "corrupt and faulty."

"Innocent Landscape," too, directs attention to a special artistic experience in which form exorcises meaning:

> Here is no peace, although the air has fainted,
>   And footfalls die and are buried in deep grass,
> And reverential trees are softly painted
>   Like saints upon an oriel of glass.

3. Oscar Wilde, "The Decay of Lying," *Intentions* (London, 1913), 1.
4. James Abbott McNeill Whistler, *The Gentle Art of Making Enemies* (1890; reprint, New York, 1967), 143; Wilde, *Intentions*, 30.
5. Edmund Wilson, Jr., "The Bronze Trumpet of Fairyland," *Bookman*, LIV (1922), 579.
6. Wilde, "The Critic as Artist," *Intentions*, 201–202.

The pattern of the atmosphere is spherical,
   A bubble in the silence of the sun,
Blown thinner by the very breath of miracle
   Around a core of loud confusion.

Here is no virtue; here is nothing blessed
   Save this foredoomed suspension of the end;
Faith is the blossom, but the fruit is cursèd;
   Go hence, for it is useless to pretend. (123)

The "innocence" of this landscape, art, is its mortal flaw; for it is not the serene, inclusive vigor of true art but the exclusive, simplistic harmony won by technique exercised for its own sake and by disengagement. Its "peace" results from the suspension of life. The sounds of human footfalls "die and are buried" in the grass of a Pre-Raphaelite-like scene whose trees are not growing things but "reverential" images on "an oriel of glass." The pattern of this landscape is "spherical," recalling Coleridge's pleasure dome and Shelley's "dome of many-coloured glass"; but "bubble" is a word adequate to describe its evanescence. The very order of this art, its repression of the "loud confusion" and genuine aspect of life, are indeed "miracle[s]." But such miracles do not last. The "fruit" of the landscape is "cursèd" because it is a pretense of the harmony of true art. The poet urges, "Go hence."

Wallace Stevens, whose poems were sometimes accused of Aesthetic excess and whose readers, Randall Jarrell says, sometimes resented his "spending his time collecting old porcelains" in them instead of "Fords,"[7] writes in "Poems of Our Climate" a lyric whose theme is essentially similar to Elinor Wylie's in "Minotaur," "True Vine," and "Innocent Landscape." His poem also warns against the seductions of pure form and the heartlessness of empty elegance. In it, Stevens presents a scene which, like Wylie's in "Innocent Landscape," has been "simplified" of rich colors. Wintry, a world of "cold porcelain," it signifies the "concealment" of the "evilly compounded, vital I" even as in "Innocent Landscape," "loud confusion" is suppressed in a glassy atmosphere (like Stevens' "world of white") in which trees become "saints." For Wylie's sphere, there is Stevens' bowl, also "brilliant" and

7. Randall Jarrell, *Poetry and the Age* (New York, 1955), 123.

"round" with nothing in it but "clear water" and plucked, hence perishing, "pink and white carnations." His conclusion, like hers in "Minotaur," reminds us that "the imperfect is our paradise"; that one "want[s]" and "need[s] more" "than a world of white" while the "fiercer grain" of flesh she speaks of in that poem finds a cognate in his defense of "flawed words and stubborn sounds."[8]

Like the Stevens of "Poems of Our Climate," Elinor Wylie shows herself highly concerned in *Trivial Breath* with the ideal nature of art. Whistler once argued that only an artist can be a competent art critic.[9] Appropriately, Wylie chose in her poems to subject the art with which she herself was identified to critical scrutiny.

It is fitting that *Trivial Breath*, whose chief themes are art and human imperfection, should begin and end with poems addressed to Wylie's perfect artist, Shelley. Poems within the volume also celebrate his art, personality, or both.

The four sonnets of the book's "Dedication" relate the history of Wylie's love for "song," which is intertwined with her discovery of Shelley's poetry. "When I was seven years old," she writes, "I had a primer." (At seven, she tells us in her essay "Excess of Charity," she read "The Cloud" and "To a Skylark" in her Third Reader.) The "pellucid truth" and "balsam" of "the mother-tongue" were first dispensed to her by Shelley, the first poet whose voice enchanted her. His poetry was a "cup of pearls dissolving into dimmer," an ethereal language rich with visions. Yet, her second sonnet explains, though the "ceremonial supper" of Shelley's art "refreshed [her] childhood," she has never been able to repay him in verse worthy of his own. The imagery she uses in these sonnets is efficient if awkward-sounding in paraphrase. Shelley is a merciful lord, a (Castilian) knight "whose sacred hand unbuckled / Extreme Castalia for a careless child." By making a poetic feast for her, the Shelleyan language is related to that maternal source, the language itself, which feeds the speaker with "cream." The image of Shelley as knight Wylie developed in other poems and in the figures of Shiloh and Hazard. In "Dedication" as in the rest, she presents herself as his follower: "she is your vassal while she is a

8. Wallace Stevens, *Poems*, selected and with an introduction by Samuel French Morse (New York, 1959), 93.
9. See Whistler, *Gentle Art*, 5.

woman"; "the woman never wandered / In vile devotion to a lesser prince."
"Dedication" makes clear that Wylie's love for Shelley was doubly prompted
by her admiration for him as an artist and by her attraction to him as a man.
The last sonnet, using images that recall Shelley's in "To a Skylark," thanks
him for the "courtesy" by which he gave her "nourishment and wine and
physic." Shelley's "rainbow clouds," his "blithe" "bird" whose song is a "rain
of melody," "a crystal stream,"[10] are implied in Wylie's encomium to his art:
"a rainbow-coloured bubble, / An innocent bird, an iridescent music, / To be
my own for all the rest of living." Shelley's poetry celebrated the unearthly,
the sublime, the free, and the good. He himself, in Wylie's view, possessed a
liberality and dignity that could never be adequately commemorated by her
"dull mortal homage of the mind" (109–11).

The sonnets of "Dedication" with their private allusions to "sacred hand"
and "prince" might be puzzling to a reader who did not know of Wylie's
devotion to Shelley. *Trivial Breath* marks the serious beginning of her poetic
recourse to a private Shelleyan symbolism and iconography. If one of the
characteristics of a genuine artist is that he create a recognizable personal
world and have a proper vision of it, then Wylie is genuine. The cool
landscape of her earlier volumes, with its occasional burst of gay color, the
sharp forms and glittering rhymes that made her famous and imitated are
achieved once again in *Trivial Breath*. And now, with a confidence bred of
indifference to critics of her infatuation, she established the figure of
Shelley—prince and later "archangel" and mystic lover—in her firmament.

Four sonnets entitled "A Red Carpet for Shelley"—votive sonnets, undistinguished in imaginative content—articulate what remained a major
anxiety of her career: that, despite industry and skill, she lacked the "soul"
requisite to true poetry and that the frivolous aspects of her nature would
keep her from greatness and from patterning herself on Shelley's image. She
can offer him merely "devout affection," a brilliant wish: "I would unroll the
rounded moon and sun / And knit them up for you to walk upon" (157).

Elinor Wylie's desire to be associated with Shelley, man and artist, appears
not only in these devotional sonnets but in her use of such Shelleyan titles as

10. Percy Bysshe Shelley, *The Complete Poetical Works*, ed. Thomas Hutchinson (London,
1948), 602–603, "To a Skylark," lines 33, 1, 2, 35, 85.

"'Desolation Is a Delicate Thing'"[11] as well as in two mournful poems, "The Coast Guard's Cottage" and "Lament for Glasgerion." In the former lyric as in several poems in her earlier volumes, Wylie writes about death by water and invites a drowned ghost to "come home" to her bed (149). The poem regrets the "unequal wrong" whereby the speaker is left alive while the dead man has been "murdered." And though he is not obviously Shelley (the speaker says, "I'll never ask if you were beautiful / In life, or straight and slender" [150]), her lament that he is dead while she lives relates this poem to Wylie's elegy for Shelley, the volume's penultimate poem, "Lament for Glasgerion":

> The lovely body of the dead,
> Wherein he laid him down to rest,
> Is shrunken to corruption's thread;
> The blood which delicately dressed
> The flying bone, the sighing breast,
> One with nothingness is made.
>
> The darling garment is outworn;
> Its fabric nourishes the moth;
> The silk wherein his soul was born,
> Woven of flesh and spirit both,
> Is crumpled to a pitiful cloth:
> His soul lies naked and forlorn.
>
> So one that walks within the air,
> Who loves the ghost below the ground,
> Rejoices fervently to wear
> A body shaken and unsound;
> A brow divided by a wound;
> A throat encircled by a care.
>
> Shall I go warm above the cold
> Wherein he sleeps without a shroud
> Or shred of beauty left to fold
> About the poor soul's solitude?
> The vanishing dust of my heart is proud
> To watch me wither and grow old. (165)

11. Wylie often used phrases from Shelley's poems as titles, both in fiction (each chapter heading of *The Orphan Angel*, for instance, is a line from Shelley) and verse. This title is from *Prometheus Unbound*, line 772.

This dignified and tender poem is perhaps Wylie's loveliest poetic tribute to Shelley. Her vision of herself as "one that walks within the air, / Who loves the ghost below the ground" does not distract (as it sometimes does in other poems) from her vision of Shelley. Rather, it is integral to the tension between real and ideal, flesh and spirit, that her devotion to him suggested to her in her last years. As she herself—perhaps not unwittingly—moved toward death, Wylie meditated in her last novel and final volumes of poetry on Shelley's death. That he had lived at all seemed to her a paradox for he was the supreme incarnation of two opposing forces: mind and body, spirit and flesh. She was to meditate more and more on this incarnation in the Elizabethan accents of "This Corruptible" and "Hymn to Earth" in *Angels and Earthly Creatures*. In "Lament for Glasgerion" she describes Shelley's aristocracy—"the silk wherein his soul was born"—as defeated; he is "one with nothingness" who once was "flying bone, and . . . sighing breast," the apotheosis of the adventurous and suffering Romantic artist. She is, unfortunately, alive but still the Elinor Wylie who suffered from headaches and a heart condition, "a brow divided by a wound," "a body shaken and unsound." She is glad to walk toward death and thus enjoy the prospect of union with his beloved "ghost below the ground."

"Lament for Glasgerion" is an accomplished lyric which shows Elinor Wylie's special ability to create a kinetic metaphoric world in which flesh and spirit metamorphose into one another, proving the solidity of the disembodied and the evanescence of the actual. In that world, in her view, the heart was already "vanishing dust" even while it beat; the soul could be described as "naked and forlorn" though incorporeal. This was true because for the maturing Elinor Wylie the otherworldly increasingly became a dimension of the world itself. The delicacy of her language, rooted in Aestheticism, was pressed now to state the beauty not only of frail objects or transient feelings but of a ghostly atmosphere of elusive presences. Some of these presences were abstract: shapes of love as in "Country Song" (305) or dream shapes as in "Peter and John" (134–36) or the ideal form of beauty, "shaped like a ghost, and imminent with speed" (307). The foremost was Shelley's presence: her angelic "companion," as she explains in her last poems, " 'caught in the common net, / Beside [her]' " (197). His imagined fellowship chastened her pride in accomplishment and made it seem appropriate that she call her verse *Trivial Breath*.

Yet there is nothing trivial in her vision of the ideal nature of art expressed in this volume. And the figure of Shelley, man and poet, that she describes as comforting her in "Dedication" was to appear even more effectively in *Angels and Earthly Creatures*. There Wylie would turn away from human love for the last time and fasten her attention on a world of "pure spirit" (311).

CHAPTER X · *ANGELS AND EARTHLY CREATURES*

Then as an Angell, face, and wings
Of aire, not pure as it, yet pure doth weare,
So thy love may be my loves spheare
JOHN DONNE, "Aire and Angels"

Angels might be met by the way, under English elm or
beech-tree; mere messengers seemed like angels, bound
on celestial meetings and partings; . . . All the acts and
accidents of daily life borrowed a sacred colour and
significance.
WALTER PATER, *The Child in the House*

 helley's poetry, the brilliant tale of Shelley's questing life, and the philosophy she could draw from both had served Elinor Wylie as her chief inspiration for almost thirty-six years when in 1926 she had an experience that led her temporarily to choose other comforts. Her thwarted love for Clifford Woodhouse was so painful an embarrassment to self-confidence that, though she could not give him up, she began seriously to meditate on the peace of death. Previously she had had few experiences that were not exorcised or put into perspective by Shelley's poetry. In 1926 she was as obsessed with Shelley as ever; indeed, her last volume of poems would contain at least three elegies for Shelley and a number of allusions to him. Under the spell of her love for Woodhouse and suffering the heart attacks that brought about her death, however, Elinor Wylie turned for a time from Shelley's noble agnosticism to the explicit

Christianity of Donne and the implicit Christianity of the sonnets of Shakespeare.

Friends remembered that in her last days in England Wylie carried with her the poems and sermons of Donne and that she and Woodhouse liked to discuss metaphysics. The verses she scribbled on scrap paper at Edith Olivier's were imitative of Donne and concerned with life everlasting, viewed in the orthodox Christianity of her Episcopal childhood. Her husband, writing on the flyleaf of his copy of her last poems, preserved in the Wylie Archive at Yale, recorded the origin of the title in a passage from Donne. That passage would be the subtle subtext of this last book. Readers of *Angels and Earthly Creatures*, which appeared in the spring following her death in December, 1928, found Wylie writing in an idiom indebted to the Renaissance. Stylistically, she was attempting something new, not, I think, because metaphysical poetry was becoming popular but because her celebratory imitations of Donne and Shakespeare paid tribute to Woodhouse, who admired them; because Shakespeare's sonnets described the anguish of imperfect love; and because in her advance toward death she seemed to require a different intellectual attunement. Her nonce explorations of the Elizabethan and Jacobean manner were accomplished and sincere, but had she lived they would probably have given way to other experiments in form. Even in *Angels and Earthly Creatures* the figure of Shelley as "archangel" persists; and Shelley's vision in *Adonais* (lines 460–61) that "The One remains, the many change and pass; / Heaven's light forever shines, Earth's shadows fly" is articulated there in a different style. Nevertheless, many of the poems of *Angels and Earthly Creatures* studiously attempt the complex juxtapositions of macro- and microcosm, the dramatization of contest between body and soul, sacred and profane, that are associated with Elizabethan and Jacobean poetry, and they prove again that Wylie could imitate various verse traditions for an original purpose.

The title *Angels and Earthly Creatures* is taken from Donne's "Sermon Preached to the Earl of Exeter, and his company, in his Chappell at Saint Johns; 13. Jun. 1624." The sermon's text was Apocalypse, 7:9, and among its passages was the following: "But because *Angels* could not propagate, nor make more *Angels*, [God] enlarged his love, in making man, that so he might enjoy all natures at once, and have the nature of *Angels*, and the nature of

Earthly Creatures, in one person."[1] The sonnets to Woodhouse that open the volume are entitled "One Person," thus exalting Woodhouse as combining two natures, divine and human. A strong narrative of hopeless love in various stages, they are followed by a section titled "Elements and Angels." Among these poems, "Love Song" and "Felo de Se" comment graciously yet sadly on the broken love affair, establishing a dialogue between human desire ("elements") and spiritual discipline ("angels") that allows Wylie to reintroduce Shelley as her archangelic protector and to celebrate him in several lyrics. The third section, "Earthly Creatures," is a group of frivolous lyrics suitable for *Vanity Fair* or *Smart Set* to which Wylie sometimes contributed. But it is followed by the careful poems of a final section, "Elegies and Epistles," which deliberately imitate the language of Donne in a further anatomy of the ruined love affair. The volume closes with "Little Elegy" to, I think, Shelley; though in its humility and tenderness it might also be a tribute to Woodhouse.

"One Person" is the story of an erotic but spiritual and tender attachment between a handsome, middle-aged English aristocrat and an American woman who admires and feels inferior to him despite her celebrity as a poet. It is told in a sequence of nineteen poems, all of which are true sonnets with the exception of VII (thirteen lines) and XVIII, which contains sixteen lines, the last two intensifying the resolution of the poem. The female speaker reverses the usual roles assumed by poet and beloved in the Renaissance sonnet sequence. She courts the reluctant male, confesses herself unworthy of his love, and when he eventually renounces their attachment encourages herself to hope merely for a spiritual communion. Only one sonnet suggests that the two ever "mingled breath" (VIII); yet the speaker, who admits that she had always "lived indifferent to the blood's desire" (V), declares that she has come to understand passion. Her concluding fantasy of restrained union in a small room where the lovers could "touch each other's hands, and turn / Upon a bed of juniper and fern" (XVIII) implies a fulfillment new in Wylie's verse.

In the course of the sequence, the speaker declares her amazement to have

1. Evelyn M. Simpson and George R. Potter (eds.), *The Sermons of John Donne* (10 vols.; Berkeley and Los Angeles, 1953), VI, 154.

at last fully encountered love (I); her conviction that her lover's acquaintance with suffering has made him unique (II); her sense of their moral inequality (III, IV) and of the inadequacy of her own beauty which he will not claim (V); a conversion from Platonic intellectualism to "those sharp ecstasies the pulses give" (VI) and at the same time a desire to comfort the lover both carnally and in spirit (VII); an awareness that time may kill their love and that seasons of the year will separate them (VIII); her farewell to the spirit of Shelley that, attending her formerly, atoned for imperfect loves (IX); an inability to help the troubled, older lover (X); grief at his extravagant declaration of love and at the necessary division their lives put between them (XI); the difference between their first happiness and present frustration (XII); a desire to die and be his bride in eternity (XIV); a request that the lover recall that she is a poet and has some personal virtues despite her rebelliousness at their suffering (XV); her determination never to disrupt his marriage (XIV); a wish to die with him, or if not, to live where he lives—by implication, not in her own country but in England (XVII); and, in conclusion, the dream of slumbering together under a common roof.

The identity of Wylie's "one person" is established by John D. Gordan and was set forth in the first chapter of this book.[2] Details of this story are worthy of fiction, among them the fact that Elinor sent Clifford Woodhouse's wife Rebecca a copy of the "One Person" sonnets as a Christmas present, then gave Benét another copy, cruelly dedicating it "To the onlie begetter of these insuing sonnets all happinesse." Neither Benét nor Rebecca was in doubt as to the identity of the true "begetter," whom in *The Dust Which Is God* Benét would describe as Alan Trayne, "an outdoor man," used to cold starlight and, like "one person," an owner of folds from which foxes are frightened (XV). Much about the lover suggests Woodhouse: his "sable . . . hair / Silvered" (X); his mansion with its "roof" and "cornerstone" (XVI), implying dynasty and continuum in wife and children; his chivalry, particularly appealing to Wylie in the behavior of Woodhouse (IV). Speaker and lover meet in the shadow of a beech, an oak, and a willow, as Carl Van Doren remembered of Wylie and her English friend.[3]

2. John D. Gordan, "A Legend Revisited: Elinor Wylie," *American Scholar*, XXXVIII (Summer, 1969), 34–36.
3. Carl Van Doren, *Three Worlds* (New York, 1936), 239.

The sequence, however, is interesting primarily as a study of Wylie's attitudes toward love in general. It is a set of psychological revelations and, as such, worthy of the Elizabethan sonnet sequences on whose traditional stratagems it draws.[4] The prefatory sonnet, for example, declares a complex view of human passion that does not deny its fervor but recognizes its quixotic quality. This sonnet concedes the artifice of art which in its efforts to describe feeling must ultimately be "false." It recognizes that all tales of love are "fabulous": both "fable" as narrative and, to the objective world, fable as unreality, grounded in private and romantic emotion:

> Although these words are false, none shall prevail
> To prove them in translation less than true
> Or overthrow their dignity, or undo
> The faith implicit in a fabulous tale;
> The ashes of this error shall exhale
> Essential verity, and two by two
> Lovers devout and loyal shall renew
> The legend, and refuse to let it fail.
>
> Even the betrayer and the fond deceived,
> Having put off the body of this death,
> Shall testify with one remaining breath,
> From sepulchres demand to be believed:
> These words are true, although at intervals
> The unfaithful clay contrive to make them false.
>
> (Collected Poems, 171)

One perceives in this sonnet the effects upon the poet of her late affection for a metaphysical style; for its argument urges the truth of paradox. Thus the story of love contained in the sonnet sequence will be "false" because "words" do not adequately convey reality and also because love is always a species of illusion. "In translation," however,—when the reader overlooks the distortion of language and, in a mood of belief, accepts its underlying message—the words are no "less than true" and dignified. Though love is fabulous, it is also an act of "faith." If it be an "error," and if Wylie's unsuccessful passion was an

4. For a discussion of Elinor Wylie's adaptation in "One Person" of the traditional attitudes of the Elizabethan sonnet, see Judith Farr, "Elinor Wylie, Edna St. Vincent Millay, and the Elizabethan Sonnet Tradition," in Poetic Traditions of the English Renaissance, ed. Maynard Mack and George de Forest, Lord (New Haven, 1982), 287–305.

error, nonetheless its very death ("*ashes*") proves how true it was. Lovers afterward will "*renew / The legend*" she is about to relate: a story that is both personal and general. And though all who love surrender to a sort of unreality they do so in an effort to make of it unfailing truth. The sestet of the sonnet further elaborates the idea of love as deception. It necessarily involves a "*betrayer*" and a "*fond deceived*," each lover taking turns in assuring the other of the validity of romantic affection. When both, in St. Paul's phrase, put off "the body of this death"—the life of the flesh which, like passion, implies its own demise—not even "sepulchres" can alter the truth of their experience that love is real and powerful. The sonnet's last couplet reverses the opening line of the octave, "*The words are true*," admitting at the same time the perverse infidelity of finite lovers who cannot always satisfy the high demands of Eros and in fear and weakness "*contrive*" to make the words of the legend "*false*" (171).

This prefatory sonnet attempts to place in larger perspective the specific and unique aspects of the story of love which follows in the remaining eighteen poems. The effect of Sonnet I after the introductory one is that of a tide of emotion which, however, establishes a premise: that this particular love is ultimate and the poet is wholly committed to it:

> Now shall the long homesickness have an end
> Upon your heart, which is a part of all
> The past no human creature may recall
> Save you, who are persuasive to unbend
> The brows of death, and name him for a friend:
> This ecstasy is supernatural;
> I have survived to see the heavens fall
> Into my hands, which on your hands depend.
>
> Time has prepared us an enduring bed
> Within the earth of this beloved land;
> And, lying side by side and hand in hand,
> We sleep coeval with the happy dead
> Who are ourselves, a little earlier bound
> To one another's bosom in the ground. (172)

Remembering the awkwardness and even the resentment with which Elinor Wylie recorded efforts to love in "Sequence," "Little Sonnet," and others, one understands her use of the word "homesickness." All are "homesick" for what they imagine as complete devotion. But for her, whom her sister described as a "still chilly Botticelli Venus" despite an attachment to two husbands, a woman whom Mary Colum called "not at all . . . erotic or amorous,"[5] it is clear that the word "homesickness" has particular poignance, suggesting the delayed fulfillment of one who had yearned to achieve it. In this poem the speaker imagines the lover as the sole person who understands her earlier frustrations; he can do so because he is unafraid of death, the phenomenon love deplores yet counts upon for its own importance. The concluding lines of the octave affirm the speaker's triumph over lesser attachments—"I have survived"—and her characteristic vision of carnal love as also spiritual: the "heavens" are now her portion, supported for her by the beloved's interest. The sestet, sadly and with premonition of heroism, transcends the idea of physical communion. Time, which in the course of the sonnet becomes a villain, here assures the lovers of "an enduring bed." Even in this early sonnet it seems apparent that the speaker cannot expect to share a real bed with her lover. Therefore, her thoughts turn toward death and their possible if reductive union in the soil of a land dear to each.

In Sonnet II, Wylie describes the lover, whose beauty has been wrought by "the barbarous force of agonies." The description is idealized as all who knew her agreed that her view of Woodhouse was idealized, and owes some of its aspects to Shakespeare's description of the Friend of his sonnets. (She acknowledged a debt to Shakespeare with the inscription on the title page of a first edition of *Angels and Earthly Creatures*, preserved in the Wylie Archive of the Yale Collection.) In the lover's face, there is "the shape of danger": "danger" as in the French *dangereux* which implies both adventurousness and sexual charm. The lover's beauty is "the work of wars / Between the upper and the nether stars"—a reflection of the universe. One is reminded of Shakespeare's lines, "Mine eye and heart are at a mortall warre, / How to devide the conquest of thy sight" (Sonnet 46). And in this comparatively quiet sonnet, Wylie's lover is seen to be both "touching" and awesome.

The third sonnet represents the speaker as overwhelmed by the lover's

5. Nancy Hoyt, *Elinor Wylie: The Portrait of an Unknown Lady* (New York, 1935), 337; Mary Colum, *Life and the Dream* (New York, 1947), 341.

mercy and wisdom. It begins in recollection of his casual comment that children and dogs like him and develops its text upon the speaker's "inferiority" by comparing her to "a brute" tamed by his love and to an "infant" in need of his support. The fourth sonnet amplifies this theme, calling the speaker "Orson" and the lover "Valentine," names from an old romance in which one of two twins, Orson, is carried off by a bear and after he has become savage is reclaimed by the polite Valentine. The speaker "choose[s]" that she shall "be Orson" to the lover's Valentine, seeing herself untutored and unsophisticated by comparison with him:

> For how should the uncivil brier grow
> Germane in nature to the noble vine?
> The savage should be servant to the fine;
> The falcon fly superior to the crow;

and declares,

> O dear my lord, believe me that I know
> How far your virtues have outnumbered mine. (175)

The distinction between *vine* and *brier*, *falcon* and *crow* doubtless derives from the different nationalities of the lovers; Wylie chooses to see herself as a rude American beside the polished English squire. The sestet of the sonnet in which Wylie names herself the lover's "vassal" recalls, both in language and feeling, several of Shakespeare's sonnets wherein the Friend, with like extravagance, is called "Lord of my love, to whome in vassalage / Thy merrit hath my dutie strongly knit" (Sonnet 26) or in which, as in his Sonnet 58, the speaker is called the lover's "vassail."

In the fifth sonnet the uncommon situation in which the speaker finds herself is directly confessed. She knows she has been "allowed" a certain beauty; but in this phrase the self-portraits of other poems are qualified since, the speaker says, it has "never been enough to make me proud." She could not be so, having

> moved, companioned by a cloud,
> And lived indifferent to the blood's desire
> Of temporal loveliness in vain attire:
> My flesh was but a fresh-embroidered shroud. (176)

She has been dismissive of love and heretofore preoccupied by the ideal presence of Shelley, the "cloud" whom her own body newly represents. Thus Shelley is implicitly a rival to the beloved; or more particularly, her sense of communion with Shelley's Platonism challenges him. Now, however, she willingly abandons this earlier commitment, and in the last couplet, which reflects Shakespeare's requests of the Friend that he marry and have issue, she begs the lover "ere it is too late, / To stamp your superscription on my heart" (176). This plea for sexual union is also a plea that she be allowed to bear the lover's child.

The sixth sonnet continues to extol the "miracle" of passion yet records that its power remains "remote and exquisite" because the love affair is unconsummated (177). For that reason, the speaker suddenly desires that her flesh become completely "subliminal," "a stream of air" to "comfort" the lover when she is absent. The seventh sonnet, labored in diction, establishes philosophical distinctions as it makes an attempt to arbitrate a difference between shadow and substance:

> So would I cherish you a loving twice;
> Once in a mist made matter; once again
> In my true substance made ethereal:
> And yet I cannot succour you at all
> Whose letter cries, "My hands are cold as ice,"
> The while I kiss the colder air in vain. (178)

It is apparent in the seventh poem with its image of the letter and vision of empty air that the lovers of "One Person" must endure petty separations that prefigure a final parting; and Sonnet VIII, with language commemorative of Shakespeare's, affirms the anguish of these ruptures. Quite conventionally, the lovers are together in spring and summer but autumn and winter part them, as indeed the winter season parted Woodhouse and Elinor Wylie, who spent her winters in New York. The speaker has read her Renaissance sonnets well and knows that only the mind can triumph over seasons and then only by illusion:

> O love, how utterly am I bereaved
> By Time, who sucks the honey of our days,
> Sets sickle to our Aprils, and betrays

189

To killing winter all the sun achieved!
Our parted spirits are perplexed and grieved
Severed by cold, and change that never stays;
And what the clock, and what the season says
Is rumour neither valued nor believed.

Thus absence chills us to apparent death
And withers up our virtue, but together
We grow beyond vagaries of the weather
And make a summer of our mingled breath
Wherein we flourish, and forget to know
We must lie murdered by predestined snow. (179)

In this poem, accents of Shakespeare's "Let me confess that we two must be twaine" (Sonnet 36) or "Ruine hath taught me thus to ruminate / That Time will come and take my love away" (Sonnet 64) or "How like a Winter hath my absence beene / From thee, the pleasure of the fleeting year?" (Sonnet 97) are present and intended. The word *virtue* is used as it might have been by Shakespeare to mean physical strength and courage. The last line with its recognition of "predestined snow" or the death of love institutes another emotional pattern in the sonnets, one that moves away from discovery and rapture toward pained but stiff acceptance of deprivation.

Sonnet IX recounts the history of Elinor Wylie's devotion to Shelley, the "archangel" who has been her guardian spirit, and resolves to "renounce / His heavenly aid forever and at once" so that she may not, in her present affection, "hang another weight between his wings"—burden him, at last free of the body, with the needs of "perishable" beings. The poem "renounce[s]" Shelley's "aid," presumably because it is no longer necessary as it was when "the arrows flew like hail, and hard" in her earlier life. The lover's "chivalry" (IV) is an adequate substitute for Shelley's "knightly" attention. Still, there is a certain ominousness in Wylie's choice of the word *weight*. It implies that her passion, like the various love affairs of Shelley himself, is problematic: a difficulty with which she must cope (180).

The language of Sonnet X is once again reminiscent of Shakespeare's sonnets. The lover is represented as a brave man "wounded in demonic war / Against some prince of Sirius or Altair," a probable allusion to the lover's hostility to seasons of the year that divide him from the speaker. ("Sirius," the dog-star, which Dryden's *Aeneid* describes as "flashing forth sinister lights," is associated with late summer's heat; and that season advertises the coming of winter and separation, which Elinor Wylie may be expressing in "Altair," the Altai mountains in Siberia being a vast territory of cold and snow.) The speaker, mindful perhaps of a disposition toward selfish vanity, wonders whether her "hand of clay / Though white as porcelain" "can contrive a touch" of comfort "So delicate" it will not hurt him. The lover is described as having "sable . . . hair / Silvered," which recalls Shakespeare's description of his own "Sable curls all silvered o'er with white" (Sonnet 12). The lover's "eyesockets," which Wylie imagines lodging "double-imaged star[s]," remind us that Shakespeare predicted the "deep-sunken eyes" of the Friend who, at forty, might regret his failure to marry and have children (Sonnet 2). Wylie's sonnet, another in this series which forms a narrative, shows a sense that she is greatly complicating her lover's life:

> What voice can my invention find to say
> So soft, precise, and scrupulous a word
> You shall not take it for another sword? (181)

Her desire, differently articulated in the eighth poem wherein she wishes her "flesh" were ethereal, is to cause him no pain by the fact of her existence; yet, of course, that is impossible.

It is clear in Sonnet XI that the lover, however discreet, suffers, too. The poem rehearses the story of his first avowal of love. It occurs in spring, which Elinor Wylie associates with qualities she herself seemed, despite her history, to represent to many: "cool[ness]" or decorum, chastity. But when the lover admits his own desire and frustration, she envisions her "innocence" disappearing. Her instinctive wariness of the physical, her admiration for Platonic love appear here with a certain pathos and with interesting psychological aptness. The fact of physical passion reciprocated causes the speaker to feel that the one gift she among women has to offer—"the veins of spring," an unawakened sensibility—has been nullified. Her "wedding dower" is, paradoxically, a deep-seated commitment to physical reticence. But when the lover speaks, her world and self—"the glass of heaven," "the bubble of [her] heart"—which, as the crystalline images suggest, compose a fragile and intellectualized vision of life, "split" and break. The lover's answering passion "destroy[s]" her in her own mind. The sonnet, with its images of trees, "leaf and flower," and of the speaker vanishing into the latter, recalls dryadic myths in which wood nymphs, frightened by the love of gods, disappear for safety. In this poem, disappearance suggests both timidity and astonished gratification of affection which results in the sense of the body melting away for joy (182).

Sonnet XII meditates on the themes of the passage of seasons and of increase, both found in Shakespeare's sonnets. The lovers have been "content" before autumn came; and the speaker has often imagined herself caring for the lover as for an infant, "loved beyond philosophy or shame." The sestet, however, clarifies a growing sense of the implausibility and necessary limitation of their love. Although the speaker once dreamed she was the mother of the lover's son, what she comes to understand is that she is "the daughter of [his] skeleton, / Born of [his] bitter and excessive pain," a wraith, an emanation of death. The last line, "I shall not dream you are my child again," effectively adjusts the various roles the speaker has envisioned. She can neither claim the lover as child in the age-old fashion of women in love nor bear his child (that role being assigned to another). Instead, she must accept herself as the phantasm of his thwarted wishes. This sonnet associates the idea of autumn and lost fertility with sober recognition of the impossibility of union between the lover and the poet. It does so with quiet drama and an economy of means. In the poem's last line, as indeed throughout the entire sestet which moves logically from the reminiscences of the octave to its own joyless acceptance of the present, Wylie shows an authority of voice which assumes resonance with the increasing anguish of her subject.

The thirteenth sonnet also betrays a tremulous but growing conviction that the love affair is doomed. But it does so in final, guilt-ridden moments. The octave of the poem is a complaint but lacks resignation. Instead, passion assumes the right to speak once more in this sequence, which alternates between control and appetite:

> O mine is Psyche's heavy doom reversed
> Who meet at noon, part by diminished light,
> But never feel the subtle balm of night
> Fall merciful upon a body pierced
> By extreme love; and I considered first
> That you, a god more prodigally bright

Than the lesser Eros, had enriched my sight,
Made your own morning, and the stars immersed.

But secondly I saw my soul arise
And, in the hushed obscure, presume to creep
Tiptoe upon the spirit laid asleep,
And slant the impious beam across your eyes;
And I believe I have my just deserts
Lacking the shadow of peace upon our hearts. (184)

The octave and sestet of this orderly sonnet describe different states of feeling, the muted *volte face* of "But secondly" revealing Wylie's skill as a sonneteer. Her choice of the Cupid-Psyche legend to describe her love for Woodhouse is poignant and apt. Psyche, or Soul, subservient to the god Cupid, or Love, is united with him only at night (that is, in the simplicity of pure, unanalytic feeling). But she yearns possessively for absolute communion: to see his face by day. The myth punishes her for testing a god with human artifice—the false day of candlelight. She is separated from him and subjected to what Wylie called "long homesickness" (172) as she wanders the face of the earth. The Cupid-Psyche legend with its ingredients of superior male figure and dependent, imprudent female, its emphasis on time and on lovemaking by schedule, and its implicit warning to the inferior lover that she must accept whatever conditions the beloved imposes obviously traced for Wylie the lineaments of her own romance.

Here, the speaker is an abject Psyche, doomed, like Wylie who met Woodhouse only at midday, to see her lover at noon. Thus the season and embraces traditional to lovers are denied her. She imagines that her greater Eros has "enriched [her] sight" and, like the Eros who together with Erebus (Night) produces Day, "made [his] own morning"; but the conceit is not adequate. She cannot forbear imagining the crucial event of the legend, Psyche's "impious" demand, because it is prophetic of her own urgency of feeling and of her own fate. This sonnet reflects a significant mood of the love affair in which the speaker realizes with shame that her intensity surpasses the beloved's.

Because of it, she begins in the fourteenth sonnet to meditate upon eternity:

> Mortality has wearied us who wear it,
> And they are wiser creatures who have shunned
> This miry world. (185)

Here, in hyperbolic accents, she imagines a wedding with the lover as an "appointed task" to be fulfilled in heaven. But the sequence returns once more to the lively aspects of a troublesome and real affection in Sonnet XV, in which she begs that the lover

>   forgive the unruly tongue
> That utters blasphemies; forgive the brain
> Borne on a whirlwind of unhallowed pain:
> Remember only the intrepid song;
> The flag defended and the gauntlet flung;
> The love that speech can never render plain;
> The mind's resolve to turn and strive again;
> The fortitude that has endured so long. (186)

The sonnet's octave describes the speaker as a soldier in life's battle, a melodramatic vision consistent with Wylie's self-image but also with the conventional Renaissance conceit of love as war. The sestet, however, with its allusions to "starveling hope" and to "frozen fingers" that desire to warm themselves at the lover's "fire," is an abased declaration of dependent need. Yet in the context of the sequence, which documents a progression from exultation to distrust, despair, and perverse hope, it is winning. All the poet's eloquence of language proves to her "that speech can never render [love] plain." Honestly she records the responses of a woman who cannot adequately please or possess the man who attracts her (186).

The complex reactions evoked by such an experience reach a crisis in Sonnet XVI, a poem that poses against the man's stable domestic life the woman's keen awareness of herself as interloper:

> I hereby swear that to uphold your house
> I would lay my bones in quick destroying lime
> Or turn my flesh to timber for all time;
> Cut down my womanhood; lop off the boughs
> Of that perpetual ecstasy that grows
> From the heart's core; condemn it as a crime
> If it be broader than a beam, or climb
> Above the stature that your roof allows.

> I am not the hearthstone nor the cornerstone
> Within this noble fabric you have builded;
> Not by my beauty was its cornice gilded;
> Not on my courage were its arches thrown:
> My lord, adjudge my strength, and set me where
> I bear a little more than I can bear.

Against the architectural images *house, beam, roof, hearthstone, cornerstone, cornice,* and *arches,* which imply the lover's participation in a continuous life of decorum, are posed words that suggest the disruptive vitality of the speaker's passion but also her vulnerability. Contrasted with the *house* of his stable marriage, there are her *bones* and *flesh,* indeed, her *womanhood,* that quintessential personality which is like a tree that can be "cut down" at wish. Implicit in this contrast is the conviction that houses, like marriages, last longer than bodies—or "that perpetual ecstasy," the radiance of love, "that grows / From the heart's core." For though love be "perpetual" in the heart of the lover, it after all can be rejected even as "boughs" may be cut from a tree. The tree, image of Wylie's self and her desire, may not be allowed conspicuousness, and it must not rival the dominance of the house that represents the lover's family. In the octave of the sonnet, one hears the speaker's voice as if in tortured response or protest to the beloved's objection that she is becoming too difficult or intrusive. Read together with the preceding Sonnet XV, in which the poet pleaded with the lover to find the "charity" to "forgive" her "starveling hope" that she may share some trifling portion of his love, it is pathetically revealing. In the opening lines of the octave the poet declares that she would rather die than harm his marriage; and the declaration is made with near frantic definition: "I would lay my bones in quick destroying lime / Or turn my flesh to timber." At the same time it is perhaps not a distortion to note that trees are alive as bricks and mortar cannot be. The extravagant fate Wylie envisions for her passion—being turned into "timber" that might be burned at the hearth—suggests that the lover's stolidity is no match for her earnestness of feeling. He might be willing to sacrifice "ecstasy" for his own "roof."

Nonetheless, the sestet of the sonnet humbly recognizes limiting ties. The speaker is aware that the lover has made a "noble fabric" of his marriage, and she delicately alludes to the authority of his wife, who has cooperated with him to make it:

I am not the hearthstone nor the cornerstone
Within this noble fabric you have builded;
Not by my beauty was its cornice gilded;
Not on my courage were its arches thrown:

Consequently, the concluding couplet of the sonnet is poignant. Having offered to die for the lover, having admitted that she has no legitimate part to play in his life, the speaker nonetheless begs that he will assign her some role. Here, abandoning the prevailing, organic conceit of the tree to which she earlier compared her passionate self, the speaker asks to become some element in the lover's world of lasting houses: "My lord, adjudge my strength, and set me where / I bear a little more than I can bear" (187). On the surface, the couplet is a species of turn, imploring in weakness and devotion, relation to the beloved. Yet the idea of bearing more than can be borne suggests a number of feelings: the speaker's awareness that she cannot entirely tolerate the vision of the lover's commitment to his wife; her conviction that, at the same time, she is equal to such a martyrdom; finally, perhaps, a lingering resentment that he is capable of placing her in a position of ambiguous connection.

After this crucial sonnet, the concluding ones assume a tranquil aspect. The seventeenth sonnet envisions the speaker's death and, until its event, her exile upon "This map of Paradise," England, where the lover "burn[s] like flame upon a hearth." In the eighteenth poem, the poet once again imagines a kind of communion, this time without the piquancy of sexual need; instead, with a tired, haunted tenderness in which all the reality of desire is sublimated in a prevailing image of patient abnegation.

Thus the penultimate Sonnet XVII requests death upon the speaker's "heart, which is the heart of all / My late discovered earth and early sky." Once again the influence of Shakespeare is apparent. Elinor Wylie speaks of the lover's voice as her "passing bell, in passing by," even as Shakespeare alludes to the "surly sullen bell" which will proclaim his death (Sonnet 71). The "continent" upon which she has become acquainted with her lover, the "map of Paradise," is, as the Friend's cheek is for Shakespeare, the "map of days" (Sonnet 68). The poet forswears physical love for death, embracing the only remedy violent passion seeks. Here, either death, placed first in the octave, or exile, toyed with in the sestet, are the choices she must make; and exile is an afterglance. We know from accounts of Elinor Wylie's last days that she planned permanently to leave the United States to live in England. She wished to be near Woodhouse, though at the end her love for him had altered. The concluding couplet of Sonnet XVII with its echoes of Shakespeare's *King John* shows that she had chosen England as a country in which she might achieve happiness. If, for her, the beloved "burn[s]" like "flame upon a hearth" that conceit can be by no means comforting. "Hearth" means home; and Wylie is aware that the lover's home must exclude her (188).

Describing their meetings to Mary Colum, Elinor Wylie said that she and Woodhouse usually spoke of philosophy.[6] One may read Sonnet XVII without that knowledge; for the octave poses against the troubles of the lovers a hierarchy of metaphysical values which are apparent antidotes to the problem of their attraction. In the opening lines of the eighteenth poem, there is a certain impatience:

> Let us leave talking of angelic hosts
> Of nebulae, and lunar hemispheres,
> And what the days, and what the Uranian years
> Shall offer us when you and I are ghosts; (189)

The two lovers, both sophisticated, have marshaled arguments to assuage their desire and to make their self-denial more resolute. And yet, at the close of the sequence, the poet can utter only what is true in mind and body and not what is wished. The last eight lines are scarcely passionate. What they ask is indeed an embrace; but an embrace that, despite the word "exile," is without that excitement which fear, lust, or a sense of forbidden ecstasies can confer. Indeed, they implore the repose most often achieved in domestic love, the very aspect of love to which the speaker and the lover cannot aspire. One is reminded in reading them of the yearning of Algernon Swinburne's speaker in "A Dialogue" for "Some low sweet roof where love might live, set free / From change and fear and dreams of grief or guilt":

> let us creep into the smallest room
> That any hunted exile has desired
> For him and for his love when he was tired;
> And sleep oblivious of any doom

6. Colum, *Life and the Dream*, 339.

> Which is beyond our reason to conceive;
> And so forget to weep, forget to grieve,
> And wake, and touch each other's hands, and turn
> Upon a bed of juniper and fern. (189)

At the close of this moving sequence, the speaker returns to a consideration of restrained affection, to Platonic love.

"One Person" is an interesting collection, not only for its expression of superb passion—unique in Wylie's work—but for its capable employment of the various rhetorical stratagems of the Renaissance sonnet tradition. Other writers, particularly women, and of them, particularly Edna St. Vincent Millay in *Fatal Interview*, would imitate "One Person" by describing love affairs in sonnets evocative of the Renaissance and, indeed, of "One Person." [7]

The poem "Love Song" from "Elements and Angels" immediately and properly follows the sonnets to "One Person." It is a final, philosophical judgment upon the lover's rejection of the speaker. The title is ironic because, although the first two stanzas argue the honesty of her defeated but sincere love, the last stanza declares renewed commitment to an ideal love that may (once again) suffice her in crisis; and that love cancels her earthly one. Hence "Love Song" is addressed to two men, one living and one—Shelley—dead:

> Had I concealed my love
> And you so loved me longer,
> Since all the wise reprove
> Confession of that hunger
> In any human creature,
> It had not been my nature.
>
> I could not so insult
> The beauty of that spirit
> Who like a thunderbolt
> Had broken me, or near it;
> To love I have been candid,
> Honest and open-handed.
>
> Although I love you well
> And shall for ever love you,

7. See Chapter IV, note 2.

> I set that archangel
> The depths of heaven above you;
> And I shall lose you, keeping
> His word, and no more weeping. (193)

"Love Song" declares the dilemma all who love better than the beloved must face: the game of concealment. And the speaker explains that so cynical a game is not her "nature" to play. The spirit of the thunderbolt that has nearly broken her is Eros', here given the force of Jove's; in the seeming afterthought "or near it," one feels a degree of pride as well as acceptance. The last stanza, with its proclamation of fealty to Shelley, reverses the decision made in Sonnet IX of "One Person." After the defensive proviso of the first two lines, the last phrase, "and no more weeping," is purposeful as though in dismissal of a yearning that lingers (193).

The directness, the determined absence of dialectical intricacy with which this poem is written, defends a candor that appears again in "Felo de Se"; but that poem attempts a more complex manner to express a devious purpose:

> My heart's delight, I must for love forget you;
> I must put you from my heart, the better to please you;
> I must make the power of the spirit set you
> Beyond the power of the mind to seize you.
>
> My dearest heart, in this last act of homage,
> I must reject you; I must unlearn to love you;
> I must make my eyes give up your adorable image
> And from the inner chamber of my soul remove you.
>
> Heart of my heart, the heart alone has courage
> Thus to relinquish; it is yourself that stills you
> In all my pulses, and dissolves the marriage
> Of soul and soul, and at the heart's core kills you. (198).

The poem's title, taken from Anglo-Latin, means "Suicide" or theft of oneself. According to Sir William Blackstone, one who "deliberately puts an end to his own existence, or commits any . . . malicious act, the consequences of which is his own death,"[8] is guilty of *felo de se*. Thus the title illumines the poem's

---

8. Quoted in the *Oxford English Dictionary*, IV (Oxford, 1933), 147.

focal paradox: ostensibly the lover is killed in the last line, but in wresting him from her heart the speaker "kills" herself. The poem is written with a graceful complexity that illustrates the near-classical contemplative preoccupation of Wylie's last days: she separates the proper actions and spheres of *soul* or *spirit*, *heart*, and *mind* yet shows that such separation is murderous. Moreover, since she and the lover are one soul, married to each other by desire, her desire to "please" him by forgetting him makes her complicit in his murder. The poems in "Sequence" of *Black Armour* betrayed the fear and guilt of a speaker caught between the love of two men. In them the poet's voice was troubled and intense and the images it selected were grotesque and emblematic. But the weight of her feeling found its linguistic equivalent in rhetorical emphasis:

> I shall submerge my body in the mud
> I shall submit my spirit to the storm
> I shall bend down my bosom to the snake. (83)

In "Felo de Se," the passion of love is opposed by the desire for self-denial. Generosity of affection must become generous relinquishment. Thus a train of paradoxes is set forth in a set of antitheses.

The energy of the speaker's voice and the counterpoint of her language do not, however, permit comparison to the fiery involution and convolution of the metaphysical style. "Felo de Se," like many of the love lyrics of *Angels and Earthly Creatures*, may more properly be compared to certain love poems of Yeats, always Wylie's master, in which verbal repetitions are balanced against each other or inverted to create a sense of irony and mystery. Thus, for instance, Yeats's "Into the Twilight" with its lines "Out-worn heart, / In a time out-worn" or "The Heart of the Woman": "My heart upon his warm heart lies, / My breath is mixed into his breath." The comparison to Donne, inevitably invited by the title of Wylie's collection and certain aspects of her style, really rises in this case as in others from her subject matter and from its treatment: a treatment that predicates Christian values.

So, for example, the dissolution of love and self recorded in "Felo de Se" is followed in the next poem, "O Virtuous Light, " by the speaker's prayer that reason—that power every Christian must militate against sense—may outwit recalcitrant passion. In this poem the ancients' view of love as both insanity and splendor appears with suasive force. Against it the poet pits industry, courage, and the "virtuous light" of intellect:

A private madness has prevailed
Over the pure and valiant mind;
The instrument of reason failed
And the star-gazing eyes struck blind.

Sudden excess of light has wrought
Confusion in the secret place
Where the slow miracles of thought
Take shape through patience into grace.

Mysterious as steel and flint
The birth of this destructive spark
Whose inward growth has power to print
Strange suns upon the natural dark.

O break the walls of sense in half
And make the spirit fugitive!
This light begotten of itself
Is not a light by which to live!

The fire of farthing tallow dips
Dispels the menace of the skies
So it illuminate the lips
And enter the discerning eyes.

O virtuous light, if thou be man's
Or matter of the meteor stone,
Prevail against this radiance
Which is engendered of its own! (199)

It must be remembered that immediately before she died, Wylie arranged the order of poems in *Angels and Earthly Creatures*. Appearing after "Felo de Se," "O Virtuous Light" has the power and dimension of a prayer for strength before the (conceded) "radiance" of love. Love is a "private" madness that basks in its privacy, its indifference to opposition; and it may easily triumph over "the pure and valiant mind" whose sphere is public, responsible, and opposed to idiosyncratic whim. Having determined to exercise the powers of the soul against love in "Felo de Se," Wylie meditates now on what passion— "star-gazing eyes"—has been able to do to intellect and to the powers of the artist, committed to shaping "slow miracles of thought" into "grace." Love's spectacular radiance, which can "print / Strange suns upon" the "natural dark" of obtuse human vision is nonetheless "destructive." For it rises from the "sense[s]," which are really "walls" that impede "growth." Passion is a "light begotten of itself," in Wylie's case, most certainly, since it is opposed to virtue. And thus it has set itself, a false light, against the "light by which [the artist] live[s]." Wylie's poem marshals against "the menace of the skies"— the power of Eros—a force apparently puny: "the fire of farthing tallow dips," the industry of the poet. Yet that fire uses the love-menace to make the poet's "lips" and "eyes" "Discerning"—knowledgeable, now, not for the purposes of lovemaking but for those of art. This poem's final quatrain is dignified by anxious fervor and by a plea that the poet herself be sustained against passion by intellect. Though no ostensible allusion to religion is made here, religious feeling is clearly apparent in the poet's juxtaposition of the Christian antitheses of spirit and matter, mind and sense, and in her election of the powers of reason above those of appetite.

The concluding poems of this section, "Hymn to Earth" and "This Corruptible," bring to able fulfillment that meditation on spirit and flesh, sacred and profane love, which the sonnets to "One Person" inaugurate. "Hymn to Earth," continually anthologized, is a finely modulated poem that fuses colloquial cadence with inherited Renaissance accents, an enlargement of the crisp tones of Elinor Wylie in the service of a traditional vision. "This Corruptible," the Pauline title indicating a Christian context which it explores, attempts a modern rendering of the medieval "Dialogues" among personified faculties. In this case, Wylie spends effort and tenderness on the despised body, put in its place by all the poems of *Angels and Earthly Creatures* which precede this one, yet to be pitied and—in a profoundly biblical context—respected.

The Shelleyan values implicit in "Hymn to Earth" have been demonstrated.[9] I should like to remark on the cadences employed in that poem. It is a hymn to all those humble sensual responses embodied in Earth as element which Wylie has subjected to inquiry or else discarded in a volume that considers the cost of illicit love. Since sensual love is the subject of her book and since she understood the theological amplitude of the Renaissance idiom, it is, I think, no accident that Wylie chose Miltonic overtones in her "Hymn." She writes,

> Farewell, incomparable element,
> Whence man arose, where he shall not return;

9. See Julia Cluck, "Elinor Wylie's Shelley Obsession," *PMLA*, LVI (1941), 842.

And hail, imperfect urn
Of his last ashes, and his firstborn fruit; (200)

Surely, no one can fail to remark the parallel with *Paradise Lost*, Book I, lines
249–52:

Farewell, happy Fields
Where Joy for ever dwells: Hail horrors, hail
Infernal world, and thou profoundest Hell
Receive thy new Possessor.

Underlying the lines of her hymn, a celebration of Earth, are accents that
speak of the fallen aspect of all that is human. Using those accents to celebrate
the seductive loveliness of Earth, of "the kind embrace of clay," Wylie
accomplishes a subtle irony: she commends the sensual (rare for her) yet in
accents that undermine the commendation. Pledged as they are to spiritual
experience, her lines show her growth in objectivity:

Hail, element of earth, receive thy own,
And cherish, at thy charitable breast,
This man, this mongrel beast:
He ploughs the sand, and, at his hardest need,
He sows himself for seed;
He ploughs the furrow, and in this lies down
Before the corn is grown;
Between the apple bloom
And the ripe apple is sufficient room
In time, and matter, to consume his love. (202)

Similarly in "This Corruptible," Wylie manages a plausible modern version of the old medieval dialogues, her subject disclosing her interest at last in
last things. "This Corruptible," like "Hymn to Earth," celebrates that "unlucky slave," the body, which *Angels and Earthly Creatures* chooses to subdue. In
it, the body, despised, is also "the wheaten bread of the Mass; / And the fabric
of the rain, and the lightning" (206). She alludes to the body here as the "grain
of God in power," superior to the heart and the mind in its vulnerable
patience (207).

This contemplation of the ordinary precedes Wylie's light lyrics, "Earthly
Creatures," and the "Elegies and Epistles" which conclude her volume. This

last section presents two poems, "The Loving Cup" and "The Broken Man," that anatomize the love affair with an idealized Woodhouse that is recounted in "One Person": and they do so from a psychological point of view.

"The Loving Cup" is a busily metaphysical poem, written in couplets, which voices the envy and jealousy that might be expected to display themselves in a doomed love affair. Probably autobiographical, it analyzes an unpleasant incident which, by means of argument and hyperbole, it attempts (laboriously) to translate into a happy one. The lover, angry and eager to hurt the speaker, declares that he will not drink her health except from his wife's glass. The insult to the speaker is apparently trivial yet symbolically serious, for she knows what the wife does not—that she and the husband are lovers. Yet she has committed herself to the preservation of their marriage so that, acting in the interests of both, she becomes the "chattel" of each, divided, like the wine in the cup, "into share and share." But the wife is not stupid, and the speaker discerns that *she* drinks the latter's "death" in the "loving cup." Repeating the conceit of Sonnet IV of "One Person," the speaker regards both herself and the wife as the lover's "vassals," each "bound" to him by different "oath[s]." Thus—in a nice off-rhyme—the women become, like the cup, his "vessels," because the lover like a predator takes from both. After a good deal of complex argument, the speaker convinces herself that she and the wife drink "health" from the cup only because it has kissed the lover's lips (230–31). "The Loving Cup," regarded by Thomas A. Gray as Wylie's "only successful imitation of the metaphysical style,"[10] is also less her own than any of her other poems: it is tortured and awkward, lacking in the grace of apprehension and line that is usual in her verse.

Nevertheless, it shows her trying to comprehend the psychological dimension of her love affair with a symbolic man—Woodhouse—who at the end of her life seemed to her the composite image of all the dangerous and elegant men whom she had loved. "The Broken Man," a clear and witty poem in couplets, summarizes the psychological development of Wylie's life. It traces the poet's fascination with a "broken man," a damaged china figure as well as (ultimately) an emasculated lover, to whom the speaker feels committed as child and adult. The "real" man whom she loves at last was

10. Thomas A. Gray, *Elinor Wylie* (New York, 1969), 103.

prefigured by this china figure, his "double," whom she "pilfered" from a stranger. The china figure (like Woodhouse in "One Person") has hair that is "sable silvered." The speaker has loved him since she was seven, even as she loved Shelley; he has remained, despite her vicissitudes, her "lover, waited [for] and welcome" (225).

Yet to those familiar with Wylie's writing, "The Broken Man" isolates those features of her imagination that both explain and remark her peculiarity. Thus the "broken man" is a Platonic entity, apparent to the speaker under various guises of "air, or alabaster stone"; she has once "translated [him] into glass," refining him but making a mockery of him: the refinement into nonentity to which, as woman, she submitted her husbands and, as writer, she submitted her heroes. The "broken man" is both lover and child of the speaker (as husbands and lovers are in Wylie's verse), and she comes to him like the speaker of "Viennese Waltz" who appears in "feather[s]" of snow, (255), as "feathered snow," a symbol of virginal disinterest (225). He is particularly attractive to her because, like Shelley or Woodhouse, he seems "too fine for [her]" (226). She smashes him at last, even as Wylie ruined her husbands in one way or another and as she imagined herself afflicting her angelic protector Shelley. In "The Broken Man," it is her father who complacently remarks that the china boy is broken and sweeps him into a bag, only to have him mended later but in such a way that he becomes unattractive, a man of iron instead of porcelain. The poem makes clear that any man who is loved by the speaker must be scarred and thus able to be Shelley to her; it also demonstrates that Wylie had developed a consistently self-expressive pattern of images, of which the idea of broken porcelain, emblematic of her taste, was preeminent.

Angels and Earthly Creatures contains one poem, "Chimaera Sleeping," whose vague and evanescent atmosphere and evocative landscape commemorate the atmosphere of Shelley's visionary poems, where light and shade often strive with each other. Its speaker sees the "holy ghost" of Beauty fleeing before her as an apparition yet remaining behind, a "body pale as glass." The body is Shelley's, turned to petals which "softly stir / As seaweed under seawater." The fragile sea motifs, the "exact and plain" grass, crystal, the spirit of the "fox or fawn," "the lightning flash," the idea of silver in the "silver ash," all are summoned to describe the figure of Shelley, a chimera partly dead yet wholly alive, after whom the poet must remain in pursuit (194–95). *Angels and Earthly Creatures*, primarily the narrative of Elinor Wylie's unfortunate romance, is the story at last of her commitment to Shelley. The final poem in the volume, "Little Elegy," is written, I think, to no human lover but to the abiding spirit of one she had never known and always missed:

> Withouten you
> No rose can grow;
> No leaf be green
> If never seen
> Your sweetest face;
> No bird have grace
> Or power to sing;
> Or anything
> Be kind, or fair,
> And you nowhere. (233)

AFTERWORD

linor Wylie's sudden death in her forty-third year occurred at the height of her fame and at a turning point in her life. Had she lived, she intended to leave America and to settle permanently in England, thus numbering herself in a company of expatriate American artists with whom she shared various insights: Henry James, James NcNeill Whistler, Edith Wharton, T. S. Eliot, the young H.D., and Ezra Pound. Her desire was in one way personal. She fantasized a romantic return to the English countryside where she had once been happy with Horace Wylie. In another, it was strictly professional. She wished to escape Manhattan and to conduct a more ascetic life in which her art could develop.

Wylie was, as she knew and said, a distinctly American writer "down to the Puritan marrow of [her] bones" (*Collected Poems*, 12). Her poetry described the landscape of Maine, Maryland, Virginia, Delaware, and Pennsylvania as well as the streets of New York City. In *The Orphan Angel* she "recreated" most of the United States. She was proud of what she thought a johnnycake side. Yet, like Edith Wharton's, her personal elegance, breeding, and assumptions were those of an American upper class that had read widely, traveled much, and felt at home in great houses. Like Wharton, Eliot, and James, she was cosmopolitan, often setting her scenes in a Europe as familiar to her as her own country. With the great James, in fact, she shared more than this urbane or patrician taste. A few of her themes recall his own—conflict between art and life, the dangers of overrefinement, especially the antagonism between sophistication and innocence expressed in the dominion of a worldly man over a naïve girl. Still, her devotion to foreign places, especially England, never drove out her passion for a wilder land. Perhaps more than James or Eliot, who became British subjects and were, like Wylie, snubbed as Americans by the Woolf circle, she regarded her roots as inalienably Yankee. Proclaiming herself "an American in England," she qualified her sympathetic allegiance to the land of her forebears yet confessed her keen need at last of the comfort it offered: "Let the divided heart come home" (297). Wylie's contemporary, Ezra Pound, who never wholly forswore the Aestheticism she shared, sought English shores to escape Idaho and American provincialism. Wylie had settled first in England to escape moral censure. Yet, like Pound's, her English sojourn in the early 1900s put her in close touch with a literature she could learn from and react against. Like H.D.'s, a few of whose Greek poems she imitated in *Black Armour*,[1] her career was partially formed by English influences.

Well-traveled in France and Italy, Elinor Wylie was nonetheless anglophile in her serious tastes; for her the Continent was primarily a setting for fiction. Hating what she thought the white neon glare of Paris, she separated herself from the large group of Americans from Whistler and Wharton to Williams and Gertrude Stein who sought nourishment there. Still, as I have suggested elsewhere, the relation between her art and Whistler's is succinct. His wistful romanticization of English scenes, particularly in the *Nocturnes*, finds its analogues in her own, especially in *Mr. Hodge and Mr. Hazard*. England was not wholly kind to Whistler as an artist but it was for him as for Wylie a challenge, a test, made by an older yet related civilization, of his creative powers.

Had she lived to become what she planned, an expatriate in England, Wylie might have joined those Americans whose imaginative careers resembled her own. Yet her life and art pose challenges to a settled view of her. At her death Wylie was planning to live near Henley-on-Thames and to write a novel about the witches of Salem, one of whom was her ancestress. Her interest in magic, like her devotion to fairy tales, had always been pronounced and became clear in *The Venetian Glass Nephew*. Had she lived, she planned to combine it with a typically Aesthetic fascination with curious religious prac-

1. See the last poems in that volume, for example, "To Aphrodite, with a Talisman," "On a Singing Girl" ("Musa of the sea-blue eyes, / Silver nightingale . . ."), and "To Claudia Homonoea" (Elinor Wylie, *Collected Poems* [New York, 1932], 100, 102, 103).

tices in a novel about witch-burnings. Thus England would be her home; early America, her subject.

Much has been said in this book about her debt to English writers because it is evident and immediate. Yet a consideration of Wylie's themes shows her bond with such earlier American writers as Nathaniel Hawthorne and Edgar Allan Poe. Hawthorne's Puritan suspicion that art provides undue, perhaps dangerous, satisfactions was not shared by Wylie to whom great art was holy. Nevertheless, in stories like "The Artist of the Beautiful" or "The Prophetic Pictures" and especially in *The Marble Faun* Hawthorne concerned himself with what he considered the generative antipathy between brute fact and imagination and with a reconciling theme of metamorphosis. For him as for Wylie, life and art were opposed but could have mutually nutritive and affective powers. Hawthorne's "artist of the beautiful" who attempts to "spiritualize machinery"[2] prefers delicate small objects as do the subjects of Wylie's poems. That preference both exalts and ruins him as it does the usual Wylie protagonist. Strikingly, Hawthorne provides in *The Blithedale Romance* the vision of Zenobia, a gorgeously seductive woman, who is, at one point, in one view, "transformed . . . into a work of art." That she becomes so horrifies yet pleases Hawthorne's narrator, Miles Coverdale, even as Rosalba's transformation is appalling yet ultimately acceptable to those who love her. Hawthorne's interest in female sexuality—indeed, in women's rights in *Blithedale*—expresses itself in emblematic transformation, as does Wylie's in the poems and the *Nephew*. He, too, was attracted like the Wylie of *Jennifer Lorn* to the theme of "the miraculous power of one human being over the will and passions of another."[3] Furthermore, Hawthorne clearly imagines that art has mysterious occult powers, a vision embodied in the Wildean story of the "Prophetic Pictures," a story whose interest in cosmetic transformations provides a true analogue to Wylie's story of Virginio and Rosalba.

The "American" art of Elinor Wylie may be related to Poe as well. His preoccupation with lovely, enervated women and his delineation of the antagonism between life and art recall her own. In his "Oval Portrait," for

2. Nathaniel Hawthorne, *Mosses from an Old Manse*, "The Artist of the Beautiful," in William Charvat, Roy Harvey Pearce, and Claude M. Simpson (eds.), *The Centenary Edition of the Works of Nathaniel Hawthorne* (14 vols.; Columbus, Ohio, 1962–80), X, 465.
3. Hawthorne, *The Blithedale Romance, ibid.*, III, 164.

instance, the struggle between the power of life, represented by the painter's radiant young wife, and the genius of art, symbolized by the painter himself, calls to mind *The Venetian Glass Nephew*. Poe's painter must nullify his wife's vitality in order to achieve the exuberance of the painting; as she starves and dies, the painting comes to life. This terrible exchange, accepted so docilely by the female model, is what Wylie describes in her novel. It testifies to a preoccupation with the problem of art that transcends time and country but was as American as it was European.

In a sense Wylie had two careers, one as a fabulist, the other as a poet. How and what would she have written had she lived beyond her forty-third year? Her unfinished manuscripts in the Wylie Archive—the *April, April*, fragments about Shelley, a romance about Henry VIII's sister Mary, a symbolic tale about the "Moon" and "Starr" sisters of Philadelphia—suggest that in fiction she would have continued to write fantasies. She looked forward to beginning her "witch" novel with an enthusiasm bred, I think, of a precise understanding of her own powers. Her passion for history, her fascination with magic, the surreal, and the occult (a fascination shared by her hero Shelley and her admirer and supporter Yeats) would doubtless have resulted in tales that were more and more austere philosophically and increasingly shrewd in nuance and invention. Her last poems, *Angels and Earthly Creatures*, might suggest that her poetic style had taken new directions. Yet though she said she liked, in her last days, to "enjoy with Donne a metaphysical frolic" and spoke of Thomas Browne as her "brother," I do not think she would ever have become a true "Daughter of Donne"[4] (276, 302). Her interest in metaphysical and Elizabethan verse was timely, wrought not of Eliot's fashionable prescriptions but of her love for Woodhouse, who admired it, and of her suspicion of the advent of death. Good scholar that she was, she associated last ends and fatal loves with that school of poetry which had most richly

4. For a different view see Herbert S. Gorman, "Daughter of Donne," *North American Review*, no. 169 (May, 1924), 679–86. Allan Tate in his *Collected Essays* (Denver, 1951), 329, declared that there was "as little evidence of the influence of Donne" in Wylie's poetry "as one might derive from Tennyson." The metaphysical attribution is widely made, however: George Dillon called her imagination "metaphysical . . . in the rare, true sense" (Tate, "A light never on land or sea," *Poetry*, June 29, 232); Louis Untermeyer spoke of her "metaphysical" imagination (*Modern American Poetry* [New York, 1950], 295); and Dayton Kohler compared her to Donne ("Elinor Wylie: Heroic Mask," *South Atlantic Quarterly* XXXVI [1937]).

expressed them. *Angels and Earthly Creatures* was on the whole a "nonce" volume, struck out with a special purpose. Her real vision was Aesthetic and comprehended the nature and problems of Aestheticism. Her two great subjects—art and her personal deficiencies—were related to the tensions between the pure Romanticism of Shelley and the Neo-Romanticism of the Aesthetes.

That she had evolved a highly personal style as a poet in the seven years of her professional career became apparent in the parodies of that style written most effectively by Edmund Wilson in poems such as "Nocturne: To Elinor." [5]

> The foxes wink their onyx eyes;
> The tranced witches twitch their wigs;
> The pixies snap, like startled pies,
> Their frozen filigree of twigs.
>
> Ice-sheeted crofts, close-hedged with thorn,
> Confront Diana's dinted shield;
> The watch-dog's bellowing, forlorn,
> Chills sharper sharp-chilled stream and field
>
> Then come! in some deep-sunken hole
> Below the drifts you shall be kis't;
> Or, crouching in some hollow bole
> Snow-cushioned for the hidden tryst.
>
> Cold bone shall ring against cold bone;
> The skeleton like flint shall spark;
> A high thin thrilling javelin tone
> Shall glance like ice-beams on the dark . . .

Had Wylie lived, she would not, I think, have been able to abandon this personal style. On the other hand, that quest for grander utterance especially in spiritual matters that appears in her later poems would no doubt have grown. A considerable number of the poems in her last two volumes concern the Christian mysteries. The "Birthday Sonnet" chosen by William Rose Benét to conclude the volume of her *Collected Poems*, which first appeared in 1932 and is still the standard edition of her verse, poignantly reveals her old sense of personal delinquency. It speaks of her pride as an artist, a role she

5. Ms. 207 in the Wylie Archive.

clearly felt might ransom her spiritual faults. Deeply confessional, it rehearses the stages and attitudes of her life: her need to be protected from the "secular danger" that sometimes overtook her; her awareness that she was inadequate as a woman; her desire to "preserve Thy gift," her creative powers. It begins with language reminiscent of the Book of Common Prayer she read in childhood, "Take home Thy prodigal child, O Lord of Hosts!" and ends with a phrase that some who knew her ill could not have imagined her using: "Defend Thy prodigal" (311). This sonnet with its alternate conviction of guilt in life and salvation through art is almost classically Aesthetic. Its extreme intensity as well as the increased number of religious poems in Wylie's last books lead me to speculate that had she lived she might have turned her attention not only to the problem of art and the self but to the problem of God and the self. Had that happened, she would once again have behaved like an American artist: like T. S. Eliot or Wallace Stevens, the first of whom per-plexed her and the second—so like her in taste—whom she never knew.

But Elinor Wylie did not live beyond 1928. She has left to us a surprisingly large body of poetry and prose as well as the myth of her translation from a woman limited by social position into an artist, independent and self-aware. Both have lasting attraction. Her determination to achieve a life of meaning in a cosmos of trivial appearances resulted in her concern with the problem of art, a concern that was characteristically modern yet typically American. That concern produced her fables, her experiments in lyrical form—elegies, bal-lads, dialogues, epistles, couplets, sonnets—and the respect for literary tradi-tion that enabled her mimetic exploits in verse and fiction. True Aesthete, she never wholly suppressed an idiosyncratic spirit as Eliot would command poets to do. But, rewardingly, her spirit commended the language of art above every other good.

INDEX

Adams, Franklin P., 13
Aesthetes: their art significant to EW, 9, 17, 18, 37, 42, 45–46, 48, 49, 54, 56–57, 60, 63, 68–69, 73, 78–83, 101, 103, 108, 179, 208, 209, 211; criticism of, in EW, 36–37, 45–46, 99–101, 109, 111, 119, 157–59, 163, 166, 171–76; their manners as influence on EW, 17, 42, 78
Anderson, Maxwell, 128
Arno, Peter, 33
Arnold, Matthew, 120, 120n–21n
Auden, W. H., 65
Auslander, Joseph, 3
Austen, Jane, 9, 44

Bankhead, Tallulah, 34
Beardsley, Aubrey, 2, 37, 99
Beaton, Cecil, 17, 31, 103
Beckford, William, 37–38
Beerbohm, Max, 3, 37, 40, 42, 48–49
Benét, Colonel James, 28
Benét, Stephen Vincent, 138
Benét, Teresa, 17
Benét, William Rose, 4, 7, 12, 13, 14, 15, 16–18, 20, 23, 24, 25, 27–29, 31, 33–34, 37, 50, 75, 92, 94, 96, 110–12, 129, 182, 184, 211. See also Wylie, Elinor: marriage to William Rose Benét
Bernhardt, Sarah, 19
Blake, William, 3, 66–67
Brontë, Emily, 3, 60
Brooks, Van Wyck, 10, 10n
Browning, Robert, 24, 154
Brummell, George Bryan ("Beau"), 42
Bynner, Witter, 12

Byron, George Gordon, Lord, 66, 88, 123, 131, 133n, 145, 149, 150, 151–52

Cabell, James Branch, 18, 51, 56, 129
Canby, Henry Seidel, 13
Carriera, Rosalba, 104
Casanova de Seingalt, Giovanni (Jacques), 1, 104, 106, 112
Cather, Willa, 3n, 113
Clairmont, Claire, 127, 141
Clark, Emily, 138
Cluck, Julia, 134
Coleridge, Samuel Taylor, 80–81, 98, 115, 116, 142, 174, 175
Collins, William, 40
Colum, Mary M., 13, 15, 18, 33, 187, 197
Colum, Padraic, 13, 15
Cooper, Lady Diana (Manners), 103
Corot, Jean Baptiste Camille, 81
Cowley, Malcolm, 84
Coyle, Kathleen, 16
Crouse, Russel, 20

D'Aurevilly, Barbey, 42
Decadence (Decadent movement) 36, 45, 53, 57
De la Mare, Walter, 21, 31, 62, 108
Deutsch, Babette, 64, 171
De Vere, Aubrey, 117
Dickinson, Emily, 3, 10, 59, 59n, 76n
Dobson, Austin, 45, 79, 104
Donne, John, 9, 32, 181, 182–83, 200, 210
Dowson, Ernest, 47, 60–61, 77
Dryden, John, 191
Duse, Eleanora, 31

Eliot, T. S., 8, 60, 207, 208, 212
Emerson, Ralph Waldo, 163
Exquisites, 2, 31. *See also* Aesthetes

Faulkner, William, 3n
Firbank, Ronald, 2, 31, 42
Fitzgerald, F. Scott, 56, 128
Fragonard, Jean Honoré, 39
Furness, Henry Howard, 21

Gautier, Théophile, 42, 69, 79, 102
Gershwin, George, 30
Gilbert, Sandra M., 78
Godwin, Mary (Mary Shelley), 118, 123, 127,
    128, 130, 133–34, 135, 150
Godwin, William, 125, 127, 128
Goldoni, Carlo, 109
Gozzi, Count Carlo, 104, 104n, 105, 106,
    109
Gray, Thomas A., 3, 107n, 204
Gubar, Susan, 78

H.D. (Hilda Doolittle), 64, 207, 208
Hawthorne, Nathaniel, 102, 209
Heffernan, Jo, 38, 38n
Hemingway, Ernest, 4, 30
Herbert, George, 61
Hergesheimer, Joseph, 54–56
Hichborn, Philip II (EW's first husband), 14,
    15, 23–24, 25, 26, 27, 38n, 50
Hichborn, Philip III (EW's son), 6, 14, 16,
    17, 23, 26, 118
Hickey, William, 45, 45n
Hogg, Thomas Jefferson, 117, 123, 127, 135,
    137, 149, 151
Hopkins, Katherine (Mrs. Horace Wylie),
    14, 24, 25, 26
Hough, Graham, 12
Howard, Brian, 31
Hoyt, Anne McMichael (EW's mother), 14,
    21, 22, 27
Hoyt, Constance (Baroness Strumm, EW's
    sister), 14, 22
Hoyt, Henry Martyn (EW's father), 21, 22
Hoyt, Henry Martyn, Jr. (EW's brother), 14,
    22, 26
Hoyt, Morton (EW's brother), 14
Hoyt, Nancy (EW's sister), 4, 14, 18, 20,
    58, 160

Hugo, Victor, 79
Huxley, Aldous, 117, 139
Huysmans, Joris Karl, 48, 53, 73

Ingpen, Roger, 31

Jackson, Holbrook, 63, 77
Jarrell, Randall, 175
Johnson, Lionel, 47, 77, 79, 85, 86, 151

Keats, John, 86, 120, 121, 132
Knopf, Blanche (Mrs. Alfred), 13

Lamb, Lady Caroline, 152
Langner, Lawrence, 30
Lardner, Ring, 52
Le Gallienne, Richard, 77
Lehmann, Rosalind, 31
Lewis, Sinclair, 9, 21, 34, 51
Longhi, Pietro, 109
Longworth, Alice, 22
Lowell, Amy, 28
Lowndes, Mrs. Belloc, 31
Luini, Bernardino, 103–104

Machen, Arthur, 31, 54, 107
McMichael, Morton (EW's grandfather),
    21, 22
Martz, Louis L., 1
Medwin, Thomas, 117, 133
Mencken, H. L., 21
Millay, Edna St. Vincent, 13, 16, 21, 61, 64,
    84, 84n–85n, 125, 198
Milton, John, 127, 135, 140, 142, 147
Mitford, Nancy, 109
Moore, Douglas, 13
Moore, Marianne, 64
Morley, Christopher, 13
Morris, William, 99, 127
Munroe, Harriet, 26

New Republic, 3
New Yorker, 29, 63
Nicolson, Harold, 15
Norris, Kathleen, 17, 18
Norton, Caroline, 150, 152

Olivier, Edith, 17, 33, 182
Olson, Stanley, 4–5, 27, 129, 159

Parker, Dorothy, 8, 22, 30, 63, 164
Pater, Walter, 102, 181
Peacock, Thomas Love, 34, 117
Pearsall, Martha (Mrs. Paul), 16
Poe, Edgar Allan, 56, 209–10
Poiret, Paul, 13
Pope, Alexander, 171
Porter, Katharine Anne, 29, 29n
Pound, Ezra, 2, 58, 60, 104, 104n, 108, 207, 208

Ritchie, Charles, 31
Romantics. *See* Wylie, Elinor: and the Romantics
Roosevelt, Theodore, 20, 37
Rossetti, Christina, 59, 60
Rossetti, Dante Gabriel, 84

Sackville-West, Victoria (Vita), 15, 31, 128–29
Saint-Pierre, Bernardin de, 39
Satterlee, Henry Yates, 23
Sergeant, Elizabeth Shepley, 36, 49
Shakespeare, William, 9, 182, 187, 190, 191, 192, 196
Shelley, Mary. *See* Godwin, Mary
Shelley, Percy Bysshe, 20, 31, 59, 98–99, 175; his art as influence on EW, 11, 22, 89, 121–22, 141, 156, 163, 176–80, 181, 202; his life as influence on EW, 5, 18, 30, 87, 88, 116, 118, 121, 122–24, 127, 128, 145, 156, 164, 181, 210; as imaginary lover of EW, 23, 30, 114–16, 128–30, 177, 179, 190, 198–99, 205–206; as protagonist in EW's works, 113, 116, 118–19, 127–43, 145, 149–62, 176–80, 198–99, 206
—works: *Adonais*, 116, 120, 121, 151, 182; *Alastor*, 116, 130–31, 133, 135; "Boat on the Serchio," 151; "Buona Notte," 137; "The Cloud," 115, 176; *Epipsychidion*, 15, 113, 114, 116, 117; "Exhortation," 140; "Julian and Maddalo," 131; *Letters*, 114, 135, 137–38; "Ode to the West Wind," 142; "Rosalind and Helen," 151; "Stanzas Written in Dejection," 142–43; "To a Skylark," 115, 116, 176; "Two Spirits: An Allegory," 134
Sitwell, Edith, 2, 17
Sitwell, Osbert, 17, 31

Sitwell, Sacheverell, 17, 31
Smart Set, 29, 183
Speyer, Leonora, 25
Stein, Gertrude, 208
Sterne, Lawrence, 1
Stevens, Wallace, 2, 60, 119, 163, 175, 212
Stoker, Bram, 22
Sutton, Denys, 101
Swinburne, Algernon, 197
Symons, Arthur, 77

Taft, William Howard, 24
Teasdale, Sara, 17, 30
Tennant, Stephen, 31
Tennyson, Alfred, Lord, 155–56, 157
Thompson, Francis, 77
Town Topics, 14
Trelawny, Edward John, 115, 131, 136
Twain, Mark, 140

Untermeyer, Jean Starr, 17
Untermeyer, Louis, 76, 78

Van Doren, Carl, 4, 13, 18, 78, 103, 111, 122, 128, 138, 159, 184
Van Doren, Mark, 84, 84n
Vanity Fair, 28, 128, 183
Van Vechten, Carl, 17, 19, 30, 42, 51, 54, 56, 107
Velásquez, Diego Rodríguez, 59
Viviani, Emilia, 114, 117, 130
Voltaire, François Marie Arouet de, 1

Walsh, Thomas, 29n
Watts, Isaac, 59n
Webster, John, 64
West, Rebecca, 18
Westbrook, Harriet, 118, 130, 135, 136, 150
Wharton, Edith, 4, 10, 22, 23, 109–10, 207
Whistler, James Abbott McNeill, 38, 38n, 42, 65–66, 81, 86, 99, 101, 103, 143, 157–58, 174, 176, 207, 208
Wilbur, Richard, 8
Wilde, Oscar, 42, 47, 56, 75, 77, 99, 102–103, 157, 174, 209; "The Decay of Lying," 174; *The Picture of Dorian Gray*, 42, 46–48, 65, 66, 69, 71, 102; *Vera*, 42
Williams, Jane, 141
Williams, William Carlos, 22

Wilson, Edmund, 4, 13, 20, 28, 30, 64, 104n, 211

Wolfe, Thomas, 17, 19

Woodhouse, Henry de Clifford, 4, 32–33, 110, 164, 181–205

Woodhouse, Rebecca, 32–33, 184, 195–96, 204

Woolf, Virginia, 2, 5, 8, 31, 208; *A Room of One's Own*, 130; "Not One of Us," 127; *Orlando*, 128–30; *The Voyage Out*, 144; *To the Lighthouse*, 5

Wordsworth, William, 66–67

Wylie, Andrew, 14

Wylie, Elinor: ancestry, 21; art, her interest in, 6, 22, 26; birth, 21; children, 4, 6, 26, 30; courage, 15, 35, 94–96; death, 13, 33, 207; dedication as writer, 34, 113, 160–62, 209; education, 21–22; and the Elizabethans, 179, 182, 185, 185n, 194, 198, 200, 210–11, 210n; feminist accents in, 2, 5, 25, 111; frustrations of, 17, 25, 30, 32, 85, 110, 113, 145; funeral, 12–14, 15–17; ill health, 26, 30, 164, 179; legend of, 4, 8, 10, 14–15; marriage, attitude toward, 7, 34, 95, 109–10, 113; marriage to Philip Hichborn II, 4, 23–24; marriage to Horace Wylie, 4, 14–15, 24, 26–28, 30, 50, 58, 94, 110; marriage to William Rose Benét, 4, 28–31, 33–34, 109–12, 113, 184; maternity, attitude toward, 90; perfectionism, 18, 114; and Platonism, 114, 130, 205; pride, 5, 13, 15, 18–20, 96–97, 161–62, 163, 166; religious faith, 13, 15, 96–97, 182, 200–203, 211–12; and the Romantics, 66–68, 79, 87, 89, 119, 145, 149, 152–54, 156, 158–59, 160, 174; her scholarship, 18, 37, 115–16, 138–39, 182, 210; sexuality, 5–6, 88–97, 114, 117–18, 144, 164, 187–98; vulnerability, 18–21. *See also* Aesthetes; Hichborn, Philip II; Hichborn, Philip III; Benét, William Rose; Shelley, Percy Bysshe

—essays: "Excess of Charity," 115–16, 176; "Jewelled Bindings," 99–100

—novels: *Jennifer Lorn*, 5, 6, 10, 11, 28, 29, 31, 34, 36–57, 75, 84, 90, 109, 111, 129, 141, 146, 156; *Mr. Hodge and Mr. Hazard*, 30, 119, 128, 129, 131, 139, 144–62; *The Orphan Angel*, 19, 30, 31, 70, 113, 116, 117,

125, 127–43; *The Venetian Glass Nephew*, 2–3, 17, 45, 57, 75, 91, 102–12, 113, 129, 208

—poetry collections and groups of poems: *Angels and Earthly Creatures*, 8, 13, 32, 164, 179, 180, 181–206, 210; "One Person" sonnets, 32, 33, 50, 85, 164, 183–98, 204; *Black Armour*, 10n, 29, 50, 84–101, 164, 200, 208; *Incidental Numbers*, 24–25, 58–63; *Nets to Catch the Wind*, 11, 28, 29, 36, 59, 64–83, 84; *Trivial Breath*, 31, 32, 116, 121, 163–80

—poems (individual): "An American in England," 208; "As I Went Down by Harve de Grace," 15; "Atavism," 26, 121; "August," 81–82; "Beauty," 65–66; "Bells in the Rain," 69; "Beltane," 32; "Birches," 63; "Birthday Sonnet," 211; "The Broken Man," 204–205; "Bronze Trumpets and Sea Water," 174; "Chimaera Sleeping," 205–206; "The Church-Bell," 69; "The Coast Guard's Cottage," 121–22; "Confession of Faith," 164–65; "Country Song," 179; "A Crowded Trolley Car," 69, 82; "Dedication," 176–77; "Demon Lovers," 98–99; "The Devil in Seven Shires," 166; "Drowned Woman," 97, 121; "The Eagle and the Mole," 35, 66–68; "Escape," 69–70; "Epitaph," 50, 91–92, 158; "The Fairy Goldsmith," 72–74, 79, 81; "The Falcon," 68; "Felo de Se," 183, 199–200; "Fire and Sleet and Candlelight," 26; "From the Wall," 25; "From Whom No Secrets Are Hid," 24–25; "Full Moon," 47, 85, 86–87, 89, 98; "The Good Birds," 54; "Heroics," 85, 86, 89; "Hospes Comesque Corporis," 124; "Hymn to Earth," 179, 202; "Innocent Landscape," 166, 174–75; "The Innocents," 166; "King Honour's Eldest Son," 86; "The Knight Fallen on Evil Days," 63; "Lament for Glasgerion," 178, 179; "Let No Charitable Hope," 88–89; "Little Elegy," 10, 183; "Little Sonnet," 81, 91, 186; "Love Song," 183, 198–99; "The Loving Cup," 32, 204; "Minotaur," 166, 171–73, 175; "Miranda's Supper," 166, 167–71; "My Best Content Were Death," 35; "Nebuchadnezzar," 96–97;

"Nonchalance," 97; "O Virtuous Light," 200–202; "On a Singing Girl," 208; "Peregrine," 86; "Peter and John," 166, 179; "Portrait in Black Paint . . ." 50, 118; "Preference," 50, 88, 89; "Pretty Words," 240; "Prophecy," 50; "A Proud Lady," 12, 64, 82; "Puritan's Ballad," 166; "A Red Carpet for Shelley," 119–20; "Sanctuary," 69–70; "Sea Lullaby," 81, 121; "Self-Portrait, 98, 161–62; 163; "Sequence," 92–96, 186, 200; "Silver Filigree," 26, 80–81; "Song," 81, 97, 121; "Sonnet," 4; "A Strange Story," 166; "This Corruptible," 179, 202, 203; "This Hand," 87, 91, 92, 93; "Three Wishes," 50, 97, 158; "To Aphrodite . . ." 208; "To Claudia Homonoea," 208; "To Paolo and Francesca in Purgatory," 63; "Tragic Dialogue," 116, 124–25; "Unwilling Admission," 164, 165–66; "Valentine," 82–83; "Velvet Shoes," 17, 26, 75–78, 79, 81; "Viennese Waltz," 205; "What Did You Buy?" 73–75; "Where, O Where?" 164–65; "Wild Peaches," 70–71, 101, 207; "Winter Sleep," 69–70, 82; "With a Bare Bodkin," 20
—unfinished manuscript: *April, April,* 127–28

Wylie, Horace, 4, 6, 14, 16, 21, 24, 26–28, 50, 58, 60, 64, 92, 94, 110. *See also* Wylie, Elinor: marriage to Horace Wylie

Wylie, Katherine (Mrs. Horace). *See* Hopkins, Katherine

Yeats, William Butler, 2, 3n, 12, 35, 61–62, 66, 70, 73, 77, 85, 100, 200, 210

Young, Helen, 159